There Is Only YOU
Beholding YOU

A Spiritual Journey of Never Ending Invitations

To Rosalie and Greg, in
celebration of our long
lasting friendship.
With love and gratitude
for your presence in our
lives   Berta Ellen Canton

Thomas A. Leemerts

2/2008

There Is Only YOU
Beholding YOU

A Spiritual Journey of Never Ending Invitations

by
Thomas A. Leenerts, Psy.D.
and
Berta Stella Cantón

Foreword by Henry Grayson, Ph.D.

Mill City Press

With
profound gratitude
for Life

For more information contact:
Permissions
Mill City Press
212 Third Avenue North
Suite 570
Minneapolis, Minnesota 55401

info@millcitypress.net
www.millcitypress.net

ISBN: 978-1-934248-84-3, 1-934248-84-3
LCCN: 2007943719

Cover Design by Jenni Wheeler
Interior Layout by Tiffany Laschinger

Printed in the United States of America

TABLE OF CONTENTS

Acknowledgements

I am deeply grateful to Brenda Schumacher, a dear friend of Berta and I, who read the first manuscript. Her encouragement, enthusiastic support and detailed feedback on how the reading of the text impacted her gave me inspiration and motivation to continue writing.

Others read later drafts as the book unfolded. Jim Riley, a professional writer, offered valuable suggestions; Courtney Hann pointed out how to bring the story across in a way that gave it greater authenticity as a personal life experience.

Among those who supported me and expressed assurance of rewarding outcome are: Lucha Corpi, a novelist and poet, Aldo Hugo Cantón, historian, Edgardo Cantón, author of *Abuelo de Pajaros*, Max and Aida Grevstad, Rev. Michael Gerdes, Mari Wilson, Dr. Margaret Merrifield and Michael Booth.

My thanks to Robin Ireland, sagacious editor that believed in the book and helped to develop the literary side of the manuscript over two years. Her persistent questioning and requests for more examples added to my own clarity and the readability of the text.

In the initial undertaking, I had editorial assistance from Sue Chin. Her coaching added to my determination to complete the project. One final editing and readings was done by Virginia Sliman who helped me know when to say "the manuscript is finished."

General support and encouragement through tireless reflections about spirituality for more than 15 years was had from Tom and Leslie Hatcher. Thank you for being in my life.

The impact of these above mentioned individuals and countless others was tremendous. However, none of them individually or collectively can actually compare to my loving wife Berta for being present in a myriad of ways. She has a common sense, coupled with deep wisdom that I could and did access at any time of the day or night. Because she willingly read and reread the different versions of the text with careful thoughtfulness and full attention to details, I found the energy to carry on.

Thomas A. Leenerts, Psy.D.

Prelude

A Fable from 3001

The new millennium was one year old, yet the citizens of Circle 41 had led their lives within the boundaries of the city for at least eleven generations. Circle 41, a member city of Earth Power II Confederation, sat on a broad plain in a sunny valley that had once, long ago, been called California. Its citizens, farmers of the Confederation, grew produce for the empire.

It was a stable society. Life had a simple design. No one lived there who had not been planned and who had not been bred for the exact purpose of tilling the soil. All needs were met, and no one was burdened by choices. In genetically selecting for this Circle, the Confederation designed physically robust people with a psychological tendency to conform. All were blue-eyed and blond. Most of the men were eunuchs, and the women not chosen for breeding were sterilized at a young age. The citizens had no need to concern themselves with food or shelter or care, for the Confederation provided these for all who lived within the Circle.

Predisposed by design to conform, the residents accepted the status quo. In the event that questions might arise, multi-dimensional entertainment distracted their minds with bright images and sounds, and reinforced the advantages of the system. The inhabitants of Circle 41 were happy because they were told they were happy. And with their physical needs met, they knew they must be content.

However, the Confederation left nothing to chance. The residents knew Circle 41 was twenty-four miles in diameter and that an impassable barricade around the city kept out monstrous mutations that wandered through the valley. The barricade itself consisted of two concentric circles, the outer one of which was a 30-foot-high stone wall. In between the fenced areas roamed ferocious guard beasts placed there as extra protection against those of the outside. The residents were grateful for this. But they still feared the monstrous guard beasts. They had seen news films in their scheduled recreation time that showed what happened when an individual had wandered into the fenced area by accident, or even once or twice by design in a misguided attempt to leave Circle 41. The beasts tore them apart and devoured them. *Foolish, foolish people*, thought those watching the film. *Why would anyone want to leave a place where we are so cared for? So safe?*

Sleeping quarters for one group of men sat about 100 yards from the barricaded area on the north end of Circle 41. Though they lived close enough to see and hear the beasts behind the first fence, the men knew better than to approach the area. The movies had assured that.

One hot evening, long after the sun had set and the lights of the night sky had passed far along their courses, a young worker called L28 tossed and turned on his bed. He could not sleep. Finally, he rose and slipped outside in search of freshness. He stepped into the silent night and looked around, realizing that he had never been outside alone - so late. He looked up at the sky where only a small piece of the moon glimmered. Everywhere else a sea of sparkling stars spread from horizon to horizon. He gasped in wonder. Slowly, he walked around, his eyes fixed on the spectacle above him. After meandering around for about half an hour, he sat on the still warm ground and just gazed up, his heart filled with deep appreciation.

Time passed. It was perhaps an hour later when he glanced around and froze—not even daring to breathe. He couldn't believe what he saw. He was sitting in the middle of the fenced-in area. He had crossed the barrier in the dark! The wild beasts were all around him, gnashing their teeth, rising on their hind legs. He looked back toward the sleeping quarters only a short dash away, and saw he could not reach the edge of the area without passing two of the beasts. This, he knew, had to be his death. He looked around from beast to beast to see which one would come for him. But none did. He checked each one again, tense in readiness. But not one beast looked at him. They stood, they thrashed, they gnashed, but they did not seem to see him. Perhaps, he thought with flickering hope, it was because he was sitting so still, because it was dark. Perhaps, if he moved very, very slowly, he might reach the fence and safety.

Inch by silent inch, he crawled toward the wall until he was finally near enough to climb it. With a surge of relief he put his hand out to touch it, but missed. He tried again. His fingers slid right past it. Startled, he reached again farther, thinking that in the dark he had misgauged its distance. Still his hand slid through the air with no resistance. Again and again he reached for the fence. Again and again he felt nothing.

Distracted by this puzzle, L28 did not notice as one of the animals walked up to him. A sudden roar spun him around in time to see this massive, shaggy beast right at his back and moving fast toward him. As he froze in horror, the beast reached him in one step and then...walked right through him. L28 looked down at his hands, reached for his neck and face, felt his chest. He was unharmed. It could not be, but he was unharmed. He spun around to see the beast moving away from him now, still clawing at the night air, still growling. What was happening?

Another growl drew his attention and L28 jerked to his left. A beast was heading straight toward him, but instead of running from it, he stepped toward it and reached out to touch it. His hand went through empty air. He reached with both hands toward its head, its stomach. He tried to catch its clawing paws. Nothing. Neither the animals, nor the fence, had substance. They were nothing more than images.

He turned to look at the great wall on the other side of the fenced-in area. He could not comprehend the scale of this deception, nor its purpose. Almost involuntarily, he began to walk toward the final barrier that had surrounded him his entire life.

L28 reached the wall and stopped. He raised his head to see it tower above him, massive, hopeless. He didn't know which he feared more—that it was real, or that it was not. Slowly, he raised his hand. Gently, he reached for the wall. But instead of stone rough enough to scrape flesh, his hand felt nothing but air as it moved past and through. The wall wasn't real. Like the inner fence. And the monsters roaming the circle. This barrier, too, was only an image.

What did this mean? How could these things keep him and his brethren from harm if they were only a mirage? The thought settled hard on him that all this time they'd thought they were safe, when anything could have come through these walls as easily as his arm had passed. They had never been safe. They had only thought themselves so. It had all been a lie.

Sucking in his breath, he stepped all the way through the wall to the other side. He looked around at the wide plain in which Circle 41 stood. By the light of the stars he could see a vast country. Off in the distance, mountains darker than the night stood in silhouette against the sky. He walked back and forth through the wall five or six times just because he could. He stopped on the outside of the wall and looked at the staggering emptiness before him. Suddenly, it was all too much. He couldn't comprehend his discovery.

He stepped back inside the wall and ran back to his sleeping quarters. On tip-toe, he entered the dormitory. Everyone was still asleep. He sat on the edge of his bed, and thought again of what he had discovered. The barricade was a lie. The monsters were a lie. The news films, then, were also lies. His whole life he had been surrounded by circles of lies.

He began to laugh. He could not contain himself. It was so absurd. His laugh grew so loud it disturbed the others sleeping in his barrack. They crept to his side, drawn by his glee. "What's wrong?" they asked, but all L28 could do was laugh. Soon, one or two others started to chuckle in spite of themselves, then others joined in. In moments, the whole place was ringing with laughter. No one knew why, and all L28 would say was, "It's all a big joke....it's all a big joke." Finally, their mirth subsided. They pressed him for an explanation, "What's a big joke? Was it a dream? Tell us." He couldn't answer. How could he explain something so big? All he could do was shrug his shoulders and laugh with each question. After an hour, the others had all gone back to sleep. L28 lay on his bed, staring out into the dark, listening to the sound of thirty breaths being drawn and let out, drawn and let out. Finally, he, too, closed his eyes and slept.

During the next three weeks, L28 tried to explain to some of the workers with whom he was closest what he had discovered. They did not believe him. They would not believe him. He could see the doubt in their eyes. He could see their fear ...of the idea ...of him. To make them see, L28 invited them to go with him to the barricaded area, but none would go. They turned away from him, uncomfortable with the change in him. Those with whom he had slept and eaten and worked for so many years were suddenly different from him. They felt it, and so did he. His experience had changed him and he could neither share what he had learned, nor undo it.

One day, when the men in L28's barracks woke, they found L28 was gone. They looked at one another wordlessly. What had happened to him? Had he gone back to the wall and been eaten as they'd expected he would be, or had he been removed as an undesirable? They did not know how to ask the question, much less find the answer. A whisper traveled from field to field that L28 had lost his mind and must have been eliminated. Yet the Confederation authorities said nothing of the matter, and L28 did not return.

At dinner several days after L28 had vanished, the Confederation overseers of Circle 41 confirmed the rumor. They said it was for the best. No one person, they said, could be allowed to disrupt the harmony and safety of the Circle, jeopardizing all who lived there. All around the mess hall people nodded their heads and said, "Oh, yes. That is what's best. Such an insane person does not serve the common good of Circle 41 and the Earth Power II Confederation."

Still, one thing left some workers troubled. Since L-28 had been eliminated, they wondered in their most secret thoughts Why were his possessions still in his locker for five days before a Confederation representative confiscated them? When a worker rejected confederation teachings, the clothes had always been taken away the same day the person was eliminated. Maybe, they comforted themselves, someone had forgotten.

The workers followed the Confederation guidelines and never mentioned L28 in their conversations. But those few who had wondered about his clothes could not look at the barricade again without wondering, if even for a moment, "Is it possible that things are different than they appear?"

Foreword

Psychotherapists often give us useful insights and spiritual teachers present us with profound truths. Many, however, fail to provide us with the practical tools necessary to integrate and carry out these insights and truths in our lives. Thomas Leenerts, a psychologist and a spiritual teacher using his own life journey, shows us the circuitous paths our lives may take, but which lead us to deeper and deeper understandings of Truth. He has the understanding that the best of spiritual thought is profoundly psychological and that the best of psychology is clearly spiritual. And most importantly, he provides us with very practical tools for the journey.

All too often we think that one who is enlightened just happened to be that way—perhaps even born with evolved enlightenment. Leenerts, quite differently, shares so openly his life journey, and how his continual dedication to discovering Truth helped him use his diverse life experiences for learning and spiritual growth. Such an account inspires us all to use our life's journey, whatever form it might take, as the occasion for such growth. Otherwise, life might be much like a student attending a great school, but pays no attention in classes, sees everything as irrelevant, and eventually leaves the school with little more knowledge than he came in with. Such would be much like Socrates described as the "unexamined life which is not worth living." Some might think, "My life was not like Leenerts with such safety and structure. My life was filled with the pain of rejection, loss or abuse. How can I learn from that?" Yet, as one woman once said to me, "If I had not been married to such a critical and verbally abusive man for those fifteen years, I would never have learned how to keep myself centered and at peace regardless of external circumstances. I feel like I attended an advanced graduate school!"

Dr. Leenerts has been deeply influenced by the *Course*, as have many well known authors such as Wayne Dyer, Marianne Williamson, Gerald Jampolsky, and countless others. Even though I have studied many diverse spiritual systems, both Western and Eastern, the *Course* is undoubtedly the most profound psycho-spiritual work I have encountered. While it uses much traditional Christian language, the meanings given to the words are quite different than taught in most churches and synagogues, taking us totally out of dualistic framework into a world of unity and Oneness. This work was scribed by Dr. Helen Schucman, hearing an inner dictation, with the support and aid of Dr. William Thetford, both professors of psychology at Columbia University's College of Physicians and Surgeons back in the 1960's. It has since been translated into almost 20 different languages. Leenerts does a wonderful job of bringing the central teachings of the *Course* into practical applications. Getting us past our illusion of separateness and our tendency to blame others with our projections, he reminds us with his title, *There Is Only You Beholding You.*

~Henry Grayson, Ph.D. author of "Mindful Loving"

Introduction

Stories can be catalysts for the heart's desire for meaning. They impart an energy that is broader, more comprehensive than the individual narrative itself. Stories can melt defenses and allow us to tap into our own intuitive knowing. Sometimes they act as mirrors, and we silently give ourselves permission to see our limitations, imperfections and imposed restrictions reflected in them. They can also awaken our hunger and thirst for that which is real.

I started writing my story ten years ago. At first it was easy. Over time, I noticed that discerning the meaning from life events gave me more of a sense of who I was beyond the events. Combining hundreds of intertwined stories of my life, including "A Fable from 3001," into a single book eventually became more challenging, yet the process enhanced my awareness of the constraints I had believed in and abided by for so long.

In the first half of this book, events of my life illustrate how we are sung to sleep by the culture into which we arrive precisely because we lack the awareness to see it for what it is. We find ourselves "programmed" or "conditioned" to respond to life in certain ways that soon become deeply ingrained, and we live our lives unaware of these scripts.

My story suggests that our programming grows more vigorous with every successively larger ring of culture as we expand from family outward to schools, churches, communities and careers. Gradually, I came to understand that the decisions I made in life were not so much choices as they were the result of ways of thinking that I had acquired unconsciously from family and society and of which I was unaware. In my case, early experiences contributed to my judgment of myself as inadequate. And as a result, I felt compelled to seek ways to prove my adequacy. Once the script was in place, it was outside of my conscious awareness and I acted as if it were true. I acted it out without ever noticing it.

The events, teachers and practices that led to my growing awareness of the script and, eventually to a deeper understanding of conditioning and the True Self are also chronicled in this book. My hope is that by sharing my journey, describing the steps I took and the ones I avoided, others will be able to shorten their own.

The second half of the book focuses on material my wife Berta and I have used for the past fifteen years in our Wellfolk workshops and weekend intensives called "Dialogues on True Identity." We designed the course work to uncover layer after layer of automatic responses that a human being accumulates in a lifetime of unexamined acculturation.

These exercises are meant to increase your awareness of scripts that might be influencing your life. When we are able to look at past programming without judgment, we experience a state of mind that connects us with a self that is beyond scripts. May this book serve as a light by which to see your own life through that clear lens and find the path you were meant to travel.

~Thomas A. Leenerts, Psy.D.

Part One: My Story

My teacher said that there is only one true choice in a life; all the rest is conditioning. That one choice is to turn your back on everything to see that which is prior to it all.

~Eli Jaxon-Bear

Foundation

That Into Which I Came

My life began in a small German-Catholic community in the Midwest in 1933. At that time, Humphrey, Nebraska, had less than 1,000 residents, and it was the epitome of small-town America, complete with front porches, curbed streets, fire station and schools. In the center of town—and equally at the center of people's lives—stood the St. Francis of Assisi Catholic Church. The church could be seen for miles across the flat, rich farmland of Platte County, its beautiful spire topped with a twenty-foot cross pointed toward heaven. Its clear bell rang every fifteen minutes throughout the day, a persistent reminder to center your life in God. Our family home, which my parents built in 1929, stood a block away from this hub in the community wheel.

My father, a large animal veterinarian, lived and practiced in Humphrey his entire life. My mother was his second wife; his first passed away. He had a daughter and a son prior to his marriage to my mother, and together they had three girls before I was born, followed by two more boys and three more girls, for a total of eleven children. They were gentle people, not given to harsh emotion. In fact, they actively discouraged such extremes. If we felt anger, we were expected to quickly set it aside. If we felt sadness, we were expected to remove ourselves from the group until we could regain self-control.

I remember an instance at the dinner table when my mother began to cry. Without a word, she left the table and went to her room. None of us said anything, and certainly, my father made no comment. I didn't know why she was crying then, and I still don't. Whatever it was that reduced her to tears in the public setting of the family table remained unarticulated, and perhaps unaddressed. That was simply how extremes of emotion were handled. In a large family, things needed to proceed as smoothly as possible in order to meet everyone's needs. Strong emotions, if indulged in public, presumably impeded that, so family culture made them a taboo. If we required corrections to our behavior, they were administered in nonviolent ways. Three examples demonstrate my parents' respective styles.

Father discouraged us from any kind of blame. In a typical situation, my brother Jerry, who was one year younger than I, complained that I had pushed him. Father asked in a tone most serious, "Tom, did you push Jerry?" I admitted that I had. Dad said, "The next time you do that, then, it will be the second time, right?" Dad did not side with Jerry as he had hoped, nor did he correct me, as I had feared. He stated a fact and dropped the issue. Both Jerry and I nodded in agreement. Father made it clear he would not be bothered with our childish ways.

A second example is how he would handle verbal conflict. If two of us butted heads in a quarrel, Father gently grabbed us by the back of the necks and insisted that we kiss and make up. That always served to derail us at once, and most frequently we ended up laughing. My mother had a different method. She always found a way to touch our sense of honor. In a household with thirteen people, everyone had assigned tasks. One of my sisters came home from school one day, and my mother inquired, "Today is Wednesday, do you want to dust and vacuum the upstairs bedrooms?" My sister, perhaps full of some new-found sense of self, said she didn't want to do that. My mother quietly said, "All right. I will do it, and you will see how I do it." Mother then went upstairs and sat my sister in a chair in the first bedroom while Mother dusted and vacuumed the floor. She did the same thing in each of the four upstairs bedrooms. The sight of Mother doing the work that she herself had been assigned so shamed my sister that she never, ever, denied a request of my mother's again.

We kids were guided into accepting the culture of the home in a fashion that reinforced it without damaging it. My father found a creative way to deflect the energy in moments of conflict, either through active discouragement or through humorous diversion. My mother used a form of self-sacrifice to motivate obedient behavior. Her underlying message was that work needed to be done, and she was not asking anything of us that she herself would not do. Her actions shamed my sister, and shame was an appropriate tool when used justly, as it was in this case. It showed my sister the consequences her self-centered behavior in a way she never forgot.

Learning that our actions, both those we took and those we withheld, had a direct effect on those around us was one of the hallmarks of maturity, not to mention civility—certainly the first rule of a successful relationship whether with family or mate. Both of my parents, in different ways, also reinforced the idea that order and authority were for your own good, and if you didn't obey them, you destroyed the whole structure. I learned to believe that a system is destroyed when chaotic energy is allowed to move in unrestricted fashion, and it isn't any fun to live under chaos's rule. The subtext to these examples was that life remained peaceful and coherent as long as we obeyed our parents, and by extension, the Church, and ultimately, God.

Other values picked up by osmosis in our environment stressed self-sufficiency, that we all had a role to play within the community, and that a father's role was to always provide for his wife and children. Whining and complaining, so tempting to children, were always nipped in the bud.

It was understood without question that children were of value, and their welfare was always paramount. To provide for his family, Father had his veterinarian practice, but he also had some land in another area of town. On it he kept a cow for fresh milk and calves raised for beef. But in addition to meeting the direct needs of putting food on the table of a large household, my father always kept a pony or a horse. This was strictly for the children's enjoyment. We had a little pony cart and rode around town in it and entered our pony and cart in the annual town parade. On those acres we had a large garden, including a strawberry patch, so the needs of the stomach were equally balanced with the spirit's needs for delight and play.

It is hard to remember now what this safe, self-contained world was like. Our lives were defined by seasons and holidays. We moved through the year in anticipation of Sundays on a small scale, and autumn with Halloween, winter with Christmas, spring with Easter, summer with Fourth of July, and birthdays on a larger scale.

A feast of the senses began on Saturday when Mother baked her breads, rolls and cookies. The whole house was filled with the smell of these, an olfactory cue that Sunday was coming. During Sunday Mass, at times I thought of crispies, a homemade pastry waiting for me at home, and I looked forward to reading the Sunday funnies. Even this was a ritual, for it was customary for the elder children to spread the funnies out on the floor and read them to a younger sibling.

Easter had its traditions of new clothes, and the Fourth of July brought a family picnic. We began thinking of Halloween weeks ahead of time and spent hours planning and preparing our costumes. Christmas anchored the year, both figuratively and literally. On the first day of December, each of us wrote our names on a small card and dropped it into a hat. We took turns drawing cards and the name on that card was the person we gave a Christmas gift. Sometimes this posed a great challenge, and I developed the habit of turning to my mother for a secret consultation about what to get the person on my card. I once drew a card for one of my sisters. I didn't have any idea what to give her. When I consulted with Mother, she told me she had bought that sister a dark green dress and suggested I might buy her a pair of dark green socks to match. Mother always knew what each of us needed, often, before we knew ourselves.

On the weekend before Christmas, the children gathered in the kitchen while mother baked cookies in different shapes to be decorated and used as tree ornaments. Surrounded by the smell of freshly baked pastries, we added flourishing touches of colorful designs to stars, balls, Christmas trees, angels, little cookie boys and little cookie girls. It was great fun, and I recall an intense feeling of intimacy and security as we worked together and "ooh-ed" and "aw-ed" over one another's creations. We also strung popcorn on long strings to garland the tree.

Father bought our tree at the end of November. He or my elder brother mounted the tree on a sturdy stand and left it outside until the week before the twenty-fifth. When it was time, Dad put the tree in the living room. Using the old decorations retrieved from the attic and that year's new creations, we festooned the tree with lights, garlands and hand-made ornaments. Each of us who decorated cookies hung them where we wanted. I placed mine on the lower branches so I could sneak a bite of cookie now and then over the next few days.

On Christmas Eve, we gathered around the piano as Mother played and we sang carols. When Father said Santa was about to arrive, I nearly exploded with anticipation and excitement. He sent us downstairs to the basement to wait while Santa did his job. We strained our ears listening for Santa's footsteps, and nearly stopped breathing the moment we heard them coming down the stairs to the basement. Silence filled the room, our eyes glued to the entrance. Father always entered first, followed by Santa. When he came in with his "Ho-ho-ho" and good cheer, our eyes popped wide and our mouths hung open in a round and silent "O."

Santa told us he had left his gifts under the tree, but "before we go upstairs I want to know two things." This was the moment of peril for us younger children. "Were you good during the past year?"

"Oh, my yes," we of course answered.

Looking directly at the older children, he asked, "Do you know your prayers?" It was always a relief to me that he did not ask me to recite prayers. I hated to think the biggest source of my yearly happiness depended on a perfect recitation. Fortunately, he only visited this test upon the older children. After one or two said the Lord's Prayer, Santa led us upstairs. He told us he had to be on his way to see other children. "Merry Christmas to all of you," he'd say, and he left as mysteriously as he had come.

I had a sense this might not really be Santa as I grew older, but I went along anyway for the pure pleasure of the excitement and fun. It wouldn't have worked without all of us participating in the charade, which I later realized was true of many other dynamics in life, including in the Church and in society as a whole. We agree to agree in order to experience the benefits of belonging. The Santa ritual reinforced the culture of the whole by making our obedience a condition for the rewards Santa represented. The well-publicized theme was that we needed to earn them—and not just by refraining from "bad" behavior, but also by being able to recite our prayers, which tied Santa back to the Church.

After Santa left, we tugged the gifts from under the Christmas tree and stacked them on the dining room table. No one touched them until Mother started distributing the presents one by one. Then we tore into our gifts. Another tradition occurred on Christmas Day, when Father took a picture of Mother with us gathered around her in front of the tree. That practice continued through the years even if only one or two of us were present.

As calendar days passed, we were constantly in motion with whatever event shimmered on the horizon, autumn after autumn, spring after spring. I felt connected to this cycle of life and the family in ways that simply aren't possible anymore. This is not a nostalgic thought, for as sweet as that life was, the very security of it depended on an unquestioning acceptance of everything in it. This unquestioning attitude was to become one of the central themes in my spiritual and personal development. These small and large, familial and communal celebrations made me feel comfortable—part of something larger than me. To maintain such a pleasant sensation, I clung to what made me feel secure, often compromising myself in vigorous ways, making adjustments and shifts that threw me further and further off balance. I became desensitized in some areas to protect myself from jeopardizing my comfort. And in other areas, I grew ever hungrier.

There's no question that comfort and security are of value. But life is not static. By its very definition, it involves change from second to second, year to year. Over time, a culture that doesn't accommodate or encourage growth calcifies. Actions that support the culture lose their meaning and the people in it begin to feel imprisoned, or worse, hollow. The same occurs on an individual level. It happened to me as I grew up. Without being able to question, I did not change or grow. I became a robot acting out programs, instead of a living being responding to and interacting with life and the inner spirit.

That Which I Was

The world into which I arrived was peaceful, stable and loving, with a place or a role for everything and everything in its place. I came with a temperament to match. According to family lore, I rarely cried, and when I did, it was exactly on time and little more than a small whimper. My older brother Gordon remarked that the household could set its separate and combined watches by my cries. I was quiet, aesthetic by nature, and had a disposition inclined to accept whatever was going on around me. Even as a small child, I had a sense of witnessing life, of paying attention to little details of my internal play

When I was about four, I played a game where I sat in my bed in my room at the top of the stairs after dark and watched what I called "ghosts" coming up the stairs toward me. I felt frightened and, at a certain point when the "figures" reached me, I shouted "Boo!" and they dispersed, re-formed at the bottom, and came up the stairs at me again. I did this over and over again. Even though I was playing a game of being afraid, I wasn't deeply bothered by these things that seemed to be trying to scare me. I delighted in beating them to the punch.

The cyclical quality of our lives captivated me. I loved our holiday traditions and I loved nature. Some of my fondest memories are of the four o'clock flowers in our backyard. These little flowers only bloomed at sunset, and when they did, fireflies flocked to the blossoms. My brothers, sisters and I knew when it was time for the plants to bloom, and we waited on summer evenings for the fireflies. They were invisible until they lit up like little stars come down to earth in our backyard. We caught them in the palms of our hands, being careful not to harm them. We put them in a jar with a perforated lid and sat and watched them turn their lights on and off, winking in and out of blackness. Before going to bed, we let them free. Watching these amazing creatures light up was such a memorable experience, it inspired an awe of nature in me that never dwindled.

The firefly tradition expanded into another part of the seasonal calendar when my mother had us gather seeds from the four o'clock plants every autumn. She kept the tiny black seeds in a jar next to the cookie jar in the kitchen where the mere sight of them promised a summer to come. In the spring, we planted another row of flowers that—in a couple of months' time"—magically called up the fireflies from of the darkness again.

My love of nature was where I connected most with my father. He had a natural curiosity about life and he shared it with us by showing, rather than telling. He once isolated three hens in separate pens and had us feed them colored water, one with green, another blue, and the third drinking red water. Each hen began to lay eggs with yolks the color of the water she drank. We kids spread the surprise by luring visiting, and hopefully unsuspecting, neighbors into cracking open one of these special eggs to find a red, green or blue yolk inside.

Father always took one or more of us on his rounds to neighboring farms, often to watch someone's sow, mare or cow give birth. Few things have been more incredible to me than watching a piglet, calf or foal enter this world. On one occasion when I was with Father, he pulled out a calf and turned to me and said, "Now, there's another one in there that wants to be born, but he needs a little help." He tied a rope to the second calf's front feet, and the farmer and I pulled on the rope. The calf popped out and dropped onto the straw-covered floor. As Father previously instructed, the farmer and I quickly set to work rubbing the delicate creatures with burlap sacks. In a short time, both calves began to move. What a moment that was to feel life begin to course through them, and to see them wake up to this world. The mystery and power of that resonated deeply in me, and like the tradition of four o'clock flowers and fireflies, it has never left me.

The gentle rhythms and traditions of this home where I lived reinforced my natural tendencies to notice and accept. The sense of security led as well to a kind of somnambulance. It never occurred to me to question this life because for the most part, its "slings and arrows" were few. The pressures to conform were gentle ones, and my easy-going temperament made that pressure all but invisible in those years before I started school. I never questioned anything; the world had never given me any reason to distrust it. I and it "just were," and that was enough.

*Nothing is wrong with you but the ideas you
have of your self are altogether wrong.*

~Sri Nisargadatta Maharaj

Walls

From the moment we are born, our lives expand outward in concentric circles of influence and complexity. First, it is our mother's face at the center of our existence, and then we notice the father or other siblings, if such people are present. Person by person, and experience by experience, we develop a sense of who we are by our interactions with our expanding world. These interactions reflect the values of the environment and over time, mold the personality into a structure that fits that environment—either by assimilation or by force.

A family's values are expressed by the behavior of those in charge of the household. Sometimes these are articulated verbally (that's not how we do things in this house), or through repetition as in the examples given in the previous chapter. More often, however, values are so deep that they aren't part of an oral tradition or directly expressed. Rather, they create an atmosphere that permeates every activity, the family culture, as it were. A child acquires the values through absorption, watching the behaviors modeled by others in the group and mimicking or harmonizing with them. It is as if we are hard wired to do so for our survival.

The family culture can be so pervasive—and we are influenced by it at such a young age—that we may not be consciously aware of what we have learned or why. The walls it forms around us remain invisible. If we do not reach a point where we look back and examine those values, whether they are positive or negative, those walls can harden to the point of cutting off our vitality. We lose our sense of innocence and wonder, as well as our capacity to respond to the life force for goodness. We become automated, imprisoned inside our own unconscious behaviors.

Many of my parents' values were positive, and served to strengthen family and community ties. Honesty, consideration of others, respectful address, cleanliness, generosity, service to others, these things have merit in nearly any context. Of all the wonderful values I absorbed, there were three that interacted with my personality in such a way as to herd me in a particular direction. These were duty, routine and an inhibition toward expressing strong emotions.

Sense of Duty

Duty was perhaps the backbone of the Leenerts family culture touching every aspect of life. It sprang from a rural lifestyle that required sacrifice and hard work, where the needs of the whole were paramount to the needs of the individual, because the group's responsibility was to meet the survival needs of every individual in it. This structure works well when life is defined by physical hardship, but it can disregard what might be termed the softer needs of personal satisfaction, approval, tenderness, and especially the sacred yearning for knowing the Self.

My father and mother both grew up on Nebraska farms. Their parents were German immigrants who labored long hours to support their large families, battling nature, bitter winters and blistering summers. My father completed grade school, put himself through college and obtained a doctorate degree in veterinarian medicine by 1918. He opened his practice in Humphrey in 1921. It had been his dream to make enough money as a "horse doctor" to attend medical school. However, the Great Depression, put an end to that dream, and he remained a doctor only for animals.

Dad often worked fourteen-hour days attending to sick animals on farms within a twelve-mile radius of Humphrey. Many times Mother and we children ate our meals at the scheduled hour, while his food sat warming until he returned from his service calls. The message was clear: one did what one must, and the household accommodated it. Dad felt it was his duty to provide for us. He worked hard and sacrificed such little luxuries as having his meals on time so that we always had meals. We understood that implicitly.

That work and duty were the sole point of life for my father is illustrated by something my brother Bob told me. He had come back to Humphrey for the wedding of my sister Georgia, who was the last to leave home. The next morning, as my brother was leaving to return to his home in Colorado, Dad said, "Bob, all my babies have been taken care of. My duty is over. The next time you come back to Humphrey, it may well be for my funeral." A mere three months later, Bob returned for my father's funeral. Dad's purpose in life was tied to his duty. When the duty was done, so was he.

My mother arrived in this world in 1905 and left it in 2001. Her life, too, was characterized by hard work and a strong sense of duty to home, family and community. At age twelve, when the First World War started, she joined the war effort. The Red Cross had a program that provided khaki yarn for women who knew how to knit. Mother was the youngest knitter in Humphrey township. Her busy needles turned out gloves, vests, sweaters, inner helmet warmers, and scarves for American soldiers fighting in Europe.

After high school, mother followed her duty and stayed home for three years, learning how to maintain a household and working the farm with her father, who had only one son to help him. Later, in 1925 and 1926, she had what was a rare opportunity in those days. She went away to school in Philadelphia to attend the Coombs Conservatory of Music and take drama classes at the University of Pennsylvania. In the fall of 1926, she moved to the University of Nebraska. On June 2, 1927, she had two final examinations, one in the morning and another in the afternoon. Right after she'd finished her last exam, she married my father at the rectory of St. Joseph's Church in Lincoln, Nebraska. Duty first, loves second.

We kids understood that we also had to work. This ethic began with household chores and expanded as we grew older. The girls picked up greater responsibilities in the domestic arena while the boys managed the yard and livestock. We helped Father by unloading Purina feed from railroad cars, stacking it in his warehouse, and later delivering it to farmers. We planted trees for wind breaks for farmers, and two of my brothers had paper routes. One year, Father obtained employment for me de-tasseling corn for seed companies, and another year I worked with a wheat thrashing crew. Embedded in every activity was the message that work was a necessary part of life. It was so ingrained that none of us expected anything different.

I was dutiful by nature and so the emphasis on duty in the home, and later in the Church, wasn't foreign to me. I had no reason to recognize, let alone reject something so congruent with my personality. I couldn't have articulated then what I felt, but I was aware of the stability this communal approach to duty created. I eventually saw, though, that by assuming duty blindly, without evaluating whether or not a duty was appropriate, or took more from me than it brought, I unwittingly sacrificed a life guided by intuition.

Routine

If duty was the backbone of my family's culture, routine was the musculature. It is organization's best friend, for what is done by habit or system takes less energy and less time. With so many people in our home, Mother relied heavily on routine to keep things running smoothly to meet everyone's basic needs. Meals occurred at the same time each day, and Mother did most of the cooking. She also did the sewing and laundry, which in so large a household had to be done on a regular schedule to keep from being overwhelmed.

My brothers and sisters and I were immersed in routines of all sorts, from our school or work schedules and household chores, to our leisure activities. On Wednesdays, the girls changed sheets on all the beds. Even that mundane task had a protocol. First, they took off the top sheet and set it aside. Next, they removed the bottom sheet and threw it in the wash. The top sheet was put on the bottom, and a clean sheet was put on top. On Fridays, the girls cleaned the upstairs rooms. The boys cut the lawn each week and took care of the chickens. Everyone was responsible for putting away their toys and hanging up their own clothes each day.

Weekdays followed a reliable pattern. Each morning before school, we attended Mass. At 3:30, we came home, changed our clothes and had a snack. The children gathered around the radio and listened to our favorite programs, a magical time that resonates in me to this day.

Weekends, too, had a steady and recurrent rhythm. Every Saturday morning, Mother baked crispies and prepared grapefruit for Sunday's breakfast. The next morning, we walked together the short block to the church to attend Mass. After that, we came home to Sunday breakfast and, of course, the funny papers. We ate the main meal of the day, which was special compared to weekdays, promptly at two on Sunday afternoon.

Routine kept the household from descending into chaos. Routine kept stress to a minimum. We all knew what was coming and what was expected of us. For me, however, the family routines had an added bonus—it brought me a special kind of comfort. It generated a feeling of "rightness," of security, of teamwork. I trusted things were going to precede a certain way and in a certain order designed by day, month, year, within the family and at church. I loved the routines in our lives. I always looked forward to the next holiday, the next Sunday breakfast, the next afternoon's radio programs. But that same enjoyment, as pleasant as it was, made me particularly susceptible to the lure of life in the Church, to taking orders, in every sense of the word. What the Church promised me was a life founded on and run by routines at every level, even God's.

Feelings

Duty and routine were necessary parts of a large household in a semi-rural environment, but attached to those ethics like a Siamese twin was also the imperative to avoid intense feelings or emotional conflict. If we children grew tempestuous or angry to the point of tears, we were instantly banished to our rooms until we could regain our composure. Even Mother, as noted before, left the room if she began to cry. The reasoning behind this was not cruelty or disinterest in anyone's well being, but rather that such emotions, if allowed free expression, were perceived as disruptive to everyone. The needs of the group had to supersede those of the individual for the household to keep running smoothly. The belief was clear: thirteen lives couldn't stop on a dime every time someone had an emotional disturbance—it would have been turmoil.

It is easy to see how negative feelings needed to be suppressed for the harmony of the group, but the curious part was that intense positive emotions suffered the same fate. Tender words, phrases of affection, caresses and exuberance weren't encouraged any more than temper. I recall that the infants received lots of hugging and touching, but as we grew older, this pattern gave way to a different style of relating. A behavioral style that, in retrospect appears to have been a form of pseudo-intimacy. Everyone was amiable, but little real sharing occurred.

My brother Bob told me that when he was small, he loved going on walks with our father. He reached high in the air and held on to one of Dad's fingers. One day, he heard these painful words, "Son, I think you are old enough now, you don't need to hold on to me anymore." It was time to let go of "touchy stuff."

In our family, we were treated according to our age, sex and the family needs. The time for letting go of "touchy stuff" was predetermined by the parent, and not dependent on the child's needs or desires. Levels of intimacy were controlled. Intimacy permitted in our family was manifested by joking. Real intimacy was replaced with teasing that relied on personal details for its punch, rather than any kind of demonstrativeness or sensitive exchange. For me, this engendered an enormous sense of isolation.

Though the family changed a great deal over the years, initially a prohibition existed against using the phrase "I love you." My parents never said it to us children, nor to my knowledge, to one another. When my brother Bob was in his twenties and living away from home, he phoned Mother almost every week. At the end of the conversation, he always said, "I love you" to my mother. He told me that she was uncomfortable saying, "I love you, too." He persisted, though, and with time this changed. Mother began to say freely and sincerely, "I love you, too." He taught her through his own persistence how to express feelings of love with words.

To School, to School

The sense of safety and security I felt within my family ended when I entered St. Francis Grade School at age six. In our large family, the parts fit together so seamlessly, that my primary understanding of myself was as a member of that group—that is, it and I were one. By contrast, at school, for the first time in my life, I encountered people who, it seemed to me, did not have the same interest in my well-being as did my family members.

I did not read and write like others in the class. We were all, to some degree, equally blank slates at the beginning, but as months passed, I did not progress as others did. Typically, my classmates and I took turns reading out loud. This turned into an agony for me. I no sooner started, when giggles spread across the class.

When I read a sentence, I gave it the correct meaning, but used different words. For example, a text that read: The big cat chased the little mouse. I read instead as: The huge cat ran after the small mouse. The teacher sensed something wasn't quite right, and double checked her own text to see if she had misread it. Some of the other children, having their own texts in front of them, invariably broke out laughing. I interpreted their laughter as a form of disapproval. An unfamiliar sense of shame crept up my spine and darkened my cheeks. I had done something wrong, but I didn't know what or why. This sensation quickly became familiar.

Today there is a term for the problem I had, and modern education has developed a protocol for teaching children with dyslexia to read. But then, patience and discipline were the only tools available to me. Order and discipline were a natural part of me, as was my need to please, so I willingly did my homework. My elder sisters and mother helped me as I struggled, particularly with spelling, which was a nightmare for me. Over the summers, I had a tutor whose unenviable job was to bring me up to grade level.

What torture this was. How acute the humiliation. Like the ugly duckling in the Hans Christian Andersen story, I couldn't help but interpret my difference from others as a lack in myself. I couldn't escape the fact that I was in some way a failure. This bitter truth wrapped me in a cocoon of fine thread and filled me with dread and a pulsing fear of rejection. For decades, whenever I looked back on those first three years at St. Francis Grade School, all I could see was a thick blanket of impenetrable darkness.

The Church's underlying message that we are all sinners fueled my shame, and added another wall to the artificial structure that trapped me in a perpetual state of inadequacy and set in motion a critical dynamic: the more inadequate I felt, the more power the Church's teaching had over me.

I later learned that I am an image learner, not a word learner. When I began to discover and honor my own approach, the intense guilt and anxiety that had always attended learning diminished somewhat. The process became more natural, something that happened without terrible struggle.

I acknowledge that my response to the stress, and to the laughter of the other children, was totally subjective. It was my response that turned it into a traumatic experience. In a curious irony, that I could not read like other children triggered my destiny. When combined with my profound need to please, my Catholic adherence to authority and my family culture of conformity, my learning disability drove me to work harder to please others, be good, accommodate, never rock the boat, and avoid feelings—especially fear and anger. It provoked the desire to become noble, good and honorable—completely above reproach or rejection. Salvation, I already knew, lay in hard work.

I awoke one wintry morning when I was eight and made a decision that informed much of my life. I got out of bed and padded to the window. A layer of ice crusted the glass and I scratched away some of it and peered out. The sun was rising, and the first rays cast long shadows on an immaculate blanket of snow. A few flakes fell in half-hearted fashion to the ground, and the world was still and silent under the soft contours of the fresh snowfall. As I sat marveling at the new day and the cold, white world in front of me, I said to myself, "I'm going to be a good boy and shovel the sidewalk. I will work so hard that someday they will make me pope."

Catholicism defined my every experience. Nothing existed outside of it in Humphrey. Everywhere I went in my little world, my desire rested comfortingly in the future, that place in time when I would be heroic, saintly. The Pope was the symbol of this goodness toward which I embarked. Because this eventuality was off in the vague future, I was not concerned with when or how it would come about. It would happen "someday." This kept me from living in the present or becoming enmeshed in the inadequacy, shame, and guilt associated with school.

Aside from St. Francis Grade School, our parish had its own Catholic high school, which I attended in my freshman year. After school was through for the week, we were all expected to attend a church service Friday afternoons called the Sorrowful Mother Devotion. In fourth grade, the boys became servers for church celebrations, incorporating us further into the culture of Catholicism.

This was also reinforced at home, where Catholic practices impregnated many of our routines, though not always in so dogmatic a fashion. A few times during Advent, Mother attempted to pray the rosary with all her children before we went to bed. It never worked for more than a week because laughter usually broke out and triumphed over the intent. At least once, she placed holy water at the entrance to the bedrooms. That stopped, though, when we children began flicking the water in each other's faces. During Lent we were expected to give up candy. That also fell by the wayside, probably succumbing to the impossibility of such a fierce denial in a household with eleven children. Instead, we were encouraged to say more prayers for the needy and to visit the church.

The practices that did stick were: praying together before every meal and at night before bedtime, eating no meat on Fridays; and regular visits to our home by the parish priest, who checked in with us at least two or three times during the week. Thus, was our deep connection with the Church.

As children, we don't always recognize contradictions in ourselves or in our environment. I was aware when I started school, and I became more aware with further formal indoctrination into the culture of the Church, that I was a sinner capable of mortal sin. That sin, the Church told me, would exclude me from heaven, which was clearly a desirable place to be, particularly for a "joiner and a pleaser" like myself. To prevent my exclusion from heaven, I had to say the proper prayers, have the proper behavior and do the proper good works. I accepted that totally. I was driven to be "good." I moved with vigor toward what my world defined as the criteria for goodness: I had to become like the parish priests.

Modeling myself after parish priests had the added bonus of satisfying my mother, with whom I had a strong attachment. Dedicating one's life to the Church was a deep part of her family tradition; I had a number of first cousins who were religious, that is, men and women who joined religious orders.

When the Franciscan missionaries came to the parish to lead a parish retreat, we gathered in the pews to listen to them talk about their lives. In the hierarchy of our world, these men were akin to bold knights of the Round Table—they fought the good fight against evil and heathenism, upholding the faith wherever they went. I hung on their every word.

"It is said," one told us, "that mothers who have a son who joins a religious order or becomes a priest, or a daughter who becomes a nun, are guaranteed a ticket into heaven." When I heard that, I determined with youthful ferocity that I would do that, and so merit a place in God's kingdom for my mother. I felt honor-bound to ensure her salvation.

Another subtle reinforcement occurred a few months after the missionaries visited us. The pastor of the parish came to speak to our third grade class. He looked around the rooms and asked, "Who among you wants to be a friar, nun or priest?" My hand shot up. *That's me*, I thought with pride. *That's what I'm going to do!* The pastor's eyes met mine, and therein I saw something I was hungry for and didn't often find in the classroom—approval.

Besides ushering me to a seat in the priesthood, my Catholic education influenced me in other areas. Catholicism is a rich and overwhelming culture that extends backwards in history for centuries. Over those centuries, it has become adept at seeking out and plugging every nook and cranny in a person's pantheon of needs with a decree or requirement. As happened with L28 and his companions in the fable, the Church tells one what to think and do. It is understood that there is no aspect of a person's life that does not come under its purview and authority. This creates both a sense of security in the individual and an equally strong sense of God's, and by extrapolation, the Church's omnipotence.

Often, chief handmaidens of religion are guilt and its cousins, fear and sin. In my Catholic education in the 1940s, I learned Adam and Eve's disobedience caused all subsequent evil in the world. Their behavior closed heaven to humankind. If that weren't bad enough, to appease the heavenly Father's anger and reopen heaven to humans required a ransom fee. Jesus, "His only begotten son," paid this debt with a bloody, painful sacrifice, making heaven once again accessible to all of us. But that, it turned out, wasn't quite enough. We still did not automatically go to heaven. So, how *did* we get there?

According to the Church, we could enter those celestial gates only by saying the right prayers, receiving the proper sacraments, and performing good works as established by the Church. The straightforwardness of that appealed to me. I liked a well-defined path, and this was nothing if not well-defined. It never occurred to me to question the path. The Church insured against that by stressing acceptance as a primary ingredient for being a good Catholic.

The Church taught that sin was the act of doing bad things. And naturally, the Church, through its proprietary access to God, defined what constituted "bad." The effect of sin, we were told, separated us from the divine. There were the small sins, called venial; there were the really big, bad ones called mortal. Thoughts, desires and acts of a sexual nature were sinful and reflected one's depraved nature. For any venial sins I might commit, God would punish me with purgatory. For the mortal sins, I would end up in the eternal fires of hell. Only a fool would want to go there. The Church also made it clear, at the same time, that I was blessed. Our merciful God gave us the sacraments, especially penance.

With my obedient nature and attraction to rituals and tradition, I embraced that doctrine. My temperament and the thickness of the Church's influence seduced me into accommodating its moral code. I became more and more absorbed by it and was, conversely, less and less open to my own inner voice. Even as I reached for further participation, I grew more alienated from real, heartfelt inspiration, and became more a victim of my German-Catholic conditioning.

I knew how to be good. I could see a path not only to acceptance, but to salvation—which I understood as the whole point to life. I embraced it with eagerness and dedication. I became an altar boy. Since I lived so close to the church, the priests frequently called upon me to help out. With great pride and satisfaction, I cleaned the church when needed or prepared flowers for the altars. To increase deposits in my heavenly savings account, I attended many extra religious services during the summer months, such as the Sorrowful Mother Devotion on Friday evenings. I sang from the depths of my heart so often that I remember to this day the refrain of one of the songs:

> *Mother Dear, oh, pray for me,*
> *Whilst far from heaven and thee,*
> *I wander in a fragile bark,*
> *Over life's tempestuous sea.*

The song reflected the heavy emotions of inadequacy, of not measuring up. Mother Mary seemed a sympathetic ally, and the words urged me to reach out to this heavenly being. I was comforted by the compassion she had for my suffering despite my unworthiness. This devotion, as with other Catholic practices, registers with the universal human condition of presupposed separation and emotional pain, and therein lies our susceptibility to it. What relief and comfort this brought to a sinner like me.

From the catechism I learned: "We came here to know, love and serve God, and thereby gain heaven." The teaching was explicit. That made my goal equally so. I understood the duty inherent in the instruction. I was willing to make whatever sacrifice was necessary to avoid sin. My familial culture prepared me for this, and I assimilated Catholic doctrine as only a sensitive, impressionable and dreamy boy could. I felt I understood it, that it was somehow written just for me— a powerful elixir by itself. Church teachings gave me something to aim for: becoming a self-sacrificing friar and dedicated priest.

Anger was a sin in the eyes of the Church as much as it was discouraged in the home. Because I was committed to being good, I didn't express it. Paradoxically, without an awareness of anger, I had little sense of any other emotions either. I had no way to discern what I wanted apart from what others wanted of me. I lived outside of myself.

The 1998 movie *Pleasantville* depicts the world I entered in late childhood and remained in for much of my adult life—one that used routine and duty to compensate for a sense of inadequacy. The story is of two teens trapped in a circa 1950s town where there are no thunderstorms, fires, lost basketball games, deaths, or signs of aggression, hate or anger. Everything is, well, pleasant. To represent this monotonous atmosphere, the movie is filmed in black and white. Pleasantville has no colorful birds, blue skies, green grasses, red roses or passionate kisses. Everyone knows and follows the rules for living, and enjoy the approving smiles from the residents of Pleasantville. Then, something out of the ordinary occurs only when the two teens begin behaving in ways that violate Pleasantville's rules and customs. And in doing so, they begin to see color everywhere. By the end of the movie, their passion has spread, awakening everyone in town. They all can see life in bright colors and begin to feel joy and follow their dreams.

If youth's task is to assimilate tribal values and follow the lifestyle of the community, I deserved high marks. The busy and industrious atmosphere in the Leenerts home, and later in the minor seminary, where I attended some high school and the first two years of college, masked my growing feelings of alienation. And the Church culture reinforced in subtle ways my gnawing sense of inadequacy. Keeping busy with physical and intellectual activities suited me well and dimmed these feelings. I mistook busyness for enjoyment and saw it as a sign that I was where I belonged. Gradually, however, as I became more dedicated to pleasing others and reaching arbitrary goals, I grew more and more disconnected from my intuitive self. Those things that formed the foundation and walls of my past—the need to conform, love of routine, sense of duty, obedience to community—automatically kept me focused on the future and out of the present moment, the Now.

Years later, with the advantage of layers and years of perspective, I saw the first twenty years of my life unfolded with little conscious participation, without true choice. Like L28 and the other laborers of Circle 41, my life course was set before I ever whimpered a sound or spoke a word. And like L28 and his co-workers, I never questioned it. I blindly accepted a specified description of the world around me without ever looking to see if any of it was false, or at the very least, not quite true.

With that acceptance, the walls around me began to solidify, locking me inside. I lost my capacity for spontaneity, which is the place where real joy can exist. The happy, accepting nature of my childhood faded. My world changed from color to black-and-white, and I barely noticed in my preoccupation with achieving and proving, proving and achieving.

As I looked to authority for definition and approval, I separated even more from my feelings. I had to do this to avoid internal conflict. I maximized my ability to stifle emotions, thinking that would make my environment gentle and safe. Disconnected from my feelings, I had no alternative to, or defense against, the conditioning of the seminary.

In the years that followed, the pattern of stifling my emotions continued. If I became aware of any discomfort, my only thought was to do what I was already doing, only more so, which only served to intensify the walls around me. It was to be years down the road before I managed to live in color again.

... the neurotic process is a problem of the self.
It is a process of abandoning the
real self for an idealized one.

~Karen Horney

Roof

It is clear that my rural Nebraska, German-Catholic conditioning and personality orientation were firmly implanted by the time I was sixteen. As a direct consequence of my decision to become a noble, Franciscan priest, I would go to minor seminary, which involved high school and the first two years of college, then to the novitiate, on to the major seminaries of philosophy and theology, and finally to life in Brazil as a missionary. I felt compelled to pursue this path. In time, I came to see how Spirit used all of this to awaken me and allow my conditioning to be undone.

The Minor Seminary

At sixteen, I entered St. Joseph, a Franciscan minor seminary in Westmount, Illinois, as a high school sophomore. St. Joseph was a boarding school, and I came back home for two weeks at Christmas season and three months during the summer.

I was away from my home and family for the first time in my life. Even though they were the center of my universe until then, I did not have strong homesick feelings for my parents or siblings. Studies consumed my attention through three years of high school and two years of college as I prepared to enter the Franciscan order and priestly ordination.

Seminary life was like my home life, close living with many people, the same rituals and the same overriding faith. I enjoyed the hard work and discipline in the classrooms, study halls, dormitories and chapel. The

Church knew well enough to keep seminarians as busy as possible. I studied English, Latin, Greek and German, and had classes in music appreciation, choir, band, public speaking and drama. In addition to scholastic pursuits, there were organized sports, including baseball, basketball, touch football, bowling and tennis. Study, prayer, play and work punctuated each day in a pleasant routine.

As soothing as the routine was, the environment provided plenty of intellectual stimulation as well, with many educational and culturally enriching activities. I felt blessed to be a part of it.

Novitiate: The Franciscan Family

After minor seminary, I entered the Franciscan Novitiate in Teutopolis, Illinois. Entering a religious order is, in many ways, similar to entering the armed services or any organization where the intent is to remold you into a functioning unit of that organization. The old you is discarded and a new you is created, custom-tailored to fit the organization's needs, complete with look, language and a firm position within a well-defined hierarchy.

The first step of training in the religious family is to mark each transition in a way that leaves no doubt that things have changed. At the novitiate, again as in the armed services, a profound physical change initiates the process. Every Franciscan aspirant was given a hair cut and a uniform, the plain brown robe with white corded belt that identifies Franciscans. The brothers then assigned new names by which the aspirants were hence forth known. The name bestowed upon me was Leigh, to which I answered for the next eight years.

In spite of the clear demarcation between secular and ecclesiastical life, I don't recall any sense of loss in leaving home, family or self behind. I was so focused on achieving status, so conditioned to rely on routine for comfort that my thoughts simply did not drift back to my rural Nebraska home or the twelve people there. I was so sure of life, and so confident that the best path through it lay in ecclesiastical study.

I loved routine and simplicity, and the novitiate provided it in double-handfuls. The religious culture permeated every waking moment. The day started at 12:05 a.m., when the brothers assembled in the chapel to chant the Divine Office in Latin (a collection of hymns, psalms, lessons and readings) and meditate for thirty minutes. After the meditation we returned to our rooms to sleep. At 6 a.m., the brothers were summoned from bed a second time. Even the act of waking up novices was done with a specific ritual. The one assigned to wake up the others knocked on each cell door and called out, "Ave Maria" (Hail, Mary). The novice in bed had to put his feet on the floor and respond, "Gratia plena" (full of grace). By 6:15 a.m., we gathered in the chapel (where each friar had his own prayer stall) for morning prayers, Divine Office, and Mass.

I can't describe how intoxicating it felt to witness the order in this world where everything had a place. I know nothing in today's world that quite compares to that delicious sense of knowing where you belonged, and what it was you were to do with your life. At the same time, it was highly constricting to believe the world was so rigid. I had a place, albeit one founded on satisfying my own insecurities. Feeling that I was where I should be was a rich human experience, especially since I felt so inadequate. I saw how precise religious life was, how it flowed in certainty from one action to the next, and back to the central core of worship. I took this certainty as confirmation of my path.

At 11 a.m., we walked the novitiates' garden paths reciting prayers and psalms to the Blessed Virgin. At 11:45 a.m., we returned to the choir and again chanted the Divine Office. We had lunch at noon. After lunch, we went to the chapel for a "particular examination of conscience." This was a fifteen minute, individual review of the past twenty-four hours to ascertain if we had experienced any anger, bad thoughts, and distractions or had not stayed focused in prayer. At 4 p.m., we returned to the choir to chant the Divine Office again and meditate for thirty minutes.

There were four classes each day: two on the Rule of St. Francis, one music class and a class on the English translation of the Divine Office. Kitchen, gardening and cleaning duties, or reading and study filled any gaps in our days. Each evening at 8:30, we gathered in the classroom for a lecture on spirituality read by the master of novices. Promptly at 9:30, we retired to bed. We took daily meals in the friar's refectory at 7 a.m., noon, and 6 p.m. and we were not allowed to converse while we ate. Instead, one of the friars read aloud to us from a religious text. We were permitted to speak to one another for one hour each day, between 1 and 2 p.m., except during times of special penance, such as Lent or Advent, when we observed total silence.

We slept in cells furnished with a simple bed, desk and chair. On the wall in each novice's cell hung a discipline cord. It was a light whip made of four or five strands of cords with knots tied to the loose ends. After supper on every Monday, Wednesday and Friday that did not precede a first or second-class feast day, the novice master recited prescribed psalms out loud.

While he did so, we heard him in our cells and were encouraged to take up the "discipline cords" and beat ourselves in accordance with our individual spirit of sacrifice. This was a wonderful opportunity, we were told, to lessen our time in purgatory by days, or even years, if our vigor was sufficient.

I wondered as I saw how this culture of perpetual unworthiness mixed and married with my own acquired sense of inadequacy. It was so precise, so efficient a tool, and was so effective at tying me even closer to the shelter of the Church's arms through my gratitude at being loved in spite of my weakness and sinful nature.

In retrospect, I know I chose this thought system out of a sense of fear and inadequacy. It was an exquisite learning experience, one I have only grasped after decades of reflection. From my experience being absorbed in those teachings and that way of life, I came to understand more clearly a universal spirituality that has nothing to do with organized representations. But I also see that I needed to submerge myself in that thought system, before I could break free of it.

In novitiate, the days may have been heavily circumscribed, but the surroundings were beautiful and spacious. We had a large, walled-in space with a tennis court, vegetable garden, and numerous shade and fruit trees. We harvested thirty-five bushels of peaches and 180 bushels of apples the year I was there. While we had assigned duties, there was also some room for creativity. Once, when a large, old tree fell over, another novice and I took on the project of making a bench from its wood. We drew up plans and built it, using only dove-and-tail and wedges. It was the custom for Franciscans to make their own rosaries, which we did during the last six months at the novitiate. Whatever the intended significance of making my own rosary might have been, it was not important to me. What was enjoyable was the craft work. Just like making the wooden bench, this task allowed me to do something concrete with my time in contrast to abstract religious studies.

After we finished our twelve month training, my classmates and I took three-year vows of poverty, chastity and obedience. With these vows, I pledged to stay on my predetermined path and committed myself to the values and spirit of St. Francis. I had become a Franciscan friar, and had the brown habit, the white cord with three knots on one end (one for each of the vows we had taken), and the attached large rosary.

In the early 1990s, I told my mother I was writing the story of my life. Unbeknownst to me, she had saved every letter I sent her from novitiate. Hoping the letters would assist me in writing, she gave them to me.

Reading those letters, I scarcely recognized the boy who wrote them. It saddened and embarrassed me. My words were empty. It was obvious to me that I had performed rituals and routines like a trained seal. Those rituals kept me deeply asleep to the spirit within. I was not fully alive. In my defensive stance and naiveté, I had willingly taken on austerity and denial in place of simplicity and joy. I gave up my birth right, my sense of innate peace and happiness, for a bowl of cold porridge. I had defined what I was, and this was a primary block in knowing who I was—and am.

That life so easily drew me in. Everything reinforced its containment, from my love of routine and ego-driven sense of spirituality, to the Church's influence in my life; from my desire to please, to my need to achieve.

Philosophy and Theology

After novitiate, I traveled to Our Lady of Angels Seminary in Cleveland, Ohio, for three years of philosophy. All the students were Franciscan clerics studying for the priesthood. In addition to philosophy, we attended classes in education and the hard sciences. A number of active sports rounded out the curriculum. As clerics, we again recited the Divine Office as we had done in novitiate, but we no longer had to attend midnight choir.

The students around me were intellectually bright young men dedicated to high ideals. We were embarked on a life of high service, and equally mesmerized with a romantic vision of ourselves as specially chosen for God's work. Many of the students had talent in music and drama. I have fond memories of staging Gilbert and Sullivan's productions. One year we performed *The Mikado*. I took the role of the Mikado. At six-foot-six inches tall, I delighted in strutting about the stage and bellowing, "A more humane Mikado never did in Japan exist, to nobody second, I'm certainly reckoned a true philanthropist." Simple pleasures, to be sure, but my memories of these events remain fond ones, and those simple pleasures contributed to the feeling of belonging.

The question of my sexuality, and any accompanying attitudes and morals, surfaced continually. I was, after all, a healthy young man. As was my habit, however, I sublimated such thoughts and related desires to conform to Church standards. That, too, was part of being "good." I learned to block that part of my life in exchange for perceived security and approval by the community. It seemed a prudent and profitable action, for by doing so, all my needs for food, shelter, companionship and even health insurance were generously provided. I was as deeply immersed in the Catholic culture as one could be, so it was easy to convince myself to accept and follow those directions. I still thought it was my idea, and I took it up willingly.

At the end of three years of philosophy, at age twenty-three, I took my perpetual vows. After that, my focus was on completing theological courses, which meant a return to Teutopolis, to the Franciscan Theology House for four more years of rigorous theological study, including dogmatic theology, systematic theology, moral theology, sacred eloquence (the art of preaching), biblical studies, Church history and canon law (codified church laws).

Every once in a while, a question arose in me about what I had done and planned to do, just a shimmer of doubt about whether I was on the right or wrong path. But I had been taught to view my inner voice as a whisper of temptation from a realm outside truth, rather than a source of truth itself. I had been equally trained to run away from such temptation, and so I did. What a remarkable system I chose. By identifying freedom from all conditioning as the enemy, I created the strongest defense possible to remain under my own religious programming. Any and every attempt the inner voice for freedom made to break free was instantly diagnosed as evil and promptly exorcized.

I hid from myself by staying fixed on another aspect of my life goal, and that was to do missionary work. I was drawn to being heroic, and the work of missionaries fit this ideal, particularly since the only missions the Franciscans, with whom I was associated, had were in the jungles of the Amazon River in Brazil. In my second year of theology, Franciscan officials notified me that I was to be sent there after ordination. I recall feeling particularly inflated by this news, for it meant I was accomplishing what I had set out to do.

In preparation, I began to learn carpentry, electrical wiring and welding, all skills that would be of use in a poor and underdeveloped population in the Amazon Valley of Northern Brazil. At times these skills related to survival, and at other times I would be able to use them to help the local people build schools and churches.

In December of 1959, I was ordained as a deacon. Six months later I was ordained as a Roman Catholic priest. I celebrated my first Mass that month in the parish of my birth in Humphrey, Nebraska. I had worked hard and given thirteen years of my life in preparation for that moment. Yet, I remember a moment during the deaconate and sacerdotal ordinations ceremonies when something in me broke free to the surface, and I asked myself, "What am I doing here?" But I had been so long in the culture by then, that I ignored my own inquiring voice. I was twenty-eight years old, and by then had twenty-two years of Catholic education: nine years at Saint Francis Grade School in Humphrey, five years at St. Joseph Seminary, one year of novitiate, three years of religious philosophy, and four years of theology. I had assimilated a vast amount of information, all of it designed to turn me into a well-organized cog in the giant wheel of Catholicism. I had learned well the culture of responsibility from my parents, and in my mind at the time, I had no choice but to carry on with my commitments if I wanted to follow God's will for me.

On an intellectual level, I believed my education represented truth, the right path to a meaningful life, and literally to salvation. The Church was, after all, the source of infallibility and correct morality. I was so invested in it and it in me, that I confessed to no small sense of pride in my path and achievements. I had abandoned the real self for my idealized one. It had been difficult, yes, but I had done it. This filled me with a dangerous sense of confidence. I was exactly where I had planned to be, and actually thought it was my own doing, my own abilities, that had brought me to that happy confluence, rather than the larger desire of the Church to lead me there. I thought I was safe in the arms of God. Such distorted thoughts generally invite the world to balance them, and such was the role that beautiful and mysterious Brazil played in my life.

We do not succeed in changing our desire,
but gradually our desire changes.

~Proust

Windows

Brazil. Beautiful, mysterious, sensual Brazil. I could not have picked a place more opposite to the world where I grew up. Where my world was quiet and orderly, Brazil was noisy and chaotic. Where my culture pivoted on the reassuring qualities of reason and logic, Brazil was whimsical, passionate, and one of the most intuitive cultures in the world. Where I had lived most of my life apart from the daily lives and struggles of others, Brazil immersed me in the lives of others in every conceivable way: from the high infant mortality rate, to the subhuman living conditions that lacked even the most basic nutritional and hygiene resources. The poor, who made up the majority of the population in northern Brazil, lived in appalling poverty.

In August of 1961, my arrival in Brazil was the fulfillment of a dream, the consequences of methodical planning on my part. I stepped off the plane in Belém into air hot and heavy with moisture. It seemed too thick to breathe without drowning. I looked around at palm trees, graceful colonial homes and the many shades of people. I was not in Nebraska anymore.

The name I had been assigned upon entering novitiate could not be translated into Portuguese. My given name of Thomas could not be used because another Brother Thomas already lived in the Franciscan community. After some deliberation, my confirmation name, Lawrence, won the honor, and I became Frei Lourenço— Portuguese for Father Lawrence. For the second time in my life, I adopted a superficial shift in identity. This was only the beginning.

Part of settling in included learning Portuguese. The national language of Brazil, though other languages were also spoken there, particularly among the tribes in the interior. The next class, however, was not scheduled to start for another two months. In the interim, the Order sent me five hundred miles up the Amazon River to Santarem. This city was the seat of the Catholic diocese with the largest territory in the world, and it sat, steeped in poverty, in the midst of the jungle.

It is hard to describe the impact this area had on me. There was impossibly dense vegetation, exotic sounds and smells that hammered at my senses, and in the thick underbrush, poisonous and dangerous creatures posed lethal threats. But the people themselves...how can I describe the contours of this level of poverty? I have never known anything that quite compares to it. In the slums, or *favelas*, sanitation didn't exist. The homes were little more than shacks.

I had been immersed for thirteen years in an intellectual environment that had been sanitized of all that was dirty, dangerous or unclean. My chosen lifestyle had alienated me even from my own culture, let alone the squalid world in which I found myself in Santarem. This place sent my senses reeling with excitement and overwhelming surprise. These people *lived*...on the keen edge between life and death.

I stayed in Santarem for two months, entering the *esprit de corps* of the friars, who, as a group, where fun-loving and high-spirited men with a sense of independence and practicality. I spoke as much as possible with Brazilian children as I walked all over the city and waterfront, assimilating whatever I could. Still, I was impatient; I could not wait for the language school to open. Finally, I flew to Annapolis, near Brasilia, the capital of Brazil, to enroll. I spent the next three months undergoing intensive language and cultural training.

Linguists well understand how a language can shape a person's psyche. I experienced that first-hand. When I learned to speak Portuguese, my whole manner of expression changed. English is a linear language, each thought growing out of another to express intellectual function. Portuguese, on the other hand, seemed all about expressing feelings and making an emotional impact. For the first time in my life, I not only had a forum for my emotions, but I had to rely on a language that insisted I express them. I began to use gestures when I spoke.

From the very first, Brazil gave me a new name, new language and new culture, and even then, she was not done with me yet. The next breach in the walls of my conditioning came in the form of the director of the language school, Monsignor Ivan Illich. Much to my good fortune, Illich did not reinforce the ecclesiastical party line. He was provocative and passionate, and forced me to go within and question my motivation for becoming a missionary—something I had never done before, and certainly had never been asked to do.

A brilliant man of great compassion, the Monsignor saw culture as a living organism, deserving of the same fundamental respect or rights as any life. He felt that the identities of all people, and especially the poor of Latin America, were rooted in their culture, which had existed for many generations. These cultural identities were bound up with and included all spheres and elements of life: work, fire, air, water, religion, food, music, death, sex and family. All these elements combined form a flavor that differentiates a Russian, who bakes in the summer and freezes in the winter, from a Polynesian who breathes the sea every day.

We foreign missionaries came to Brazil with a diametrically different cultural background, one rooted in intellectualism. Ours was a rational, logical approach to life, marked by authoritarianism and a strong sense of independence. Brazil's culture, by comparison, was rooted in feelings, intuition, spiritualism, egalitarianism among the masses, and a sense of predestination or fatalism. The way the people expressed themselves in their popular religious celebrations with music and dance contrasted with the traditional religious ceremonies I had known since childhood. For example, the following common expressions developed from the way the people experienced their lives: "It's God's will." (*É a vontade de Deus.*); "That's my destiny." (*É meu destino.*); "Yes, if God so wills." (*Si Deus quiser.*)

Illich believed that foreign missionaries could unintentionally cause great turmoil by uprooting the Brazilian people from their culture, their identities, their sense of self. Missionaries might create more problems than they solved from a faith perspective. This was a radical viewpoint, for it considered the effects of our missionary work within a larger, cultural framework. I immediately understood that his perspective was beyond Church dogma and religious practices. I believe, in hindsight, that through my association with Illich, my ecclesiastic orientation softened, and I started to grow more broad-minded in my thinking.

In dialogues with Illich, both in the classroom and in our off hours over the course of three months, I began to question who I was, and what I was doing in Brazil. It was not that I did not belong there, rather, I began to see that my assumptions for being there were wrong. Illich stretched the walls of my understanding and opened a new aperture through which I could view the world. The simple act of learning to question assumptions—so long discouraged in my formative years—eventually became so much a part of me, that it influenced my decision to become a psychologist after I left the Church.

Once I began to question myself, challenging and tracing every thought to its source, it was only a small step to apply the same process to everything I encountered. This is the demarcation between sleeping and waking. Life changed dramatically. I discovered places and conditions I could no longer endure within my new understanding. My debt to Monsignor Illich runs deep.

His influence on my life did not end there, however. He also introduced me to the pedagogy of Brazil's world-renowned educator, Paulo Freire, who has had a great impact on political and educational thought both in his own country and abroad. His book, *Pedagogia dos Oprimidos (Pedagogy of the Oppressed)*, has been translated into more than two dozen languages. His ideas eventually drew the attention of the Brazilian politicians and military who judged him subversive. Freire had been forced to leave the country before I arrived. His educational system was geared toward awakening people to their ultimate power to change the status quo. The ruling politicians and military feared this approach would destabilize the country by inciting uncontrollable uprisings.

In simple terms, Freire believed that every man had within his own experience and culture all the knowledge and ability he needed to understand and transform his world. Freire developed an educational approach to facilitate this process. Education was not the acquisition of facts, but rather a process of discovery through which an individual identifies how society functions and what one can do to change that society. Once this discovery takes place, action follows, and the subsequent reflection on actions and their outcomes.

As a result of Freire's ideas and encouragement, I began to reevaluate the type of education I had accepted during the last twenty-two years. My initial forays into that process yielded insights that were almost incomprehensible. They suggested an arbitrary acculturation process of profound magnitude. My behavior, from my earliest days, had been influenced unremittingly by what met the needs of others, with almost no thought for what met my own needs. That was not to say that those things expected or asked of me were necessarily deleterious. On the contrary, some of the values, as mentioned earlier, were positive ones, both in their application and their effect. But without examining them, I could not have chosen whether or not to access them, much less could I have known how to appropriately apply them.

I had gone to Brazil in arrogance to help people I thought were less fortunate than myself, and found instead that I was the one being transformed—far more than I realized at the time—in the deepest levels of my being. The key, in hindsight, was my willingness to allow myself to question what I had presumed to be the truth.

After completing the language and cultural course, I returned to Santarem. From there, the Order sent me to the parish in Belterra. A former rubber plantation built by the Ford Motor Company, Belterra had been turned over to the Brazilian government to run when the Americans no longer had an interest in South American rubber.

Compared to Santarem, Belterra was sparsely populated with a well-organized parish. There was a grade school and a high school, and three chapels to attend to. All were within four miles of the main parish church. I spent several months there perfecting my Portuguese and learning how to run a parish in accord with local traditions and culture. Although Catholic, this area had more feast days in honor of the Blessed Mother and the Sacred Heart of Jesus than I was accustomed to celebrating. And each celebration included long processions that had to be organized.

At the end of my first year in Brazil, the diocese appointed me pastor to the parish in Boim, a town 100 miles up from Santarem on the Tapajos River, the largest tributary of the Amazon, with a width of about three miles. Besides the main parish, nine river villages or communities were scattered up and down both sides of the river. My duties included regular visits to each chapel and work with the village catechists. We discussed many areas of their lives, including health, nutrition and schooling.

In many villages, one family became the natural leader of a group of twenty-five to forty-five families. That family gathered feedback from the community and informed me who would be the catechist. He or she was an unpaid volunteer. Responsible catechists governed each of the individual chapels and kept them clean. They also conducted Sunday services and prepared children for first communion. They were usually persons of high moral standard in the Church's eyes and held in respect by their community. When approved by the local pastor, catechists received training in teaching religion and in conducting prayer services.

These river-jungle villages had no roads, only the river. The only means of transportation was by boat. There were no bicycles, nor did they have electricity. Everywhere I went—up, down and across the river—I traveled in an eighteen-foot aluminum boat powered by an eighteen-horsepower Evenrude motor. It took 30-35 minutes to cross the river. Because this area was on the equator, the climate was hot and humid. Happily, I acclimatized to it rapidly; and my skin became as dark as that of the local people.

The work in the parish was relatively easy because the priests who came before me had organized things well. As the parish priest, I visited the isolated river communities about once every seven weeks.

During previous decade, the Franciscans had provided a school and teacher for each community or village, so the majority of the younger adults were at least semi-literate. The teachers taught up to the third grade. In time, municipalities assumed responsibility for the schools and began to pay teachers. With this, the teachers' lives changed little. Since the municipalities were poor, teachers were likely to be paid in a less timely manner than they had been under the Church's administration.

The people in the area made their living primarily by hunting, fishing and farming. Most families did all three. Sometimes small groups of six or eight came together to perform activities. For farming, they cleared a small area in the forest and cultivated the same plants their ancestors had for hundreds of years before them. In spite of the fertility of the jungle their diets were incomplete, often lacking basic nutrition. It was common to see older teenagers with half their teeth missing.

During the months I lived in Boim, my fascination with how the people lived grew. My interest had neither purpose nor goal. It was akin to my delight with the fireflies of my early childhood years. It simply brought me joy to observe what was. Images of daily life in this community are still strong in my mind to this day.

The homes, for instance, were as eloquent as the people's lives and relationships. In the more isolated villages along the riverbanks, a typical home was 20 by 20 feet. The frame of the house was made with saplings four or five inches thick, and had openings for a front and back door, and windows on all sides except the back. The walls, doors, windows and roof were woven from a specific type of long palm leaves, which were attached to wooden poles. The back door opened to the kitchen, which was a veranda-like structure with only a roof, and a half wall opposite the back door. A clay stove sat on the half wall. Nearby, the family's pots, pans and tableware were kept on shelves. In addition to a rustic table and four chairs, there was always a large earthen jar for fresh drinking water.

Few in the more isolated villages had beds. Hammocks were practical because they were the coolest way of resting in a hot climate, and they occupied little space during the day. Typically, they hung from metal hooks that screwed into posts about five feet from the floor. Hammocks were one of the products sold by boat merchants; all were of heavy woven cloth and were easily washed and dried in the sun. I always slept in a hammock, and carried my own wherever I went. It was relatively easy to master the art of sleeping in a diagonal manner in the hammock in such a way that the body was always straight and horizontal. The most disturbing aspect was the mosquitoes.

Situations happened frequently that were uniquely interesting and even entertaining because I came from a different culture. On one occasion, the woman who volunteered to prepare my meals served corn— a rare treat for me. When she left the room, I noticed she covered her mouth with her hand. She was laughing. I asked the catechist with me why the woman was laughing. He also began to laugh and told me, "Here, we raise corn only for pigs. But she knows Franciscans like corn, so she prepares some for them when she has it." We both had a hearty laugh as I added, "So, corn is only for pigs and Franciscans."

Another time, four of us sat in a circle, conversing with an elderly woman who smoked a homemade pipe. Curiously, I never saw a man smoking a pipe, but I did see many old women smoking. Someone asked her, "How old is Padre Lourenço?" She looked at me, making her calculations, and said, "He is very, very old because he is very tall and he has very thick glasses." In her world, height and poor eyesight were both elements of age.

I was deeply curious about how the people hunted and fished. A friend, Carlos, showed me how they caught turtles. We bent a quarter-inch, iron reinforcement rod into a three-foot circle and attached a coarsely woven, five-foot deep net to the circle. We secured the circle to the end of a fifteen-foot wooden pole. With this hunting tool in hand, we headed out into a night lit only by a bright moon in an 18 foot aluminum boat. Carlos took me to an island and said, "There is a village of turtles living in the waters off the tip of this island. With the motor running as slow as it will run, go around and around in a twenty-foot circle. You will see what happens."

After several minutes, turtles began to surface, one here, another there. Carlos told me the turtles were curious to see what was happening. When they surfaced, we caught them with our long pole and over-sized basketball net. We kept three large turtles that night, each about thirty inches in width, and put several smaller ones back in the water.

As we returned home, Carlos said, "Many of my friends use a pole that has an iron spear tip attached to one end. A rope is secured to the spear head. My friends slap the water with their boat paddles to attract the turtles. They surface and the hunters strike, penetrating the turtle shell with their spear until the iron head lodges inside the turtle. One of the men then slowly and steadily pulls in the turtle. When it is close, another reaches for the turtle, grabs it, and lifts it into the canoe."

The river-jungle people had no refrigeration, and killed game had to be eaten within twenty-four hours. The advantage of catching turtles was that they could be kept in a fenced-in area near the home and raised in the same way as we might raise pigs, to be killed one at a time as the need arose. Large turtles were valuable bartering items. The boat masters who periodically showed up in the villages offered kerosene, matches, cloth, pots, pans and tools for farming, hunting and fishing in exchange for live turtles.

Every five weeks, I took a break from living alone and returned to community life with the friars in Belterra. I rested for a few days, something I usually needed. I also enjoyed the companionship I found there, and could receive mail and write letters during my stay. It was on one of these trips in June 1964, that I received the sad news that my father had died two weeks before. I wept openly. The loss hurt, of course, but more than that was the awful aching over what might have been, and now could never be. My father was a gentle and gracious man, and I grieved that I had spent so much time away from him. Death can teach us to appreciate our loved ones, but sadly it is too late for those whose death brings the teaching.

It has been said that if you give a hungry man a fish, you feed him for a day, but if you teach him how to fish, you feed him for life. While in Brazil, I had the opportunity to see how this worked in a real situation when I and some fellow friars met a few times a year to organize workshops for catechists and local community leaders. We prepared for the workshops by writing vignettes from Brazilian people's daily experiences. At the end of each example, we asked questions about the stories. We divided the hundred or so catechists who attended the workshops into groups of eight to discuss the vignettes and respond to the questions.

Through these discussions, local leaders learned how to express their ideas, listen to others, lead groups, and analyze the dynamics at play in a situation. Most importantly, they discovered they could define and resolve their own problems. These workshops were Paulo Freire's educational concepts in action. The experience of actually employing them and seeing for myself how they empowered people, was invaluable. I saw how learning could be a process for stimulating collective creativity and affirming people's innate sense of well-being.

As years rolled by, I became more and more dedicated to this form of adult education. At the same time, I grew increasingly discontent with traditional educational processes. By traditional, I mean a method of education wherein the teacher is seen as the one with all the answers, and the pupils are expected to passively take it all in. I realized we teach a great deal through the way we relate to others. For example, if I describe a common problem and then ask the group for their solution, I am sending a message "you are resourceful, your opinion counts." If I rigidly hold on to a more "traditional" teaching role, I also teach, but I convey a different message. If I describe a common problem and tell the group the solution without consideration for individual points of view, I imply to the members of the group that they cannot solve the problem themselves. I am really teaching dependency. Freire's concepts instead taught self-sufficiency and independence.

After working in Brazil for three years, I returned home for a vacation. I divided the time between visiting my family and friends, and preaching on behalf of the missions. When I returned to Brazil, the Order assigned me to the parish of Fortlandia, even farther up the Tapajos River. Like Belterra, Fortlandia had originally been a rubber plantation started by the Ford Motor Company and later turned over to the Brazilian government. This parish, too, had a grade school and high school. In both Boim and Fortlandia, no one else spoke English, and I was immersed in Portuguese and northern Brazilian culture.

People respond to this unique experience in different ways. Sometimes it has the effect of reinforcing one's own culture in more pronounced ways. One becomes more of an American outside of America, or more of a Spaniard outside of Spain. For me, natural joiner that I was, I moved into it, just as I had done some years before in assuming the role of a Catholic cleric. More and more, I became a Brazilian hybrid. I spoke a regional Brazilian Portuguese, had a lot of missing teeth, a dark suntan, and a great Brazilian name.

In some ways, this identity had more power over me than the one with which I had grown up. Perhaps I felt it was more my own, or perhaps it had so much more emotional flavor than the one fostered by the Church, family and community of my birth.

In early 1968, after returning from a three-month vacation to visit family in the States, I received a new assignment to the Franciscans' central friary in Belém, a city of one million, and the capital of the State of Pará. The friary was a lovely, large, old Brazilian-style home that stood next to a well-cared-for municipal park, a *Praça de San João Baptista* (The Park of St. John the Baptist), in a wealthy part of Belém. Franciscans came to the friary to rest, get medical care, and arrange visits to the States or other parts of Brazil. Priests from other countries and congregations were welcome to use the home as a stopover on trips. I served there as a guest master to visitors, facilitating their stays and providing such services as changing U.S. dollars into Brazilian currency or purchasing tools, motor parts and building materials for the friars in the interior. The job certainly differed from my previous work. I loved this way of serving, and I welcomed community living after years of living alone in Boim and Fortlandia.

The position, however, was short lived. By the end of the year, the Order appointed me as the first pastor of a new parish in Belém. *La Paroquia de San Antonio de Lisboa* (The Parish of St. Anthony of Lisboa) contained about 40,000 people within its borders. One-fourth of the parish had at least a middle class income, and the other three-quarters lived in a *favela*, or slum. Again, very little in my experience of the United States compared to the horrific, subhuman living conditions in these slums. The things I saw there held me captive. I dedicated much of my time to the people in the favela.

The parish supported me in this direction and subsequently purchased a little shack in the center of the *favela* to be my home away from the friary. I immediately started working with a Brazilian organization that specialized in building communities in poor neighborhoods. It was funded by local contributions and by the International Oxfund Foundation. I felt at home with the people from that organization because they based their methodology on a further application of Paulo Freire's work. Five Brazilian university students, who were also supported by the Oxfund Foundation, worked with me on this project.

Our work began in the *favela* conversing with residents and developing their trust. We directly or indirectly discovered what they perceived to be their problems. After two or three weeks, we asked those with whom we had conversed to come together to discuss some of the issues they had described. Ten people showed up for the first meeting, and we defined and examined the problems they identified. This process was new to most of them. Though they might have talked about the issues with one another, they had not discussed them as a group. They cited these common conditions: continual stagnant water under their homes, lack of drinking water, poor or no sanitation facilities, no medical resources, illiteracy among most of the young teenagers, and a lack of schools.

Using this type of dialogue, a consensus was reached on what the people considered the most important matters. They asked: "Do we want to meet again? Do we want to invite others? Where and when will we have our next meeting?" The next steps in the process unfolded based on their choices. The five of us who were "outsiders" facilitated the process in the beginning, and we learned much from their experiences and discussions. We could see how action fed empowerment, and empowerment fed action. The cycle was self-perpetuating.

Other questions soon surfaced: "Do we want to do anything about the problem? How? Who? When?" With every question that arose, answers were arrived at in the same way—from within the group. When I left the parish a little more than four years later, three *communidades* de base (grassroots-based communities) flourished in that one *favela*, and each one had its own center. One of the exciting ways this grew was a result of each local group wanting some of their members to begin working with communities in other parts of the city. By doing so, they hoped to form a larger organization in which ideas could be exchanged to promote appropriate action at a different level. Eventually, this came to be.

Contact and friendship with other Brazilian priests led to an invitation to facilitate weekend "reflections" with university students. These retreats offered a forum for open-ended discussions about politics, capitalism, international banking's relationship with the Brazilian economy, Catholic Church history as it related to injustices in Latin American, sexual morality, and God. These sessions exposed me to Brazilian university students who were critical in their thinking and who, in their hearts, wanted a Brazil that granted equality to its people, and was respectful of progress and freedom.

The students often brought musical instruments. Their guitars, drums, singing, and dancing were light, sensual, rhythmic, and joyous. They possessed a spontaneity and warmth far different from what I had experienced at their age. I loved working with these bright, young, university-educated men and women. I formed bonds of friendship with those who participated in these retreats, and I enjoyed a sense of community far more real than any I had previously known.

I returned to the United States for a short vacation in 1970. While there, I took a course in community development in San Francisco. One day in the city, I wandered into a bookstore and purchased a small book. *Think on These Things* by J. Krishnamurti was to have a profound impact on me over the next fifteen years.

I returned to Brazil with this book in hand, and I spent hours reading it in the months that followed. Many ideas in the book touched on aspects of what I knew, somewhere inside me, to be unquestionably true. In one section, Krishnamurti wrote about the desire to become—whether it be a great man, saint or whatever, as the kind of desire that can never be satisfied. It only grows hungrier. That, he explained, is the root cause of constant, senseless searching. I was so taken by his words that I dared not share them with anyone. To share them with friends seemed to contradict most of what I had been taught, and what my friends believed. I was not ready for that kind of confrontation.

Krishnamurti spoke to the deepest part of me. I perceived his message to be that each person is a prisoner of his or her own conditioning. For me, that meant my conditioning as a male, an American, a Catholic and a priest. I saw how my early desire had centered on "becoming" a friar and priest, rather than accepting who I am and living in the present moment, something I had known how to do in childhood. Pursuing my goals brought me acceptance and admiration from the society and culture in which I grew up, which in turn fed my ambition to continue to pursue them. Engaging in this cycle kept me locked out of myself.

While I had discussed the work and philosophies of Ivan Illich and Paulo Freire with many priest friends, I did not share the way Krishnamurti thinking impacted me. What he offered me was beyond sharing. It was revolutionary. Though his words caught my attention in 1970, it was actually many years later when they radically transformed my life.

I admired all three of these men. All three voiced what they knew and felt in their hearts to be universal. They did not follow society's edicts as I had done, but had instead responded to their own callings, meeting specific needs they identified in the world.

Over time, the combination of these influences opened parts of me that had been in hiding. Certain facets of me lost meaning in the face of these new understandings about myself, and life. Administering the sacraments and leading public and religious services were now a distasteful obligation. I wanted to give more of my time and energy to what was springing from the depth of my heart and soul.

The words used in the confessional and in the administration of the sacraments seemed steeped in a moral code that gradually had less meaning for me. I was beginning to question the theology upon which the practices were founded. Engaging in these church practices began to feel more and more artificial, even contrived, and certainly hollow. This rote ministerial work contrasted markedly with the far more vital discussions I had been having with the educated youths and adults in the country. They were all asking honest questions, such as "What is this life I'm leading all about?" or "Why care at all, since it all seems so overwhelming?" The *favela* dwellers with whom I worked were also waking up to a deeper sense of reality as they recognized the fundamental equality of all people. As they learned to work together, they found a new hope for the future. The difficult thing for me was that, unlike the intellectuals and the *favela* dwellers, I did not know how to articulate for myself what it was I wanted.

As I struggled to understand the conflicts within me, I grew more and more interested in people's lives, and the "stories" they told me, tales that instructed them in living. I collected many of them and eventually wrote two small books with these stories. I designed the books for the catechists to use in teaching Catholic beliefs and values, and published them locally with money friends sent me from the States. Several parishes in Brazil purchased them.

Both of the books had one central theme that the Kingdom of God is within the hearts of everyone. Because this was my belief, I did not like the idea of a missionary as one who indoctrinated people into a belief by imposing a dogma or moral code on others from a supposed position of superiority. Through my observations, I was now convinced of the innate goodness in everyone. I saw the Kingdom of God—a state of being that included happiness, joy, peace and egalitarianism—as the Creator's original blessing, one that even if ignored or forgotten, can never really be lost. I felt more and more strongly that a missionary's work should be to help people find a path back to their own deeper knowledge of the Kingdom of God that was within them. That's what I wanted to do, and I wanted the books to serve as a reminder of that deeper knowledge.

Months after I had left Brazil in 1973, I received an award from a German foundation for creative writing, and the foundation contributed 400 German marks to the missions. I'm not sure how my books came to their attention. I presumed some missionary from Europe picked up copies while passing through the friary in Belém, and forwarded them to the German foundation.

Also during this time, while celebrating Mass, I had another experience that shook up my traditional religious understanding. I was reading chapter four of St. Luke's gospel, in which Jesus picked up the scroll and read about the Messiah to come. He closed the scripture, handed it to the attendant and said, "Today, this prophecy has been fulfilled in your midst." I suddenly had a radical new understanding of the meaning of this gospel story. Each *individual* is the messiah! One need only to wake up to this reality. Jesus' words suggested that he had awakened to this reality. He knew we were all the same, that we are not separate from one another. I felt this truth in my heart, but I could not express that to the congregation. The intensity of my emotions left me speechless. In hindsight, I realize that these experiences, as well as my reading Krishnamurti, foreshadowed my understanding of our oneness.

My mother visited me in Brazil in 1972. The parishioners treated her as if she were royalty, which surprised and delighted her no end. It gave me a deep, yet quiet satisfaction to share my Brazilian life with her. She met my friends and we toured the parish and much of Brazil. Something about this journey with her was also a good-bye for me, though I didn't know it at the time. I had the odd, bittersweet sensation that it was the last time I would see some of the people and places. The trip was an especially poignant one for me. A radical shift in my thinking coincided with similar thoughts and changes for others in religious life and elsewhere.

Ever since I had been assigned to the friary in Belém in 1968, I had counseled nuns and conversed at length with fellow clergymen, mostly Franciscans, about their doubts, hesitations, pastoral care, and whether to stay or leave religious life and the Church. During the five years I was in Belém thirteen sisters, of the many I had counseled, opted to leave their congregations. In addition, several priests from my friary, with whom I had long walks in the park next door, decided to leave the priesthood as well. The auxiliary bishop of the archdiocese knew of my connection with those people who had decided to leave, and he was not pleased. He knew it because we lived in the same friary and we had our meals together. He seemed to view me as an irritant in the order of things, someone disrupting the status quo. I would have felt that way if I had been in his shoes, with his values and way of seeing things. He asked me to leave the archdiocese.

His request was no doubt related to the potential influence on others of my gradual change and embrace of liberation theology. This newly defined mode of thinking was growing in all levels of society—priests, bishops, the poor and the intellectuals—during the rise of populist governments and significant industrial development in Latin America during the 1950s and 1960s. These political and economic developments benefited the middle class and well-to-do urbanities. But huge sectors of the poor, living in sprawling urban slums or in isolated rural areas, became more and more marginalized under this shift. Industrialized nations benefited from this trend because they provided the know-how and capital for many projects and, of course, reaped the profits. Awareness of the disparity between the rich and poor grew among many of the educated in Latin America. Strong popular movements sprang up in Peru, Argentina and Brazil that sought social and political changes that would benefit everyone by raising the standard of living, especially for the poor.

Catholic and Protestant theologians responded to these dramatic changes. Reflecting on the realities of the poor masses, they reexamined biblical revelation and traditions. They saw liberating dimensions implicit in both sources that served as a call for churches to become involved in issues of social justice and to lessen the huge gap between the haves and the have-nots. Their subsequent writings revitalized pastoral care. Their practical applications were concerned in one way or another with the poorest of the poor struggling for liberation from socio-economic structures. This focus contrasted with the traditional approach that centered on the salvation of one's immortal soul. Many bishops criticized these theological reflections as straying from traditional doctrine. But this was the theology I was gradually embracing. The auxiliary bishop knew this, and didn't want the theology infecting his diocese.

Meanwhile, a dear friend of mine, an officer in the Brazilian army, sent a message to me through his wife that the authorities were investigating my activities. My time and energy was focused primarily on the people in the *favelas*, where I was engaged in an open-ended educational process intended to help them define and analyze problems, then take steps to resolve them. Certain members of the government and the military saw this as a threat to the status quo, and therefore subversive. It is difficult to deceive, let alone control, a population that is thinking for itself. If that population is disadvantaged, and it is to everyone else's advantage to have them remain so, the result can be explosive.

Like the government and the military, the Church is dependent upon some degree of ignorance to maintain their power. Even I could see that I was no longer thinking and acting in accord with the religious tradition in which I had been educated. It was not right for me to continue in it, thinking and feeling as I did. I decided to leave Brazil, the place I loved, whose people I had come to consider part of my family, and return to the place where I was born to find the space to ponder my life.

It was like the death of a loved one in many ways, as if half my being had been torn away, never to have or hold again. The country and its people had touched me and changed me at my deepest core, for they taught me about the heart. One of the obvious customs that contrasted with my cultural conditioning was the manner in which people greeted one another. In the States, we greeted one another, especially two men, with a handshake. In Brazil, I always met another with a hug and a kiss on the cheek. In the U.S., the appropriate psychological distance was three or four feet; in Brazil that was reduced to about eighteen inches. At every meeting then, connection and relationship were reinforced, effectively banishing isolation.

For thirteen years, I had lived rooted in Brazilian culture—so long that my own culture was but a ghostly impression. In addition to missing the warmth of Brazilian culture, when I returned to the United States in 1973, I experienced a psychological vertigo. My Brazilian face began to crack, and pieces of my American face began to reemerge. This puzzled and frightened me. Was I just an actor on a stage wearing different masks and operating from conditioned perceptions? I had felt more real as a Brazilian hybrid, but if that were so, how could that feeling have disappeared so easily? Was there, I wondered, an "I" that preceded all the thoughts that arose from my roles and cultural identity? Was there no part of me that remained permanent, unchanged regardless of time, place, circumstance or culture? If so, where was it? Who was it?

As I asked myself these questions, it seemed as if the first half of my life had been lived in a black-and-white movie, with nothing to animate my personal *Pleasantville* script. Splashes of colors, feelings of joy, emotional pain, and vitality had only begun to appear during my years in Brazil. All of my perceptions had been challenged by the people, the culture and the conditions in which they lived. There, one could not hide from life—it was too raw. Every decision had consequences, often the life or death kind. The culture of my birth had been all about minimizing risk through minimizing exposure. But that, I had discovered, minimizes the real act of living. Could there be a life in between these two extremes?

I determined I would pause and wait to see if and where life would take me. It was a switch from the way I had decided and defined, managed and mastered, my way to my desires before living in Brazil. I did not choose a new path, even though it might have appeared as if I did to the onlooker. I took a step into the unknown and waited for a path to choose me. What I did have, though, was implicit, and often explicit, intentions for my life to proceed in a peaceful, harmonious fashion. Brazil had opened a number of windows to this kind of organic approach to life.[1] By giving my life space in which to birth, it began to unfold without me having to select all the particulars. It happened in accord with my intention.

---

[1]
A curious event took place in 1990 when I spent some time studying with Denny John-son. He is a person whom my wife Berta and I consider a wonderful friend and teacher.

Denny has an abundance of intuitive information about the markings in the iris of the human eye that are connected to the mental, emotional and physical issues one has to deal with in this life, and the gifts one has been given.

He studied colored slides of my irises and among many observations he said, "Thomas, who was the woman you met when you were about 28 who profoundly impacted you?"

I thought for a moment and said, "I never met any woman when I was 28. That was the year I went to Brazil.

He responded, "Thomas, Brazil is perhaps the most feminine culture in the world. You may not realize it, but she profoundly impacted you!" Indeed I did not recognize her influence in my life until well into the writing of this chapter. Denny has written several books and lectured internationally for decades. His book, *What the Eye Reveals,* relates to this topic. His website is www.rayid.com.

The very things we wish to avoid, neglect, and flee from turn out to be "prima material" from which all real growth comes.

~Andrew Harvey

Doorway

I left Brazil with one suitcase and a small bag. It didn't seem like much to show for thirteen years of my life. And while I carried little in the way of baggage, I carried more than a little doubt: I did not know if I would return to Brazil, and I did not know what was ahead of me.

My position with the Franciscan Province of the Sacred Heart, head-quartered in St. Louis, Missouri, was also uncertain because I did not know if I would remain in the order. I requested and was granted a sabbatical to study psychology starting in June 1973 at Lone Mountain College in San Francisco. In exchange for room and board, I became a dormitory advisor.

My interest in counseling and psychology had been growing for many years, but my attraction to the field had really blossomed three years earlier in San Francisco when I had participated in the community-building training program. As often is the case in psychology, I also had personal questions that I hoped to answer through the course of study. I had noticed that many of my friends in Brazil struggled mightily for the poor and oppressed, yet they seemed as oppressive in their interpersonal lives as some of the societal structures they wanted to change. A young woman who worked tirelessly for social justice related how her lover, equally dedicated to righting blatant injustices, was given to emotionally abusing her. I was curious about such discrepancies. And certainly, I had questions about my own development that were elicited by reading J. Krishnamurti.

Going back to school so much later in life, I had a greater appreciation for the learning process. Although I relished the classes at Lone Mountain College, it was not all smooth sailing. Perhaps the most difficult things that surfaced for me were in the emotional arena. The most immediate and devastating was culture shock. I had spent my entire life surrounded by a group of people, my own tribe, as it were, both at home and with the Franciscans. I had grown accustomed to being greeted with fondness and hugged by dozens of people daily in my role as Frei Lourenço. At Lone Mountain, I nearly starved for strokes and recognition. In contrast to Brazilians, who freely expressed warm affection for one another, few people at Lone Mountain greeted or even acknowledged me.

Part of the reason for this was likely the manner in which I conversed. I interacted with others Brazilian style, up close and personal, as the expression goes. Both women and men shied away from me when I invaded their "comfort" zone. They had legitimate reasons for questioning my behavior. In this new world, such physical closeness violated a frontier sensibility of large personal space. Such a competitive society automatically excluded intimacy between equals. It could expose weakness and leave one vulnerable.

I was slow to understand this. It caused me great stress and left me feeling isolated, alienated and alone. I recall driving over the Golden Gate Bridge and being so despondent that I even thought of suicide. Such thoughts took me by complete surprise. Never had such ideas crossed my mind. I keenly missed that Brazilian sense of connection to others, and I despaired over its loss.

I experienced a kind of post-traumatic stress: my body shook with fear every time I heard police sirens. It didn't help that I knew the source of this reaction. Without exception, when going into a restaurant in Belém, my friends and I sat in the corner facing the door. This way, we could see everyone, and protect our backs. This pattern developed out of the very real danger presented by Brazil's military government that was not known for having a sense of humor or tolerance. The police had on occasions arrested and tortured individuals—including priests—who were involved in open-ended education, as I was. After all, I opted to leave the country in part because the government had taken an interest in my activities. Although I never permitted myself to fear for my physical safety while I was in Brazil, I had automatically shifted into survival mode. The fear I thought I had resisted had only gone underground. Back in the States, thousands of miles from its source, it surfaced.

Out of necessity comes invention, and one way I handled my desolation over the lack of hugs, along with my reaction to police sirens, was to form a Hug-a-Day club. We had eight charter members, and our primary rule was that we gave each other a hug every day upon first meeting one another. Instituting this practice, even within our small group, brought me a surprising amount of relief.

To deal with the more serious problem of suicidal thoughts, I entered bioenergetics therapy. The thesis of this system was that the mind and body are functionally identical. What goes on in the mind is reflected in the body, and vice versa. Unresolved issues become locked in the mind, persist as ongoing defensive thoughts, and are manifested as tension. Through specialized breathing patterns and physical exercises, one can release those areas where suppressed emotions have lodged in the body.

Following this therapy permitted intense emotional energy to surface, so that I could sense it, and let it go. I found the process eerily similar to the old game I'd played as a child with the "ghosts" that came up the stairs. It provided me a forum for dealing with emotions without taking them personally or letting them control me. This was important for me, because I'd had so little experience in the emotional realm.

Not surprisingly, much of what I released was grief. I'd had so many losses, and all of them had virtually gone unacknowledged. I'd lost the religious life I had prepared for, and had given myself to, for twenty-two years. I'd left behind twelve years of a ministry that I loved, and left the company of so many Brazilian friends. I'd lost my father, without ever really knowing him as an adult. Perhaps most importantly, I'd surrendered a childhood ideal and dream. Each of these things was a sincere loss, but somehow, I had not expected them to affect me. Ignoring them didn't make them go away. Rather, it sent them underground, to be trapped in the body where they took up space and energy.

My experience then, and certainly that of more than twenty years working as a family therapist, has shown me that when we clear out these old, unresolved emotions, we make room for something totally new and unexpected. Where Brazil opened windows, this process opened the door and allowed me to clear out my emotional house.

Through therapy, reading and classroom studies, I slowly discovered a new direction for my life. I concluded that the pain and suffering I had been feeling were due to negative scripts or conditioned ideas. Therapy helped me identify and then drop those scripts, for they were robbing me of vitality. Sure enough, when I let them go, I became more alive. It seemed to me that other people experiencing emotional pain and suffering would, with therapy, find ways to change and enjoy life as well. This thought galvanized me, and I knew I wanted to be a part of that process.

In this pursuit, my enthusiasm took over, and I forgot the lessons of unfolding that I learned in Brazil. Without realizing it, I fell back into a be-coming/achieving/goal-setting approach to life. During the next ten years, I applied the same willpower that took me to Brazil toward becoming an effective psychotherapist. I sought out the best therapeutic skills and tech-niques available in what was, and still is, a rapidly changing field. While I was certainly changing and undoing much of my conditioned self, I missed an important point. I had fallen off the wagon of unfolding and climbed on the bullet train of striving. I didn't grasp that I was using the same "doing" frame of mind that I had before, because, for the first time, the specific direction I was heading was of my own choosing. I was not living in the present moment. I was still avoiding my real self.

One thing had grown clear to me though. By the time I entered the third semester at Lone Mountain, I knew I would leave the Franciscans and the priesthood. I longed to be in a caring personal relationship. My experi-ences in Brazil had reshaped me, and I wanted to share my life with some-one who had also experienced the struggle of the poor in Latin America. It was too much a part of me to leave outside of a relationship. Curiously, not long after I realized this, a couple invited me to a Sunday dinner to meet with Latino leaders in Oakland, California. The only Latino leader who accepted the invitation and showed up was Berta Stella Cantón, my future wife.

Berta was approximately my age, single, and from Argentina. She had been a student and friend of Father Carlos Mujica, S.J., who had been gunned down as he came out of a church in Buenos Aires. When I met Berta, she was the director of *Centro Infantil de la Raza*, a bilingual, mul-ticultural children's center committed to involving parents in defining the education of their children and in the selection of the staff. As we talked, her presence energized me, made me feel alive. After dinner, we exchanged telephone numbers.

On May 1, 1975, I hung up my Franciscan habit. As I did so, I silently recalled all the years of my life. I saw the people and places I had served. My heart raced with a full range of emotions—gratitude, joy, sorrow. I cried. I was on my own. As a caterpillar pushing out of the cocoon, I felt the pain of leaving familiar, known structures. No matter how uncomfort-able they had become, I *knew* them. I said good-bye to all the security that life as a Franciscan had provided me, and I moved in with Berta.

For the first time in twenty-two years, I had to concern myself with making a living. While in the Franciscan order and priesthood, I didn't have to concern myself with finances. There I was, facing the issue for the first time at forty-two. I wondered how I could make a living as a psycho-therapist. After talking with several people, I concluded that private practice was the route to go, and for that I needed a doctoral degree.

I was accepted into the doctoral program in clinical psychology at The Fielding Institute in Santa Barbara, California. I took my introductory workshop in the summer of 1975. The students acquired competency by attending weekend or week-long workshops, reading assigned literature, and composing essays. This meant burning a lot of midnight oil. I was once again caught up in a pattern of pushing hard toward a goal. Focused as I was on the future, I didn't see the negative aspects of this way of living,—only the familiar satisfaction I derived from completing the steps to a goal, in this case, each course requirement.

I found the Fielding faculty open and challenging. The average age of the student body was forty-two. Students came from highly diverse professional areas and life experiences, which made interactions enriching. Each student worked with a faculty mentor who helped the student through the doctoral program. I selected Dr. Jerry Nims, a wise and practical man who kept me grounded and focused on my goal.

As part of my doctoral program, I worked in the field of alcohol and drug treatment at various facilities. Facilitating groups and conducting couples and family therapy brought me a lot of satisfaction, and introduced me to interactions and attitudes markedly different from those I knew in Brazil. For my dissertation, I wrote a staff training manual on out-patient treatment of alcoholism based on a philosophy of alienation. In it, I used what I had learned in my own experiences, and emphasized the notion that people's problems, addictions, or sufferings arose as a result of alienation from their innate happiness, or self.

During my second year at Fielding, I had enough credits and hours of supervision to obtain a California license as a marriage, family and child counselor.

Since my focus was on the practice of direct treatment instead of research, I trained in several psychological theories, approaches and techniques. Some of these included bioenergetics (the same system I used to access and release my own blocks), gestalt, transactional analysis, and rational emotive therapy.

In the last months of my doctoral studies, I started a search for a post-doctoral internship, a prerequisite for obtaining a license, and I accepted an opportunity in Washington State.

I received a doctoral degree in clinical psychology from The Fielding

Institute on June of 1979, while practicing in Kirkland, Washington. With what I had learned from my parents about hard work, I had completed the doctoral program in less than four years.

After several months in Kirkland, Berta and I moved to Kennewick to fulfill my post-doctoral requirement. My internship at the Mid-Columbia Mental Health Center in nearby Richland, Washington, seemed tailor made. Part of my job during those two years was coordinating the Center's educational and consultation department. In that capacity, I provided the community with courses in stress management, assertiveness and communication skills. When I had completed the two-year commitment, I was known well enough in the Tri-Cities area (Kennewick, Richland and Pasco) to start an independent practice. By August 1981, the state of Washington granted me a license to practice psychology, and the goal I had set for myself was accomplished. I could see clients privately and receive payments from insurance companies. What I had said I wanted was what I had once again become.

The problem with focusing only on goals is that the satisfaction of achieving them is short-lived. As soon as I reached a goal, life suddenly seemed pointless. Though I continued to acquire knowledge and skills from teachers who were considered outstanding in the therapeutic community, my desire to be proficient and effective remained unfilled. I spent thousands of dollars and a great deal of energy in pursuit of further mastery. Yet, the unrest within resurfaced. I began to question the necessity of seeking out new theories and techniques. I still couldn't see the real engine driving me to achieve.

In my hunger to find an answer to the discomfort I felt, I looked to experts in the therapeutic community, just as I had looked to experts in the fields of theology and pastoral care. I read their books, listened to their tapes, and watched their videos. I had initial enthusiasm for each approach, but then I sagged when I sensed what I was looking for was not in that expert's strategy. What was motivating me? As hard as I looked, I didn't know. I was only aware of some force inside that pushed me ever on.

Who knows how far and rabidly I might have searched, never finding that sense of having at last arrived? I was saved by my relationship with Berta, for that led to discovering what was truly beckoning me. Through our relationship, I finally began to walk through the door of my conditioning and into the space more suited for responding to an inner yearning for the real, the sacred.

The value of any relationship is that which is achieved
as you allow yourself to express only love.

~Tom Carpenter

Other

The human desire for intimacy is ingrained; it is a longing for connectedness. It is there for each one of us, whether we acknowledge it or not. It defines one quality of being human. For me, however, it was an especially strong desire. Years down the road, I discovered that the drive to connect with others was a key attribute in my personality. But before then, all I knew was that it remained with me even as I passed into adulthood, though I certainly learned—and was also trained—to be cautious about the drive. My ecclesiastical training had been carefully designed to move me away from close, personal attachments; we were meant to attach to God, not men, and certainly not to women. In spite of that, attachment was a motivating factor in whatever I did.

My experiences in Brazil helped me open that part of myself in ways I could not have anticipated. The culture, the people, even the politics had their influence. But one of the most influential experiences on the direction of my path was so mundane and ordinary that it might easily have gone unnoticed. But I did notice it, and it literally changed my life. I viewed it then as chance, but I have since come to a different understanding.

It occurred one day when I was serving as a pastor in Belém. I was making some arrangements, and one of the secretaries looked up at me and asked, seemingly out of the blue, "Why don't you ever say 'thank you' to any of the women?" I could only stare back at her in surprise. I never said "thank you?" My mind ran back over my past experience, and to my growing horror, I realized she was right. I did not often express thanks.

My impression of myself had always been that I was a kind and courteous person, yet here was someone telling me that I had not indulged in the simplest of common courtesies when it came to everyday interactions with women. As I thought about this, I began to realize how I had grown to see women, or more accurately, how I had grown not to see them, in order to maintain my vows of celibacy. I had developed the mental habit of erasing them from the picture. I kept them at a distance, and interacted with them in a pleasant but mostly impersonal fashion. This understanding rocked me, for it meant at some level in order to maintain the life I had chosen within the Church, I had "blocked out" half or more of the population, and I had locked up at least an equal percentage of myself as well.

This experience shifted something inside me. I began to look hard at my interactions with women, what they had been, and what I really, deep inside, wanted them to be. Any relationships I had had with females until that moment had generally been in a group context, where safety in numbers insulated me. I had not maintained any friendships, nor had I, it seemed from the secretary's question, expressed a common courtesy even in the most superficial interactions. No matter from what angle I viewed the situation, I saw my behavior as a lack in me, as something missing. I was incomplete. I sensed this contributed to the deadening that I had felt inside.

With each year that passed, I had grown more restive in the Church, and had begun to have the wholly extraordinary thought from time-to-time that some day I would marry. I knew, too, that the person would be in some way connected to the Third World, because my experience there had done so much to shape me. Looking through the rear view mirror of my life, I know the thought came from some kind of inner wakefulness that was always present, but too often shouted down by a rational, conditioned mind. And I, still asleep to it, only barely noticed the knowing, as it had passed through my mind like a short-lived comet, burning brightly and sporting a short tail, and then disappearing. That is to say, it did not get incorporated into my feverish, goal-setting, becoming mind. I had noticed it, remembered it after a fashion, but thought no more about it.

Back in the States, I had begun giving a series of talks on world hunger. One morning after Mass, a woman from the audience approached me. She was a Basque from northern Spain and was most enthusiastic about my presentation. She wanted me to come to her home to meet several other Latino leaders in the area. I accepted her invitation. The more I reflect on my life, the more I understand destiny as a thread that winds through our lives, carrying us unknowingly, and sometimes even unwillingly, to various critical points of rendezvous. That night at dinner was one of those points in my life. I had no inkling beforehand, and cannot remember if I even understood it at the time. If Berta were writing this, she would instantly say her first impressions of me carried no thoughts of destiny whatsoever. First of all, I was a priest; secondly, I dressed in a fashion that reflected my recent return from the jungles of northern Brazil, and was not at all "stylish" for the streets of San Francisco; and lastly, when I was painstakingly searching for the words to express myself, she saw me as emotionally absent.

Yet, by the end of the evening I was moved enough to have asked her for her phone number. Berta had given me her phone number. Being cautious, she gave me her work number. But I never called her. I feel a critical need to explain why. It was not because I was shy, or inexperienced, though admittedly those things applied. I just knew so firmly that this was the woman with whom I would spend the rest of my life and with that I didn't need to do anything. Or, to put it another way, no matter what I did, I knew this was what would be. Surrendering to this was not laziness or fear. I just knew.

Too often in life, I had disregarded feelings that told me when I had just stepped into a dynamic that would carry me to some new level. Bowing to environment and training—my conditioning—I had forced myself to go against the flow of the moment. That was dangerous, because I distanced myself so far from the little voice of truth, I ceased to hear it. I did not live fully, because I did not remain open to the nudges of such "knowing." Happily, Brazil had taught me a thing or two, and I had begun to see how life moved of its own accord at times. This moment, I knew, was one of those times when I could, and did, step aside, and let the process simply unfold.

Berta had not experienced the same sense of recognition that I did. Nor did she think much of anything about our meeting. Our hostess, however, had noticed right away that something was occurring between us, and was terrified she had committed a grievous faux pas. She called Berta later and wanted to know if she had done something wrong.

"Wrong? What do you mean, wrong?" Berta asked.

"With you and Father Tom!" our hostess explained.

"Oh, please!" Berta replied.

As it turned out, when I did not call, Berta thought, "Well! Why didn't he call me?" Being a bright and assertive person, she promptly called the church where I worked and left a message for me, along with her home phone number. Not at all surprised to find her message, I called her back and invited her to spend a day with me poking around the craft vendors that populated the North Beach area in San Francisco. I was forty-two at the time; she was forty-five. Neither of us had ever been married.

It's hard to say what it was that most drew me to her, but it was not hard to see how opposite we were from one another. I was quiet and took everything inside me. She was energetic, eager, and said exactly what she felt. I invited her to attend a class on communication I was teaching. I remember being impressed by two things. One, she was an engaged listener; and two, she challenged nearly everything I said. I have to say, I really liked both qualities. Each time she'd hear something that made no sense to her, she'd say, "What! What do you mean?!" Over time, I managed to convince her that I was not just making things up as I went along, and she learned to trust me.

About six weeks after we met, I invited Berta to come to Washington with me for Christmas. She told me later, her first thought was that it would take two days to get there, so that meant at some point we would have to stop for the night. Just as she was thinking about the ramifications of this, she heard herself say, "Yes, I would like to." While in Washington we went to lunch near a lake, and I asked her to marry me. Even as an obtuse male, thoroughly unschooled in the dating game, I could see from the look on her face that this proposal had not been received in the spirit in which it had been offered. I quickly amended myself, explaining I didn't mean a legal or church wedding, but that I was interested in a long-term relationship, not "an affair." Berta thought, "Well, OK, that's different." She agreed to enter a marriage that was not a marriage.

At that age in life, both of us had come to realize that a proforma marriage meant nothing. I had had a surfeit of form in the Church, and had grown to see that structure without intent was meaningless. If the intent were there, it seemed to me, the structure was not needed. Marriage was both a religious and a legal convention; in other words, it had nothing whatsoever to do with how we felt about one another.

As it happens, we did marry three-and-a-half years later, on November 4, 1978, at St. Paschal's Church in Oakland. By then, we wanted to publicly mark our pledge to one another. At the time, we were planning on moving to Washington State, and Berta wanted a celebration with her friends, so in addition to our wedding feast, it was a good-bye celebration. For both of us, it was also a way of respecting the traditions of our families, which were important to us.

Berta brought me passion. Through her encouragement and response to me, I opened up to my own creativity, and came alive in ways that had been dead to me from my first day of school. I brought her a freedom from roles that stifled her spontaneity.

That doesn't mean things were always easy. It took effort to mesh gears with another. We seldom had battles, for I just retreated in the face of strong emotion. I always came back with a possible solution, though, so it wasn't an escape. We did have had to learn about one another's styles and we had to recognize where we each employed some form of manipulative behavior.

One morning as we lay in bed, I asked Berta where she planned to be in five years. "I don't know!" she instantly answered. "I don't think in those terms." For her, life wasn't something you planned; it was something you lived as it came along. "I'll be wherever I'll be!" she said. My question was a holdover from all my years of establishing and achieving goals. But I also recognized something else in it. I was asking her because I wanted to force her into revealing her intentions in our relationship. I wanted her to say, "I want to be with you." If I had succeeded in getting the answer I wanted, it would have had less to do with the truth of her expectations, and more to do with demands of mine.

On another occasion, we were talking about emotions, as hers could be formidable to me, and she said, "If you don't like it, you can leave." I said, "OK," and very calmly got up and headed for the door. I had grown up in a household where game-playing of any kind was immediately dis-couraged, so I took her at her word. As I reached the door and began to turn the knob, she stopped me, saying, "Oh, no, no, no, I didn't mean what I was saying!"

For her, it was an opportunity to see what had been an unquestioned societal conditioning. Everywhere around us, TV, romantic novels, mov-ies, and behaviors we had witnessed were about game-playing. Women were supposed to be coy and unpredictable in order to control a man. It is the time-tested tool for those who feel they are weak against the strong.

Berta was by no means a weak person. Instead, her passionate nature had fooled her into thinking that was how it was supposed to be, all storms and forgiveness. But it was exhausting to live that way. If we had played those games, we'd have missed out on finding compassion, freedom, and the joy of an unconditional love. We'd never have succeeded in cultivating intimacy if we'd given in to manipulating one another.

Being so much older when we met presented the expected challenges of adjusting to someone else's habits, but it also meant we'd learned a thing or two along the way. We didn't need to use one another to grow up. We could be proactive about what we wanted. Shortly after I had moved in with her; I was preparing a salad for dinner. She came home from work, and not realizing I was there, sat down in the living room to read the paper, as was her habit. I made a noise or said something that alerted her to my presence, and she was aghast that I was cooking while she was sitting there reading. She thought she should get up and help me, instead of relaxing after a long day. I told her, "If this is OK for us, then it's OK!" She looked at me for a minute and then said, "Oh, all right!" and happily returned to reading the paper.

Without defiance or critical judgments about societal expectations and structures, we stepped out of predefined roles by merely questioning the conventions. We looked at every situation as it was, and asked ourselves whether it was what worked for us. By doing so, we easily moved into new patterns that grew out of who we were, and that felt comfortable to us. We were adults and could set up our routines in any way that we found helpful to ourselves and each other.

Relationships are complex organisms. They break down and build up. Mine came precisely at that point in my life when I had taken bold steps into the wilderness away from a "program" that had been in place my entire life. I'd left my home, my family, my role in an organization that was both home and family, and had begun a search to learn who I really was. Berta appeared in my life exactly at the right time and place. I was ready to experience the teachings that intimacy had to offer. We complemented one another as opposites, and yet we shared deep similarities, not the least of which was this capacity and willingness to question assumptions.

We could easily have given one another blisters, but for the habit of active listening that developed early in our relationship. This simple tool staved off many a trauma experienced in other marriages. Active, or reflective, listening is something I taught in my communications class. It is a state of engaged listening that either person can call upon with the other. It is a contract to pay attention, to *show* that we are paying attention to what we are being told.

In the first years of our relationship, we made appointments with one another to invoke it. I might say, "Berta, I need ten minutes of active listening." She would say, "OK," or "Sure, but I can't do it right now. I'll meet you in a half hour." Then at whatever time we'd arranged with one another, the person initiating the session stated what he or she needed the other person to "hear." In this way, we created a nonjudgmental, unemotional forum for exchange. Sometimes it might be a concern that had developed in the relationship; other times it might just be important information that needed to be shared and confirmed.

One of the biggest problems we encountered had to do with our respective personality styles. I was quiet, subdued and deliberate in my responses. Berta was energetic, quick and passionate. My responses often looked to her like non-responses, and she would say, "Did you hear me?" That's a question that men everywhere can probably relate to, and they undoubtedly know what's coming next. When I said, "Yes," she suspected that I was just replying in the affirmative to facilitate the discussion. She then asked me to repeat what she'd said. I did that, but repetition is not necessarily proof of comprehension, and so often does not satisfy the female, for she wants to see some sort of indication from her partner that shows the information was received. When I presented something to Berta, I might get more of a response from her than I could process. I shut down while I sorted through the emotional feedback.

Both patterns could have been destructive in the marriage, but by developing the institution of active listening, we created an environment that was safe for both of us. We both know that this saved and enriched our marriage by creating a way for us to deal with everything important in an intimate or domestic relationship—our feelings, needs, expectations, wants—in a safety zone where we were freed from the temptation to react or get caught up by a script of some sort. Gradually, we learned to laugh at our styles instead of being controlled by them. Human beings being what they are, this made laughter a fairly common occurrence in our marriage!

For both of us, life was about learning to live from the authenticity of our natural being. We found that by doing everything we could to aid one another in that task, we grew more and more successful at it, and the amazing by-product was the way our marriage deepened. This is what marriage was meant to be. Not a power struggle, a political negotiation, or a tool for one partner's expansion at the expense of the other, but a sacred space where each reaches for and reflects what is best in the other. It requires admitting and learning about one another's weaknesses so that they can be compensated for or eliminated by forming new patterns. It requires honesty and commitment, kindness and compassion, and there's not a day that I don't give thanks for the more than thirty years I have spent with Berta.

Companionship is an obvious result of marriage, but I found it went much, much deeper than just having another person around to break up the silent spaces in life. Berta and I learned to be a loving and accepting presence to each other, and the joy and satisfaction I experienced in life blossomed.

One area where this really stood out was in my life-long enjoyment of nature. I'd always loved nature, but my circumstances had never permitted me to enjoy it outside of a group; I was either with an assortment of siblings or with other brothers in the order. That kind of participation in nature diffused the experience, scattering the effect like buckshot. The times I was alone, I certainly enjoyed it, but when I was with Berta, I discovered my experience expanded to a nearly unendurable level. It was the sharing of it that brought it so alive. And this was true of every activity we shared.

Nowhere was this more evident than in the fact that we not only shared our personal lives, but our professional ones as well. Starting in the mid-1980s, Berta managed the office of my private psychotherapy practice. We were together nearly all day, every day, and under conditions that required constant negotiations over how to handle this or that situation, how patterns should be arranged in the flow of things, or what needed to be changed. The conventional view might be that we would grow tired of being around one another, that our affection would fade or even reverse its polarity. Instead, just the opposite occurred. When people learn to become facilitators of one another's souls, deep familiarity breeds not contempt, but ever more respect.

One of the things that contribute to a deadening in any relationship is when one or both parties stop growing. When that happens, one has to carry the other in some fashion, or else no new energy is introduced into the dynamic, and the relationship starves to death. Because Berta and I were committed to helping one another grow, we continued to do so. Life has become so much richer for us, but so has the relationship. There is a sense of adventure about it. As Berta and I allow barriers to fade, and we access more dimensions of ourselves, as we open to the truth within, our lives continue to expand. Our growth doesn't threaten the marriage; it strengthens it. And we welcome it. In living this way, our marriage fills us with an incredible sense of appreciation; not only for all that the other has become, but for all the other has helped us to be.

As a couple's therapist, I have noticed some people fear that if they don't maintain a controlling stance, they will lose the other person. In a loving environment, trusting the other to look out for our best interests is a source of joy. Both Berta and I learned to surrender to one another through this kind of trust. Something that occurred on a trip to Italy illustrates how this worked in our day-to-day lives.

Berta had visited Italy a number of times before we met. She was naturally quite excited to show me many things she felt were important for me to see. In Venice, she strictly organized our days to fit in the maximum amount of stops to see as much as we could. It was awful. It was grueling and tedious, and generated its own kind of stress about whether or not we would reach all the worthy goals. It totally destroyed our efforts to live consciously in the moment. Both of us began to recognize what was happening, and I took the step to change it.

We were riding in a *vaporetto*, or waterbus, and came to a stop at a bridge. I suddenly grabbed Berta's hand and said, "We'll get off at this next bridge." Though surprised because this was not on our itinerary, she said, "Okay!" and we did. Once we were off the boat, I turned to her and said, "Berta, randomly choose right or left when we come to the next street crossing."

She did this several times, changing direction only upon whim. Suddenly, as we were walking down a narrow passage, she stopped and with surprise said, "Look! This store sells shoes that are made for my narrow feet!" At first, she didn't want to go in, but I insisted we do so. Much to her delight, she found shoes she wanted. The sales clerk went next door with my Visa card to complete the sales transaction.

There we were, seemingly by chance, in this small Venetian shoe shop. Over the loudspeaker system, we heard soft, romantic music accompanying an Italian tenor. We were completely alone, and so, since it was her birthday, I took that moment, aided and abetted by the tenor, to present her with the card I had prepared. She was delighted. Everything had flowed perfectly because we let it. And the only reason we let it, was our trust in one another.

Another experience on the same trip illustrates the power of intimacy. After we left Venice, we headed to Assisi for a week. For more than twenty-five years, I had lived in dedication to Assisi's most notable son, St. Francis. This medieval village is to Franciscans, what Vatican City is to Roman Catholics. On the day we arrived, we both noticed an aura hovering over the city. We felt the sacredness of the place, as we strolled its narrow streets and visited the ancient churches, monasteries and fortress. Each morning, I rose at 6 a.m. and went into a church dedicated to St. Francis's parents, for contemplation and silence. It was beautiful. We walked in the hills around the village, keenly aware we were walking where St. Francis, too, trod in contemplation. Our experiences in this place made a deep impression on me. The paradox was that I had never felt the power of spirituality to that degree while I was in the Church; it seemed it was only possible because I was there with Berta. She had prepared me for this by teaching me to feel again.

I always had trouble finding the right gifts for Berta. One day I stopped thinking in terms of a physical thing as a gift, and instead tried to give her something I felt in my heart. I learned I could really express it in poems and stories that I created for her.

She loved these things. They often moved her to tears. Seeing how I succeeded in touching her encouraged me to continue to make the effort. Love is strange in this way, for showing Berta how much I loved her, and seeing her understand how much she meant to me, elicited more love within me. It was in this fashion, my own *Pleasantville* turned to color.

One of my early writings, called *The Pleasure of Living with Magic*, described how all the things Berta did for me in our daily life appeared as if done by magic. I never had to ask, I never had to search or wonder. From the clean and folded clothes in my drawers, to travel arrangements, things just appeared as if done by magic. Magic, it turns out, is more than a mechanism, it is a person. It is love. By showing her I knew what and why she did the things she did, and by appreciating them, she knew she was seen. To be seen, really seen by another, is the greatest gift we can receive—it is also the greatest gift we can give. The "magic" gift was one of many that touched Berta deeply.

When I was growing up, it was common to head off to the local movie theater on Saturday afternoon, where ten pennies were a passport to other worlds. The movies that resonated most in my small being were the adventures of Tarzan. Here was this wild man who lived in the jungle, and spent his time swinging by and saving people. But he was never tamed or touched by his heroics. Then one day, he encountered Jane and she tamed him with her love.

I went to the jungle to help people, or so I thought, but I did not encounter my Jane. I did not find her until I returned to a jungle of a different kind, the asphalt one of Oakland, California. We learned to simultaneously tame and free each other. She led me to my heart, which had been banished from life through all the conditioning of home, church and career. I led her to security in the chambers of my heart. We brought each other toward center, yet still grew outward at the same time. It took trust and courage for each of us, but the rewards have been incalculable, for she has been the mirror through which I learned to see my true self.

I share God's will for happiness for me.
And I accept it as my function now.

~A Course in Miracles

A Path

By 1985, Berta and I had been married for seven years, and I was well established in my own psychotherapy practice in Kennewick, Washington. We'd reached a level of stability that should have brought me great satisfaction. But somehow, something in me still was left wanting. My achievements didn't fill this void, and I might have gone on vigorously searching for more accomplishments in an attempt to fill it, but several encounters nudged me in a new direction.

Krishnamurti, Again

The path began to unfold one day when I was going through books in my library and noticed one that I did not recognize. I opened it, and seeing that many passages had been highlighted, I began reading. I discovered that some of these passages reflected almost exactly the tone and content of my own thoughts. I wondered how this author could have captured them so precisely. I checked the cover: Think on These Things, by J. Krishnamurti. Suddenly, I remembered. Besides my clothes, this book was nearly the only thing I brought back with me when I left Brazil in 1973.

I flipped through more pages, and everywhere my eyes landed, I encountered something that mirrored my deepest thoughts, those harbored secretly that rose up in opposition to so much of what I'd been taught about spirituality. Had I assimilated the teachings—at least intellectually—without remembering the source?

Even though I'd lived long in a rational, analytical society, I couldn't help but attach significance to this seemingly random rediscovery of his work. Its timing was precisely aligned with my desire to satisfy some inner yearning. Was I being invited by Spirit to speak the truth, as I knew it, rather than play it safe by repeating what others had taught me? This question reinforced my idea that the world we live in is designed in a way that is more harmonious than we think. Later, it became clear to me that all my experiences were the effects of my thoughts, intentions or expectations. I desired to know truth, to know who I was. My life was unfolding in harmony with that intention.

Spiritually ravenous, I went on a Krishnamurti binge, reading everything he wrote, listening to his audio tapes and watching him on videos. The teachings of this giant took root in my heart.

Diminutive in stature, Krishnamurti stood tall in his truth, speaking directly, forcefully and confidently to the whole world for more than sixty years. He did not conform to society's structured thinking patterns. This gave him a unique perspective from which to observe. Most of us are too enmeshed in these patterns to be aware of how, never mind why, it controls us.

In one passage he wrote:

So freedom lies, not in trying to become something different, not in doing whatever you happen to feel like doing, nor in following the authority of tradition, of your parents, or your guru, but in understanding what you are from moment to moment...there can be no freedom as long as you are merely trying to become somebody, or imitate a noble example. [1]

I knew with painful certainty he was talking about me. I'd spent my life in earnest pursuit of becoming "somebody." I'd given up trying to be saintly, as the Church defined it, but I was still giving my time and energy to becoming something else—an effective master therapist. His words helped me see my journey for what it was, not a path to freedom, but a path to greater confinement. If I persisted in it, my path would grow in ever tightening circles until I, at last, succeeded in choking the life out of myself.

In another passage he wrote:

The man who understands this whole process, who breaks away from it and stands alone, creates his own momentum; and if his action is a breaking away from the false towards the truth, then that momentum itself becomes the truth. Such men are free of destiny. [2]

---

[1] *Think on These Things*, J. Krishnamurti, Harper and Row, New York, 1964, pp. 20-21
[2] *Think on These Things*, J. Krishnamurti, Harper and Row, New York, 1964, p. 124..

Pondering these ideas provoked an unfamiliar questioning of what it was that I really knew. I'd not done that before. I had tended to accept ideas in concrete terms. I began to question my assumptions about myself and about life. What was the point behind all this expenditure of energy, all this jumping through hoops? Who was I before I had the thoughts of working hard, becoming a Franciscan, a Catholic priest, a missionary, and a therapist? I had no answers. I wanted answers, answers that I could directly experience. Truth had to be more than an abstract; it had to be something I could feel and live.

Krishnamurti awakened me. He fed me the first real, persistent spiritual nourishment I'd ever had. I had been steeped in religious training all my life, but he was the first to teach me about spirit and freedom. From his introduction, I began to seek other questions and other answers. This began my journey away from an unexamined life toward a conscious one. I write this with a deep sense of respect and heartfelt gratitude for his influence—not to mention his timing.

A Course in Miracles[3]

The next light on my path came from a book someone gave me in 1982, called *A Course in Miracles*. It has remained at my side ever since, even though I didn't open it until three years after I received it. Little did I know that it would have such an impact on the rest of my life.

The publishers of the work claimed that Jesus had dictated the entire book to a research psychologist, Dr. Helen Schucman. In light of my theological training, I approached it with caution. While traditional Christian terminology is used in the *Course*, the meanings ascribed are radically different. This factor also made it difficult for me to access. And so, the book rested on my shelf, content to slumber until something else propelled me to crack its spine, and become both a student and teacher of the material. The impetus to do so came from an unanticipated source—me.

By 1985, I knew that the now familiar state of internal unrest was a pressure I had to face, even though it didn't make sense from an ego-driven point

---

[3] Up to this point, the events that make up my story have been quite concrete. With this section, the *Course*, and most of what follows, the events become less concrete and more surprising, even for me. I encourage you, the reader, to consider that these experiences are not important in themselves; they merely continue the theme of my story. What *is* important is remaining open, and allowing your inner guide to lead the way.

of view. On the surface, my life appeared to be all anyone could ask for. Professionally, my practice flourished. I had rewarding and flattering feedback from clients, and they told others about their satisfaction. Most were pleased with the changes they made, and I was satisfied that good had been done. Personally, my marriage to Berta continued to deepen and strengthen.

Still, the awareness grew that there was a self that resided within me that was untouched by any conditioning. I noticed that few of the therapeutic techniques I used took this into consideration. They had all, as I understood it, been developed out of theoretical reflections based on a conditioned self, an ego with its own script and programming. I believed that my work with people would improve greatly if I could learn how to incorporate this idea of an unconditioned self—a unifying "one" that exists below the level of complexes, neuroses or addictive behaviors, into my therapy and my life. I began to pursue approaches that went beyond ego therapies and focused instead on the spiritual and transpersonal dimensions of life.

I grew ever more restive. My personal frustration mounted and compounded with my continued inability to break through the limitations I saw in contemporary psychotherapy. I felt like I was spinning my wheels in an elaborate and stylized dance.

One day, in frustration, I shared with Berta my quandary about the limitations I felt in my psychotherapy practice and the feeling of pointlessness this engendered. "Shared" may be too genteel a word. In a fit of pique, I showed her my driver's license and said, "If need be, I can make a living as a taxi driver." It would be a better use of my time than rote, ego-oriented psychotherapy. It was at this point that I felt enough discomfort to turn to the *Course* and, at last, to give it my attention.

The first time I read the *Course*, I examined it from a cautious, intellectual viewpoint. After three or fours months, several themes began to draw me into a more ardent study of the material. Jesus with the *Course* is not at all interested in establishing a new religion, but in helping those to whom this perspective on spirituality appeals. To them, his words are an invitation to wake up to the truth of total equality among all. This consideration was important because it contradicted the ego-driven thought that some people are essentially evil and others good.

From my seminary days, I was familiar with many of the controversies about the stories and words of Jesus in the New Testament. Scripture scholars often debated which words attributed to him were authentic, and which ones were not. In the *Course*, every word was claimed to have been recorded exactly as Dr. Schucman received the teachings from the entity that identified itself as Jesus. For me, that left no space for argument, for she did not interpret the words, she only recorded them.

Though you can purchase the *Course* in three separate volumes the combined edition contains all three volumes: the *Text*, the *Workbook* and the *Manual for Teachers*. The 622-page *Text* presents a theoretical foundation; the 478-page Workbook contains 365 lessons emphasizing experience through application; and the 88-page *Manual for Teachers* refers to the teaching of this material.

When I came back to the *Course* under the spear point of my own unrest, I had a completely different experience than the first time I'd encountered the material. I couldn't get enough of it. It was clear to me; it was Jesus speaking. The words themselves demanded I put aside my insistence on intellectual comprehension and be open to practicing the lessons in the *Workbook*.

A common theme runs through the first eighteen lessons: nothing has any meaning other than what we give it. That is, if I am hurt, sad or angry with some situation or individual, it is not the situation itself that created those feelings, but my automatic interpretation of it. As I grew more aware of this, I began to let go of dependencies that were based on a belief that worry, anxiety and sorrow were caused by things outside me.

In the past, I would have considered this thinking an abdication. But something in me had shifted. I could see that this was the start of a spiritual journey that involved examining all my assumptions, and questioning the stories I told myself. It was clear that this practice would take me beyond my automatic interpretations and reveal greater truths.

The central premise of the *Course* is: *Nothing real can be threatened, nothing unreal exists. Herein lies the peace of God.* This premise reinforced my belief that enduring happiness and peace are within all of us—that is the Kingdom of God. According to the *Course*, that kingdom is the creation of God and the extension of Divine Love. It is the Son of God or the Christ. Our bodies and the physical world are unreal in the sense of being caused by thoughts. They do not exist as physical realities except in our dream mind. They are unreal. To ego perception, the physical world demonstrates separation. Ego creates the idea of separation, projects it outward, perceives a distinction between all things, and concludes, "There is proof of separation!" After studying the explanation in the *Course's Text,* I began to work with the lessons in the Workbook and apply them to daily living.

A central theme of the *Course* is forgiveness. However, in this case, it is not about asking God for pardon and mercy, for we have never sinned against Him. It is not about pardoning others for wrongs done toward us. Instead, forgiveness is recognition and acceptance of self and all others as the perfect creation of the Father. Forgiveness is a correction of the error in thinking that tells us we are separate, that we are defined exclusively by the body, and that we are not who we truly are and will always be: the eternal, unalterable Sacred Self.

The *Course* teaches that, as consciousness, we are always moving toward remembering the truth of who we are, the one perfect extension of eternal love. So when we look in the face of others and see there the face of God, we are waking up and benefiting the totality of consciousness.

But the *Course* is not so much theological in nature as it is practical. It urges students to practice the curriculum in order to understand it. This learn-by-doing approach appealed to me; I had a surfeit of philosophies that stood apart from real living. As I studied, I found more concepts in the material that attracted me. One of these was the *Course's* purpose: to help people discover a way to find their own internal teacher. Not only did this harmonize with what I had seen from implementing Freire's concepts in the *favelas*, it was also appropriate at that point in my life. I was disgusted and in conflict with my compulsive search for teachers who would enlighten me because I knew down deep that was impossible. Enlightenment cannot be bestowed; it has to be accepted or remembered as who we are. It is not an intellectual, but a heart process.

Other topics that interested me were penance and sacrifice. The *Course* says that these things, as conventionally practiced, have nothing to do with waking up to the truth of who we are. I had done my share of both over decades in the Church and I found they did not bring happiness. They did not bring truth. They did not even bring ease. What penance and sacrifice brought was the uncomfortable feeling that I needed to do more and more of each, and still never reach a state of peace. Penance and sacrifice, for me, served to reinforce feelings of unworthiness, requiring even more penance and sacrifice. Letting go of the whole vicious cycle lifted a huge weight from me.

The *Course* was a gift intended to facilitate the undoing of the root problem, our error in thinking that we are separate. Jesus invites us to correct all our problems at the causal level by allowing Spirit to undo this error. This concept of "allowing" is critical. When I have identified with "wrong mindedness," or the false self, I can't undo the errors of my thinking because I see them as real. We can never solve a problem on the level in which it is created; we can only set up opposition, which entrenches the problem. We can, however, recognize there is an error and step aside and allow Spirit to undo it.

The *Course* gives specific ways of undoing our errors in thinking; one of them is explained next.

In accord with the *Course's* guidelines, whenever I notice something in me that is not reflective of peace, such as fear, guilt, inadequacy, vengeance, hurt or sadness, I first recognize its source, which is my identification with wrong mindedness or the conditioned mind. Next, I affirm I am Sacred Self. Lastly, I turn over the undoing of ego-generated emotions to Spirit and wait and see what occurs. Waiting and seeing are important, for with them we express our belief that it is indeed Spirit that heals.

While I was reading the *Course*, I received a written response to a billing I had sent to an insurance company. The letter stated that they would not pay because the form had errors. They did not give any specifics. Frustrated, I started to feel insecure and angry. When I recognized that I was getting caught up in a conditioned mind reaction, I identified the source of the frustration, affirmed the truth of who I was and turned the healing of the insecurity over to Spirit. With that awareness, I stepped out of the old pattern, and the negative feelings evaporated. Later, I phoned the insurance company to make sure I knew how to correct the billing error. I sent in a corrected billing form and a few weeks later I was paid.

One fundamental teaching of Christianity I learned early in life was that we are all sinners who are marked by original sin and must be baptized to enter heaven. By contrast, the vision the *Course* offers is that we are incapable of sin, because the Source created us perfect and without the slightest capability of changing that perfect nature. When the *Course* does use the word sinner, it defines it as one who has committed an error in thinking, and all that must occur is that the error be corrected. From this viewpoint, punishment is not appropriate because punishing "sin" only affirms the ego's thinking patterns. There is no eternal damnation, exclusion or retaliation. The main theme of the *Course* is the real can not be threatened and, therefore, has never changed. We are as God created us.

When we judge those who have committed atrocities as different as ourselves, we are promoting errors in thinking. We are free to see those who commit atrocities as God's perfect creation; their actions occur only within the dream state. Their actions do not change who they truly are. If we choose to see them as evil, we ignore the reality of who they are and instead reinforce the illusion. The *Course* urges us to see them as they are, to give them their just due as the perfect extension of Love.

I do not deny that horrific acts are committed. The *Course* addresses this issue from a perspective that precedes physical perception. Daily brutalities are committed by individuals, and this fits into the ego's goals. The ego thought and value system chooses to perceive individual bodies for the purpose of proving our separateness from one another and the Divine. The ego's purpose in - perceiving bodies, even though they are not real, but projections of thought, is to have us consider ourselves victims, and the atrocities further this purpose.

Through the *Course*, Jesus teaches that we were created with the ability to deny the truth of our being—but not with the ability to *change* it. We are always free to assume illusion. And, we are always free to drop it and follow what our hearts and souls have eternally known. Denying our true identity is the seat of our discomfort and the source of all problems. This false, ego-driven thought system generates *guilt* out of the sense that we have sinned, *fear* at the thought of being punished by God for said imaginary sinning, and *anger* toward what appears to be a vengeful Creator. These feelings are ubiquitous and, generally, so repressed they are almost inaccessible to us. We remain trapped by refusing to see differently.

In Chapter 3, I discussed how I felt inadequate and isolated in the first grades of school because I was not able to read and spell like other children. As a result of this experience, I felt many overwhelming emotions related to my belief that I didn't measure up. In hindsight, it is clear that I avoided those emotions when I decided to prove my adequacy and worthiness to belong. These emotions remained hidden for decades, though for decades they were also the essence of the story I silently told myself.

Consider another example gleaned from a conversation with a friend. As a four-year-old, my friend began to cry in front of his father. The father told him, "You did something really bad, and that is why you are crying." With this condemnation, the child felt intense shame and guilt, and concluded, "I am bad." Believing he is bad is a specific and concrete expression of my friend's ego-driven thought and value system. The incident was forgotten with time, but my friend's self assessment stayed with him for decades. As an adult, he felt an underlying and continuous sense of guilt that he was unable to either reach or assuage. He had no understanding of why, nor could he recollect exactly what happened when he was four. This experience from his early childhood remained deeply repressed, and it colored all his behavior and sensations. To compensate for his feelings of unworthiness, he unconsciously created a dynamic that "required" him to work seventy hours a week to prove how good he was, and coincidently, kept him too busy to recall his childhood trauma and see it with the eyes of an adult.

Artificial and suppressed guilt of this kind isolates us from the font of innate love, peace and happiness of our true nature. It has resulted in a Pandora's Box of psychological and societal ills: depression, hate, vengeance, killing, poverty, disease and war.

When we are driven by repression, we are unable to see who we really are; we can't find happiness within, because we have denied it is there. We seek happiness outside ourselves—in others or in things: a lover, children, cars, homes, career, power, etc. The *Course* calls these relationships "special" because we hope they will bring us happiness. But this is impossible because happiness is who we are, not what we acquire. When we don't find lasting happiness in other people or things, we easily slip into fear, thinking, "I'll never find it, I'll never be happy." This, in turn, transforms what we thought was a relationship of love into one of anger and resentment because it has not filled the emptiness. The special love relationship becomes a special hate relationship. When we lose hope of finding happiness in the other, we come face-to-face with more fear and guilt at our failure to be loved.

The *Course* is quick to note that the Holy Spirit has a different purpose for all special relationships. They are meant to be jumping-off places for awakening us to our true nature. Our partner in such a relationship (spouse, lover, boss or office mate) is a mirror, reflecting to us all the places where we are not living from our own Divine Nature. Relationships can be crucibles of discomfort, even abuse, but the *Course* tells us it is through forgiveness that we find our way out of the discomfort and into joy. The forgiveness is not for sins committed, but for illusions held. The voice for Truth within each of us invites us to see ourselves and all others as the Creator sees us. Spirit moves us in that direction at every opportunity. We live forgiveness when we look beyond appearance, and see all as the light that we are.

Over the years I brought to my relationship with Berta the intention to see her at all times as God's perfect creation, regardless of what was happening between us. She also brought this intention to our marriage. Seeing each other in this way has been a clear reminder of who we are. Seeing differently was a blessing for us and all of consciousness, for we are One.

In working with the *Course*, I found my mind so heavily conditioned with the meaning of traditional terms, that I needed to be alert to each line of the 1,100 pages, or I missed entirely what was being said. Besides the term "sinner," some of the other loaded words for me were: Creator, Father, Jesus, Christ, Holy Spirit, creation, penance, salvation, sacrifice, forgiveness and atonement. I thought I had quietly laid all these concepts as defined by traditional Church doctrine aside when I read and studied Krishnamurti, and in the first years of reading the *Course*. Not so. The old meanings and connotations persisted. They created a holographic image seemingly welded permanently to my brain, so that when one of the words was mentioned it immediately conjured up all the others. This made them difficult to identify and neutralize. In fact, as long as I attempted to neutralize them on my own, it was not possible. The resource I used, that we all have, was to ask Spirit for help.

According to the *Course*, Jesus took on the illusion of a body, just as you and I have. He was a human being, just like you and me. But he was less immersed in the ignorance than we are. He saw how trapped in falsehood we become when we identify with the body and the egoic thought system. Once he remembered who he was, what his innate nature was, he also saw all others as the Christ or Sacred Self. In a marked departure from what I taught as a pastor, and what many Christian churches teach, the *Course* tells us that Jesus' passion and death had nothing to do with atonement for "sinful" acts. He chose his death and resurrection as a way of teaching that what God created cannot be killed.

The *Course* offers another correction for the error of false identification with the body and all the problems that this spawns: silence.

> *In quietness are all things answered, and is every problem quietly resolved.*[4]

Through silence or stillness, we can enter into a state of mind that is without reference, where emptiness overflows with peace and a sense of our Sacred Self. In such a state, no thoughts or feelings remain to manifest as sicknesses, unwanted emotions or problems. How simple it is to be still and let all answers come without effort, watching every problem dissolve. Being still is simple, but it is not easy, because we are so profoundly identified with the body and addicted to focusing outside of ourselves. When enmeshed in wrong mindedness, there is resistance to silence because it reveals the ego's hidden and repressed issues and defenses.

A friend told me that he, on occasion, becomes caught up in a verbal/emotional battle with his wife about the best way to correct their children.

---

[4] *A Course in Miracles*, WB, 1985, 1st edition, p. 533.

This leaves him feeling frustrated. Sometimes he can just let it go, and at other times he feels as if frustration has been stuck to him with Super Glue. In those latter situations, he asks for aid from his inner guide, and reconnecting with his innate self through silence, he watches his frustration dissipate. From that conflict-free state of mind, he can talk with his wife and reach a conclusion acceptable to both of them. They step outside the dynamic of his way or her way, and move into what is right for the children as guided by Spirit.

As drawn as I was into studying the *Course*, it was a continuous challenge. Like many people, I was more comfortable when I did not focus on internal realms. I knew that staying awake to what was happening internally was a critical aspect of the *Course*'s teachings, and that without awareness I condemned myself to repeat the past over and over, focusing forever on becoming someone of importance instead of actually living in the Now. As long as I was enmeshed in this script, I was not present to what was happening within me in the moment.

After the initial focus on inner awareness, the *Course* teaches that we reach a point where there is a major shift in focus. Called the alternative to separation, it is in the mind of everyone just as is the thought of separation. It is the idea that we are One, the total of consciousness. The voice for Truth is in everyone, inviting us to change our allegiance from the ego error of separation to the truth of Oneness. That shift cannot be made by the ego, which is why we are encouraged to ask Spirit for help.

Even as I studied and practiced the lessons in the Workbook, I looked for teachers I thought would support what I was learning or expand my understanding of the *Course*. In the early 1990s, two such teachers opened up new dimensions of understanding for me. They were Stephen R. Schwartz, an American teacher and author with a national reputation, and Tara Singh, a native of India with decades of teaching experience in the States. These teachers were the architects of pivotal moments of understanding for me, though they employed very different methods. Both emphasized the importance of silence.

Stephen R. Schwartz

Stephen Schwartz first gained a reputation as a New York playwright. Later, he addressed himself to the issue of spirituality and began teaching the *Course* and published tapes and books on this subject. He worked with groups using interventions from different healing modalities, always within the context of the *Course* concepts.

His method, as I observed it, was to look for chronic blocks in people's lives as manifested in their bodies. Through the use of techniques such as breathing patterns and laying on of hands, he helped the client release whatever he or she was holding on to. In my one experience with him, he worked with a small group of no more than thirty people. Instead of lectures, he entered into dialogue with participants one-to-one.

Berta and I attended one of his workshops in August 1990, at the Breitenbush Retreat and Conference Center in Oregon. At the opening session, Stephen asked each participant what he or she wanted from the experience. I said, "I do not have therapeutic issues that I want to deal with, but I do want to meet the real Stephen." I had worked long enough with the *Course* to know that Stephen was not the body I perceived with my eyes. What he was preceded physicality. He answered that he was very pleased with my request. I presumed it was because he knew what I was requesting. After that brief exchange, I determined to be fully present and open to whatever happened during the workshop because the clarity of his response indicated that what I requested would occur. I remained open and waited.

On the last day of the retreat, Stephen invited four of us who had not yet worked with him to come to the center of the room. The rest of the twenty-five or so participants sat in a larger circle around us. I had noticed throughout the workshop that he again and again used the appropriate words for eliciting from the individual whatever they were experiencing in that moment. He asked me, "Thomas, what is coming up for you?"

"Oh, that question is right on," I responded, "So much emotional energy is coming up from my belly. It is coming as a song, Psalm 23, and it is in Portuguese. The words are, *O Senhor é meu pastor...*the Lord is my Shepherd." At the same moment, as I looked out at the participants around me in the inner circle, I suddenly saw every one of them as one light, all part of the same radiating life force. I exploded with laughter. That's the only way I can describe the sensation: Laughter came rocketing out of me with the force of a bomb. Moreover, it was contagious. The entire group began to laugh with the same powerful energy I felt pouring from the center of my being. Berta said my face had been luminescent.

I had never experienced anything like this before. I don't know what provoked it, nor is that important to me. My certainty is that I was open to directly knowing the real Stephen. This experience, as startling as it was, satisfied my request. As I have thought of it over time, I see that laughter as echoing what L28 in the fable felt—the spontaneous release of an outmoded and inaccurate vision of reality. I could have seen it as a loss of control, and in a society that places a lot of emphasis on control, that might have fractured me. But I allowed it to loosen a lot of congealed energy in my body. It felt good. It felt damn good.

After catching my breath, I said, "I see the cosmic joke. We're all expressions of the same light, the same energy. Different manifestations of *the* One, but clearly all are always one. All are the One, all are my Shepherd." To me, from years of Catholic conditioning, the good shepherd referred to one person, Jesus. In my Breitenbush experience, the idea of the good shepherd expanded to include every aspect and the totality of creation. Each of us is the good shepherd to one another, though we don't remember that truth.

I had sung the words from the twenty-third psalm many times in Brazil. It was my favorite psalm, but never had I understood the meaning of the word "Shepherd" as I did on that day and as I have ever since. This important moment marked the point when I first felt so deeply the oneness of creation. Stephen, or more accurately—Consciousness, or Sacred Self, created the right environment for me to release the "wrong minded" idea of separation and alienation and anchored me in the reality of the One.

Stephen has since crossed over, but what a gift he gave me. In our dialogue, I met him in his essence and felt him as myself. At the time I was not aware of any physical Stephen being present. He did nothing. I did nothing. The allowing presence that is reflective of our true nature brought about the phenomena. I saw first-hand how powerful it is to be in the moment, and wait, and see.

What do such events mean? Does the Universe offer us these experiences of "wakefulness" where our false identities slip from our grasp and fade to reveal the truth? Is this what is meant by "true perception," in contrast to seeing through eyes clouded by ego? Ego sees only separation, but true perception reveals the connection or oneness. It is not the particular experience that is important or even the content of the experience; it is the waking up to the eternal truth, or the Oneness, that the experience is pointing to that matters. For me, it was a knowing that behind the content in mind, there always is Consciousness or Sacred Self.

I discovered this passage from the *Course* years after my experience with Stephen, it points to some of what I felt when I looked at everyone around me in the workshop.

The Great Light always surrounds you and shines out from you. How can you see the dark companions in a light such as this? If you see them, it is only because you are denying the light. But deny them instead, for the light is here and the way is clear...God hides nothing from His Son, even though His Son would hide himself. Yet the Son of God cannot hide his glory, for God wills him to be glorious, and gave him the light that shines in him. [5]

A few months after the workshop with Stephen, I purchased one of his books, *There Is No Space Between Us*. I jumped with joy just reading the title, because it expressed so exactly what I experienced in his presence. One chapter in the book, entitled "An Ancient Ceremony," is a poetic expression of Stephen's life's work, and it is what happened to me in his workshop. Part of the poem is reproduced below.

The work that we do together in the circle
    is an ancient ceremony.
It is an act of remembrance.
We do not come to the circle
    in order to take in something new.
We do not come to seek an answer.
We do not come to gain insights about ourselves.
We come instead to invoke the Presence
    of the Great Protector,
and to take its Love
into the heart and to know it as the one and only Friend.
There is simplicity to our work.
We allow everything to come
    and we allow everything to return.
We make no enemies with the journey
    nor with the journeyman.
In the circle those who have forgotten
remember to return to the place
where they have always remained. [6]

---

[5] *A Course in Miracles,* Text,1985, 1st edition, p.185.

[6] *There Is No Space Between Us*, Stephen R. Schwartz, Riverrun Press, Piermont, New York, 1990, pp. 51-56.

Stephen's words were a great reminder to me that Creation, with its infinite manifestations, is indeed holy and blessed. Have I always known this eternal reality at the deepest level? Yes. Have I occasionally slipped into the illusion that this was not so? To be sure, sometimes for years. But this is of no consequence, for I need only be aware of the error and allow it to be dissolved.

Tara Singh

The next teacher to cross my path was Tara Singh. He had begun his spiritual work as a student of Krishnamurti and then became a student and teacher of the *Course*. I encountered his work through my own research on writings about the *Course*. I attended four of his week-long silent retreats between 1992 and 1994. I had no specific learning or behavioral goals in mind; it was more that I simply felt I needed to, and so I did. I was gradually learning to trust my intuition.

Singh's teaching style was quite different from Stephen Schwartz's more intimate approach. Singh lectured before groups of perhaps 200 participants. He often had quotes from the *Course* written on large blackboards for the audience to read. He referred to them, explained their meaning, and gave many examples to clarify his points. Frequently, his examples came from the lives of sacred men and women from India. He was open to people asking questions, but I never saw him in dialogue with an individual participant in his large group encounters.

Singh was direct and assertive. The first time I met him, he looked at me and said, "In this lifetime, you will wake up to the truth of who you are." Startled as I was by his comment, I accepted his words as coming from a knowing that was still inaccessible to me. He echoed my own desire, so I took no extra meaning from his words.

By some of the things Singh did in each retreat I attended, I came to feel he held me in warm affection. I believed our relationship was one of friendship. On one retreat, he referred to a verse in the New Testament and, unable to remember it exactly, he turned to me and asked, "Thomas, how does that go?"

Singh invited me to serve on the board of his philanthropic organization, The Joseph Foundation. I accepted and held the position for one year. Once, in a meeting of the Joseph Foundation directors, while discussing the topic of simplicity, I remarked, "It is said that St. Francis committed only five scripture verses to memory and felt this was sufficient for him."

Someone in the group asked, "What were those verses?"

"I don't have the slightest idea," I replied. "I think the point is for each of us to find what touches us, rather than pick up what was important for another."

"Yes, Thomas," Singh commented. "Very good. Find your own." This exchange felt like a conversation between old friends. Since my habit with friends is to share both my good and bad days, on a day when I was feeling "down," I told Singh about it. I had become impatient and disgusted with myself at a retreat in Florida.

I asked Singh, "Why is it I know not to judge and yet I still do it? Why is it I become impatient with myself? Why do I continue to repeat those patterns over and over? Why is my mind chattering all the time?" Singh looked at me with great intensity for a long moment, then turned away and called on someone else. For a moment, I was speechless, trying to understand his abrupt dismissal. After some reflection, I saw that he was not rejecting me; instead, he was not magnifying the grievances of my conditioned mind by responding to them. He expected me to know enough to understand my emotions were created by ego and didn't need to be given attention. In hindsight, he was correct. I continued to participate in weeklong retreats with Singh for a while, but eventually my life took me in other directions. In June of 1997, after not seeing him for more than two years, I received a flyer announcing he was going to give a weekend intensive workshop in Portland, Oregon, only 200 miles from my home. With more than a little enthusiasm, Berta and I decided to attend. Again, I had no deep objective in attending; I simply wanted to spend time with a friend.

During his second lecture, he asked a question of the 160 or so attendees, and I raised my hand to answer. He called on me by name, "Thomas." I answered with the insight the question had spawned, and to my surprise, he responded with words near to these, "You don't even have what it takes to understand it—or spirituality. You need to go back and start over from the beginning."

One could have heard a pin drop in the hall. His comment shredded me. My stomach turned in knots. Berta's immediate impulse was to defend me, but she refrained from doing so. After the lecture, she wanted to leave, asking, "Who needs this kind of treatment?" But I wanted to stay and see it through, and she went along with my decision.

Without question, Singh's treatment provoked an automatic and deeply visceral response in me, but I still had the presence of mind to take stock of my physical sensations from the perspective of "witnessing." I found I could notice and accept these acute sensations simply as facts, facts that did not require any interpretation or analysis. At the time I remembered, and I want always to remember, that nothing has any meaning outside of what I give it. I just sat with those feelings, and before long the hurt and shame lifted.

I could invent the story that he was mad at me, and that was why he had so chastised me. Or, I could assume that he spoke without any sense of its impact on me emotionally. Neither of those possible responses might have eased my discomfort. But they might have, from an ego perspective, absolved me for a few moments of any responsibility, and let me feel like a victim. None of those thoughts crossed my mind, for deep inside, I knew he wanted to wake me up to my True Self. I presumed he had nothing but the best of intentions for me. When I understood the experience from this standpoint, I saw that his words were a blessing. The knife-like sharpness of his response was the perfect surgeon's tool to cut me free from a lifelong pattern of presuming who I was. I cannot stress enough the power of that gift, even though its delivery came through pain. I might not have received it if it had come gently.

From the *Course*, I have learned what injures me is never the words of another, but only my interpretation of what is said. When I forgive, or see the truth of who I am and also the truth of the other, I then know both myself and the other as that which can never be frightened or changed. The *Course* says:

> *Only my condemnation injures me.*
> *Only my own forgiveness sets me free.* [7]

As I noted earlier, Singh stressed the importance of silence in moving into one's truth. In his book, *The Voice That Precedes Thought,* one chapter is titled "Silence." The quotation from that chapter below had such an effect on me, that I carried it in my wallet for years. It helped me remember there is no need to accomplish anything, we are already whole, already enlightened. It reminded me that the key is to simply be in the present moment.

---

7 *A Course in Miracles,* Workbook, 1985, 1st edition, p. 370.

Silence is an active undoing of wishes, knowledge,
conclusions, urges, habits, and conditioning.
Thus, Silence purifies itself,
It is an involuntary cleansing process.
You give it the space, and do not interfere.
Silence, when not imposed, has its own energy.[8]

Allowing

Interactions with Stephen Schwartz and Tara Singh offered me two important *Course* teachings in a manner outside of the intellect's conceptualizing. The first, with Stephen, temporarily altered my normal perception, and I was blessed by seeing that we all are the same light that, indeed, there is only One, and there is no space between us. I could see in that shining moment how the "real" could never be threatened, and how it was the foundation of the *Course's* curriculum.

In the second moment of distilled learning with Tara Singh, his words sliced the umbilical chord to my self-preoccupation and gave me the perfect experience with which to discover the truth that we can have automatic upsetting reactions and choose not to take them personally. We can be the witness to them, and let them be as they are. From the *Course's* vantage point, they are of the unreal world, which does not exist except as thoughts in our minds. Freedom from the unreal, or the false self, is a choice. Singh threw me into the water; I had a choice to sink in shame or start swimming. I chose to swim. Teachers are where we find them, and sometimes we learn best from what is sharpest.

The only way to take advantage of such markedly contrasting, but equally precious, experiences is by *allowing*. If we so allow, perception can be altered by Spirit. That is what happened in Breitenbush. And when we allow Spirit to lead, automatic ego reactions come and then go, leaving nothing in their wake.

When we let ego rule our lives, there is always great constriction as we react to life, creating experiences of pain, suffering, disease, greed, hate, depression and war. In allowing Spirit to guide us, we expand into

---

[8] *The Voice that Precedes Thought,* Tara Singh, Foundation for Life Action, Los Angeles, 1985, p. 89.

the infinite and eternal, beyond the discomfort associated with being mortal. Allowing is a natural expression of Being; it is totally effortless. The *Course* teaches us that to live in peace and permanent happiness...

> *...you must relinquish your investment in the world as you project it, allowing the Holy Spirit to extend the real world to you...*[9]

No matter how much I enjoyed studying the *Course*, there eventually came a moment when I wanted to consolidate what I knew and share the good news with others that I might learn to live the eternal principles at ever deeper levels, and relish the joy of teaching.

---

[9] *A Course in Miracles*, Text, 1985, 1st edition, p. 270.

*It is the function of God's teachers to bring true learning
to the world. Properly speaking it is unlearning they bring,
for that is "true learning" in the world.*

~ *A Course in Miracles*

A Vision

My relationship with Berta had taught me to open up the door to spontaneity and a creative mind. My work with the *Course* generated insight after insight into spirituality. These things met and mingled in me in the late 1980s, and I started to feel the desire to share what I had learned. At first, I wrote about spirituality, but soon, I wanted more.

I'd always found joy in sharing the curriculum of the *Course* with others, and I couldn't get enough of that joy. A strong desire to present a class to the public simmered in me. I'd shared my ideas with clients every week for some time, and had discovered ways of phrasing them that brought me much satisfaction. I'd seen how enthusiastically my clients responded to what I taught; it helped them make desired changes in their lives. This heartening result inspired and encouraged me to organize my first workshop in November 1989. I presented a summary of what I had learned from the *Course* after four years of study.

My objective was fairly simple. I hoped all participants would recognize that our true identity—the one that exists beneath and before any societal conditioning begins—is characterized by an innate sense of happiness. I wanted them to see that it is only our enmeshment in and with the conditioned mind that clouds our knowing the True Self. The key to undoing the false identification, I taught, was through expanding awareness.

I approached this aim by borrowing from Paulo Freire's methodology. First I presented examples of concepts in a story format. After reading a vignette to the group, I divided the class into small clusters to discuss questions I prepared for that concept. The groups had a set period of time to work out their answers. Once they reached a consensus, they shared their conclusions with the entire assembly.

On that first weekend, after participants had warmed up to one another, I had the spontaneous urge to write on a blackboard in large letters: "No one is broken." During an intermission a man told me that, based on his conversation with others, the idea that "no one is broken" was appreciated by everyone in the group. I knew that, like me, many had learned through their religious formation to think of themselves as essentially unworthy, guilty of some kind of intrinsic sin, and fearful of damnation. Those without religious training had simply grown to see themselves as unworthy or unlovable. Such thoughts chafe and bind us, but something in us resists them. When I affirmed the opposite thought "no one is broken," that something reached out hungrily for what it recognized as true.

The *Course* teaches that the Self is always present; always working to help us remember who we are. It is ever vigilant, and constantly nudges us to go beyond perceived differences to the unity of all creation. Self or Consciousness is always trying to help each of us remember who we are. Small things that catch our attention are often clues. When I wrote on the blackboard "No one is broken," it caught the attention of participants ready to awaken. I could read their acceptance of the statement in their eyes. I saw it reflected in their calm countenances. I recognized it in the words of those who spoke about the importance and value of that affirmation, and I found it in the nodding of other heads that signaled, "I agree."

This idea was so well received by the workshop participants, Berta and I, along with Tom and Leslie Hatcher, began to explore this further. Though the Hatchers had not participated in developing the workshop, they attended it and were familiar with what we were trying to accomplish. They were also interested in making the ideas of the *Course* available to a larger audience. We sensed we were involved in something larger than ourselves, something with a significant gravitational pull to it, something that felt like a life path. We went to work on materials we could present to the public.

Our discussion with the Hatchers focused on the three understandings I'd worked with in that first workshop. Of particular importance to all of us was finding words or phrases to use in our material that did not have any connection with organized religions. We wanted to use our own expressions to convey the concepts of the *Course* and took pains to find appropriate language that resonated with the four of us. We settled upon the following.

• *All beings are innate peace and happiness even though some may not realize it.* No one is broken. The *Course* says that we are God's perfect creation and have never changed, except in our minds. One can often detect in young children a state of being that is pure happiness and joy, an utter acceptance of themselves as they are. This happiness is an innate state, but we forget it as we are formed and molded by family and society. We may forget it, but it is never lost. It remains a permanent resource for us. The four of us felt these concepts to be true based on our own individual experiences, though it is, like other spiritual affirmations, something that cannot be proved so much as felt, believed or perhaps remembered.

We defined "being broken" as identifying with inadequacy, scarcity, limitedness, depression and suffering on emotional and intellectual levels. Since we believed happiness to be innate, we felt it should be possible to access that sense of happiness or joy even when it had been covered over by beliefs to the contrary. When we began to present this idea, the feedback we received confirmed that. People told us that we were not teaching them anything new; we were helping them remember what they had forgotten. We saw that our initial assumptions were true enough to help us make a difference in people's lives. We could help people reconnect with that undifferentiated state of bliss and bring about life-altering results.

• *Identifying with a conditioned, confused mind and its way of thinking clouds over the innate sense of peace and happiness.* In the *Course's* language, this is the world of ego. The human mind contains within it urges toward self-loathing, fear, hate, gluttony, and so forth. We can be swamped by feelings of depression, of not being good enough, or a sense of failure. We can judge others as evil, or as deserving of horrific pain. All of these, however, come from the mind conditioned by the different cultures in which we move (familial, religious, cultural, ethnic, political, and so on). It is not the content itself that obscures our innate happiness, but our identifying with it that removes us from pure and blissful being.

Participants from the workshops, as well as many of my clients, described their minds as being similar to a computer program. It seemed as if their minds were designed to automatically interpret events from a negative perspective, to harshly judge others, or to react with the same unwanted emotions all the time. They reported that they did not choose these feelings and judgments, rather they just popped into awareness. As soon as they got caught up in, or identified with, those feelings and urges in any way, they lost their innate sense of peace and happiness. They realized it was their identification with that programming that separated them from happiness. Their minds had been conditioned to respond in a way that resulted in them no longer knowing their peace.

•   *Through awareness, everyone has the ability to access the innate state of happiness.* By cultivating awareness, we can understand the process of identification with a false sense of self and learn to recognize it. Once we've seen how it happens, we can consciously ask Spirit to undo our false constructions. When at last we can let go of what we have become attached to, we return to our natural state of equilibrium, that of peace and happiness. The *Course* repeats the idea of allowing Spirit to undo our ego errors in thinking and once again access our True Being.

To illustrate how each of the three understandings[1] can affect change in a person, consider the situation of a man called Raymond. When someone called him a nasty name, Raymond's automatic reaction was anger, complete with a strong impulse to reply in kind. By stopping a moment, and allowing himself to become aware of his automatic reaction, Raymond shifted his point of reference. He stood outside of the reaction, and from there he could see how the intensity subsided when he chose to notice his impulse rather than act on it. By not indulging in the fleeting reaction of anger, his day remained peaceful.

If Raymond lived this way day after day, he would gradually discover the only things that can remove him from a natural sense of happiness and peace are those moments when he takes his conditioned mind's reactions seriously and gives them life through his actions. With time he will learn that his reactive mind acts independently from "him," and that this mind's thoughts, feelings and urges do not have to affect his sense of who he is. By being aware, he has the power to step outside the role of victim.

It is liberating to discover how to make the simple shift in identification from our conditioned mind to that of our True Self, and it is exhilarating to see how fast life changes when we do. Having both witnessed and

---

[1] During the early nineties I found several authors who were developing similar ideas to those I had developed as a result of being a student of the *Course*. Those authors were: Syd Banks, Rick Suarez, Ph.D., Rogers Mills, Ph.D., Darlene Steward, M.S., George S. Pransky, Ph.D., and Jane Nelsen, Ed.D.

experienced this transforming shift for ourselves, it is what the four of us wanted to teach others. To concretize our vision, we decided to form a not-for-profit legal entity.

Finding a Name

The next step was to come up with a name. We wanted something that captured the concepts that all beings are whole and that the natural state of existence is one of innocence. I use innocence to mean that state of radiance that is seen in small children who live life to the fullest with joy and spontaneity. Of particular importance was to not use words that suggested any other system of thought. Some spiritual traditions express similar visions with such words as Buddha nature, Christ consciousness, Divine awareness, or as the *Course* says, "Son of God," but we didn't want to be defined or limited by such associations. We wanted something that would be accessible to people from all walks of life and independent of any religious training they might have had.

One morning, Leslie, Tom, Berta and I were brainstorming a name for the organization with the above criteria in mind. We sat around a table and played with words. The word "folk" came up a couple of times, and we all resonated with it. Its unpretentious connotations appealed to us. Feeling there was power in brevity, I proposed the name "Wellfolk." "That's it, Wellfolk!" the others repeated. It felt right to us. It described what we are when we live from that innate place of goodness present within us. We named the not-for-profit organization The Northwest Wellfolk Institute.

The breadth of the vision we had for The Wellfolk Institute cannot be underestimated. Because we were outside of traditional systems, we could include anyone, anywhere, in the "remembering" process. We were working at a level that transcended differences. We knew if we excluded anyone from being "wellfolk," we weren't living in harmony with the thesis that no one is broken. Wherever we met people, whether at work, home, school, the marketplace, temple or church, our intention was to see them as "wellfolk." All four of us had come to understand the truth of the claim made by more than one faith: that in our most basic nature, we are all One.

A Teaching Method

The *Course's Manual for Teachers* emphasizes a method of teaching that contrasts with commonly accepted practices in education, whether spiritual or secular. In most realms, the teacher is the one who knows more about the subject than the students. Their roles are clearly defined and distinctly different. The teacher gives and the student receives. The teacher is the expert, enforcing that position at all times so the students will first accept the information, and second, remember it—the act of learning. This tends to be exhausting for the teacher and unpleasant for the student. Another drawback of this model is that the teacher is only engaged in the role on a part-time basis. When leaving the classroom, the lesson is also left behind. It is not an essential aspect of who the teacher is.

In the *Course*, however, that flow is reversed. One teaches in order to learn, and the students learn by teaching. *Course* learning is not the acquisition of a body of information, but instead an *unlearning* of what is associated with the conditioned mind or false self. Both students and teachers learn about the illusions of the conditioned mind at the same time, and unlearn them as they go. Both discover how to drop attachments to those illusions. This creates a circular, holistic dynamic, each part feeding the other to benefit all.

Teaching in the *Course* is not a part-time occupation, something done only at prescribed times of the day or month. It is a full-time way of living; it is walking the talk. One is not separate from the teaching, one is the teaching. Whether I am in an elevator, movie theater, or a supermarket, I see myself and others as "wellfolk," and by doing so, I convey a resonance that others can respond to.

Teaching is an acknowledgment of the one essential Self in the other, the one essential Self we all are. We teach ourselves and others every time we witness our ego-generated thoughts, emotions and judgments without taking them personally or reacting from them. We teach every time we recognize our own wholeness, and our connection to life and all creation, whether in the class or outside of it.

Over and over in our discussions, and later with the workshop participants, we found the cycle of teaching to learn, and learning to teach, occurred again and again. I recall an instance when a client came to me afraid that he had doomed himself to another divorce because he yelled at his third wife and damaged the refrigerator door when he'd kicked it. His first two wives had left him because he could not control his anger.

I explained the Wellfolk concepts to him and showed him how those urges to act out in an angry fashion didn't have anything to do with who he was. They had everything to do with who he thought he was. This, I explained, was a critical misalignment. It was an error in his thinking pattern. I showed him how he could observe those feelings without judging them as bad or good, and then he could choose to let go of the pattern of acting on them. This was a brand new idea for him, and he left the session deep in thought, determined to be the impersonal witness.

A week later he returned and spent the whole session telling me how different his life was becoming because he discovered he could be the witness and notice his urges without acting on them. The changes pleased and inspired him to continue witnessing what was happening internally. This was an exhilarating moment for my client that liberated him from his past. He marveled at the simplicity of the concept.

The learning, however, did not stop with him. I, in turn, learned from his experience that we do indeed have the freedom to just observe what is happening internally, and can choose to let go of automatic patterns of acting on impulses. Our learning extended outward to all of humanity—what he was freed from, we could all be freed from, because his experience changed the universal conditioned mind "field" for everyone. We are One; all are Wellfolk.

A huge benefit this approach to teaching is that it keeps me from falling into automatic behaviors with clients, family and attendees alike. I remain fresh and open to the potential of what Spirit would have us learn in every interaction. That makes me an open listener and far more responsive. It imparts value to this work for everybody.

In the *Course's Manual,* there is a statement that was incomprehensible to me the first time I saw it:

You cannot give to someone else, but only to yourself, and this you learn through teaching.[2]

The first reading of this may sound a bit obtuse. But if we consider that the foundation underlying this sentence is that we are all one, not separate from one another, a glimmer of sense appears. When I recognize the other as a being of peace and serenity, I affirm that I am peace and serenity as well. And the reverse of that is also true—in condemning another as undeserving of love, I condemn myself. Again, we are all connected in the dynamic, a part of the same fabric or field of being, and no one of us can change for the better without benefit to all.

---

[2] *A Course in Miracles, Manual,* 1985, 1st edition, p. 1.

The *Manual* also describes teaching the *Course* as if in a conversation:

Teaching is but a call to witnesses to attest to what you believe. It is a method of conversation. This is not done by words alone. Any situation must be to you a chance to teach others what you are, and what they are to you. No more than that, but also never less.[3]

We wanted to design our presentation of the material to reflect this idea. A conversation implies openness in our exchange with others, one that is marked by ease, respect and honesty. It is communicating with another without the need to impose our point of view or judgments. To do it successfully requires more than a rote exchange of words; it requires taking responsibility for living our lives in the full consciousness of who we are. In this way, we offer a centered, peaceful presence to the other, one that is free of prejudice or expectation. This is what it means to teach others by our mere presence. It occurs wherever we are, whether in formal or informal situations, at home or at work, at rest or at play. That's what makes this approach a being-based, not a curriculum-based teaching.

An exchange we had with an elderly woman brought this truth home to us. We facilitated a weekend encounter and an elderly woman Berta had known in Argentina, and her friend, approached my wife and said, "Berta, we don't understand anything you are saying. We keep coming for the peace that the two of you bring." Even though she didn't know what our words meant, she felt the effect and grasped the message.

As we taught the workshop material, it deepened our certainty that "wellfolk" nature is the essence of every person. We saw that if we had been totally awake to the truth of our own unconditioned nature at the start, we would never have been drawn into teaching it. But because we had our own ego-generated doubts, hesitations and inconsistencies in living the Wellfolk understandings, teaching became our path. As we taught, those doubts were burned away.

Lesson Plans

Once we formed the organization and committed to the vision, our next task was to develop a training manual. I leaned toward the pedagogy

---

[3] *A Course in Miracles, Manual*, 1985, 1st edition, p. 1.

of Paulo Freire because, as previously noted, it resembled the *Course's* suggestion to keep the teaching conversational, and I knew so well how powerful it could be. Using the methods I had learned in Brazil, I wrote the first draft of each lesson plan. The four of us worked together to create the final version.

The format was simple. For each lesson I included a small story describing a scenario that was intimate yet dealt with a universal problem, the kind many have experienced at one point or another. The draft for the first lesson included a short story about a man named Hank who lost his wife to cancer. At the end of the story, were three questions for discussion in small groups.

When I presented this draft to the other three, Berta commented about something being out of place, that the story "limped." Leslie changed the sentence structure so it had more of a flow. Then Tom tightened the language on the questions in such a way that brought clarity to the issues for group discussion. We were all delighted with how this evolved; our collaborative process created a sense of synergy. It worked because none of us tried to control the outcome, but instead focused on making the story and lesson as right as possible. We continued in this fashion on each of the lessons, and the end product was always better for having been crafted by the unique contributions of each individual.

For inspiration in the lessons, I turned to my counseling practice. I simply listened to the clients I saw every day. The problems of those I counseled were shared by many people, and in every session, I found a topic that could be addressed in a Wellfolk lesson. The content of the first lesson rose out of my work with individuals who had lost someone dear to them.

We worked to create an environment for teaching the *Course* that maximized learning from one another. We designed the lesson plans with the belief that every person has within, a basic knowledge of the Wellfolk understandings, as well as the common sense to apply it to daily life. While we did not feel it was appropriate to teach spirituality itself, we could support and nurture its development by creating a conducive environment. It could then arise of its own accord, the natural product of the innate sense of peace at the core of our being. This was what we hoped to happen in the relaxed setting of small groups. We felt that in the intimacy of such a forum, an awareness of a person's own spirituality would automatically emerge.

This small-group process was all we hoped it would be and produced some remarkable results. In one lesson, we asked each small group to come up with words that described first "conditional," and then "unconditional," good feelings, and then to make a poster representing the fruit of their collaboration. We anticipated that some groups might start out confused, and through discussion move toward agreement.

At the start, it was clear some individuals had never considered this distinction. They quickly caught the meaning, however, through other group members' feedback. In one group, a member first described an unconditional good feeling as what she felt when she'd won $100 at a bingo parlor the previous month. The group's feedback showed her that was actually a *conditional* good feeling because it depended upon an external set of circumstances. Later, she came up with a better example of an unconditional good feeling when she described how, at times, she sensed a calming gratitude for no reason whatsoever.

When each group presented their poster and insights, they were lighthearted and joyous. These feelings rose out of the power they felt in sharing from the heart. They were eager to let others know what they had learned. They became the teachers, and the rest of us were their students. By accepting their teaching role, they deepened their own understanding of what they had exchanged, and each of us participated in their discoveries and momentum.

Another concept we covered was freedom. Many in the room did not really understand what it was, or how they could experience it in their individual lives. One participant named Laura related an experience that helped all of us grasp the meaning of real freedom.

At the beginning of the session, Laura told us that during the past week she noticed her mind condemning her because she was not perfect. She said she "stayed with witnessing" the internal judgment without taking it personally on several occasions and it made a difference by lessening the intensity and frequency of the damning thoughts. "I felt so relieved," she said, "It is like I knew what freedom was all about. Mostly I could not believe how simple it really was. I know anyone can get it."

Workshop participants all smiled and gave a round of applause. Even those who had not yet understood the concept of freedom, grasped it through Laura's direct testimony. They could see how to make it part of their life. Some of them told her how helpful and instructive her words were, thus demonstrating how when one person learns something, the whole group benefits.

Besides finding topics for lesson plans by listening to clients, I used concepts from the *Course* that had been important to me, such as *Nothing has any meaning outside of what one gives it.* This concept points out that the significance of everything ultimately has a subjective flavor. For example, I lost forty percent of my retirement nest egg in the stock market in 2000 and 2001. I could have chosen to be angry or frightened, which are conventional responses, but neither could change the reality of the loss. If I had identified with the anger or with fear about the future, I would have been in a painful state of mind that could have had an adverse affect on me and those around me. I chose instead to notice those emotions, and let them go. My behavior was not controlled by the events, and I found more than a measure of peace. The event had only the meaning I gave it.

Another concept we explored was how one event can be interpreted in many ways. We wrote the following story to help individuals internalize the concept. It is fictional, but based on several real-life experiences friends have shared with me. We gave the participants the story, along with some questions, and they together came up with an understanding of the situation described.

Nancy had three children, Mickey, thirteen; Jim, ten; and Erna, nine. Normally, when the children came home from school Nancy was there to greet them. But one day, Nancy had to visit a friend in the hospital, so she left the children a note saying, "I'll be home shortly. Don't leave. Please clean up the living room."

The children came home, saw the note, and cleaned up the living room. The chore accomplished, they sat down to watch TV. They were still watching it when their father arrived home from work. He read the note his wife had left in the kitchen. In a dissatisfied voice, he asked the children, "Why didn't you clean up the living room like your mother requested?"

The children responded, "But Dad, we did clean it up."

He laughed a little and said, "Well, okay, but let me show you how to really clean up the living room. He got out the vacuum and give specific instructions to each child on what to do. In twenty minutes they were finished and sat down to the television again. Five minutes later, their mother came home. Nancy glanced over the living room and looked at everyone sitting around doing nothing. Then she said, "Didn't anybody see the note I left? Why didn't you clean up the living room?" The children looked at their dad. He broke out laughing; then the kids began to laugh as well. He explained to his wife how the kids had done what they thought she had asked, but when he had come home, he didn't think they had really done the job. He had showed them what he thought it meant to clean up the living room, and they had tackled the job again. When Nancy heard that, she, too, laughed, and thanked all of them for their goodwill.

After discussing this lesson in a class session, each of the participants in their small groups concluded the problem arose because every member of Nancy's family had a different understanding of the expression "clean up." First the children, and then their father, had thought they had done the job correctly. All of the groups also realized how the varied interpretations could have erupted into an emotional drama, complete with tears, anger and resentment. They appreciated that conflict is diminished or eliminated the more we realize that what we say may seem clear to us, but in reality may have a whole variety of meanings to others. "Nothing has any meaning outside of what we give it."

The members of each group took part in the discussion with interest because they all had had life experiences in which their words were misunderstood or they had misunderstood the words of another. Such sharing leads to the discovery that we all have unpleasant interactions, and that with awareness we can choose to act in a different way. As each group reported back to the entire assembly, we witnessed participants directly and indirectly making commitments to put into practice what the story clearly demonstrated.

By fictionalizing some aspect of living in a way that everyone could relate to, people could approach it without the emotional burdens they might have encountered if we had taken events from their own lives. And since the story worked on several levels, it gave the members of the group an opportunity to digest some of their own personal experiences in an open, safe and social context where their comments were respected and their positive conclusions were immediately validated by others.

It was also clear in subsequent sessions that this story, and the others presented, created strong images that remained embedded in the participants' memories. They continued to think about them for some time afterward, and distilled further insights. We found that the way we used the stories had a direct impact on participants by showing them how to apply what they had learned to their day-to-day lives.

This is not likely to have occurred by simply reading the story without discussion. The power of our stories came not because they were terrific stories, but because each person shared with others their perspective and their real-life experiences, which imbued each story with special meaning. We all recognize truth when we hear it, and we hear it when we have the desire to find it.

At the beginning of the second session, we found that the participants were eager to give examples from their personal lives that illustrated the lessons we had covered. Using that energy, we initiated the class by asking, "Has anyone had an experience since our last meeting that you would like to share with the group?" By the fifth session there were so many volunteers eager to tell their experiences that we could have filled the entire session time with testimonials.

Discoveries varied from person to person, depending on how each had intersected with the story and subsequent discussion. But they all reported that the teachings had helped to shift something in them. One woman said that for years she felt depressed the first four or five hours after she got up each day. No one in her family wanted to talk to her before eleven in the morning because she was so nasty and bitter. As a result of the training, she began to observe her thoughts right before she got up. To her surprise, by watching her thoughts, she discovered how the chatter of her mind persistently and efficiently discounted her with such internal commentary as "You are a failure, unlovable, unworthy...useless." Taking these thoughts seriously set the tone for starting her day. With practice, she discovered she could notice this chatter as a fact without judging it bad or good, and that is what she began to do. She didn't invest energy in it one way or another, and the thoughts lost the power to affect her mood. Shortly after this realization, a family member asked her if she had inherited a fortune because they'd noticed how pleasant she'd become, even in the early hours of each day.

Best of all, by relating her story and contributing to the learning pool, she assumed the role of a teacher, and others learned from her how to notice their own internal thoughts and stories. So it goes, each person learns and teaches, teaches and learns, for the advancement of all.

This format worked so well that I soon expanded the lesson plans with five animal stories designed to reveal, speak to, and awaken the innate wisdom I also feel is present in all of us. One story was about a young rabbit named Aldo who is ridiculed because his ears are big. His parents don't know what to do when Aldo grows so ashamed of his ears that he does not want to go to school. He even hides in the grass when the school bus passes by. Then Aldo's grandfather, whose ears happen to be bigger than Aldo's, comes to visit. He spends some time with Aldo, and tells him about how when he was young he went to school and learned to be calm in the midst of laughter and teasing by pausing and connecting with his inner peace. The tale ends on a happy note as Aldo follows his grandfather's example in a way that influences his whole life and, consequently, the lives of everyone around him.

When we used Aldo's story in a workshop, participants reported being quite moved by it, but often for very different reasons. Each person found some aspect of it that spoke just to him or her. Some fastened on the idea of slowing down and stopping in order to stay centered and "not get caught up with society's demands." Others wanted to use the story to connect with their own grandchildren. Someone else recognized in it a situation that was affecting her own family. One older person saw in it the power the elderly have to help others through the wisdom they've garnered from a lifetime of experience. The story met and sparked with each person where that person was in life.

Over a period of three years, one of my clients came to my office about every eight months to request another copy of some of the stories I collected. Each time, she opened her purse to prove to me how worn and torn her old copy had become. She told me, "Anytime I am stuck in my false self, I take out the pamphlet and read a few lines. That is always enough for me to return to knowing who I really am."

Another way we helped participants integrate the concepts in their lives was through "awareness cards." Each card contained a different thought such as, "Today, I will be aware of my thoughts that are judgments," or "Today, I will choose not to be a victim of my reactive thinking." We used these as homework assignments and handed three identical cards to every participant at the end of each session. We suggested they place them in critical areas such as on the dashboard of the car, refrigerator door, computer workstation, and so forth. We asked participants to contemplate the statement and incorporate it into their lives in some fashion before the next session.

At the beginning of the following class, students reported their experiences with the cards. What they often shared turned out to be perfect explanations of the Wellfolk understandings. When they focused on these cards, they discovered that by expanding their awareness of what was happening in their inner lives, they could live from a more peaceful state of mind. Further, they recognized they did not have to be victims of automatic reactions and could choose to step out of the past.

One man told us that when he used the card, "Today, I will be aware of my thoughts that are judgments," he discovered the majority of his judgments were related to feelings of inadequacy in the workplace. He had never observed this before. He'd gone through every day never once noticing how he was his own worst enemy, that his own thoughts were far harder on him than anything anyone else said to him. Seeing the pattern appearing again and again made it easier, he said, to merely accept the judgments and not give them power by taking them seriously. As he became more aware of how insubstantial they really were, it became easier to let those thoughts go. Eventually, he was free of them altogether. His story, when brought back to the class, increased the "wisdom fund" of all present. As he learned, so did we.

Along a similar line, others who used awareness cards noted that they could let go of their automatic urges to criticize others, and they described the relief that brought them. They had never before realized how exhausting those patterns were. By expanding their awareness, they discovered through direct experience that thinking critically of others takes far more energy than accepting them as they are. When they could let the habit go, they returned to a sense of freedom and lightness. It allowed them to put their energy into living joyfully.

We found when the participants spoke directly about their experiences, their enthusiasm and the validity of what they reported registered with everyone present. People couldn't help but change when someone else shared a truth in this way. This capacity for one person's experience to affect others who listen to it in an open and accepting frame of mind supported our own understanding that we are all one. Repeatedly, one person's learning increased everyone else's awareness. No one wakes up to the truth of Self alone. Even on those occasions when the energy of an individual's awakening does not affect anyone present, we understood, and the *Course* supports, that the person's alignment with right-mindedness takes place in the realm of total consciousness, affecting the potential for others to awaken. That potential is available and waiting to be used whenever anyone is ready. We all have a choice to remain confused about Truth or to accept it. It is there for the asking. We are Awareness, or Consciousness, and we will all awaken to this at some point.

As teachers, the use of the awareness cards repeatedly taught us that the key to transformation from victim hood to freedom is in expanding nonjudgmental awareness. The use of the cards was for the purpose of helping us to observe the mind habits that block nonjudgmental awareness. To awaken is a heart issue, the simple act of remembering who we are at the center of our being.

When an individual wakes up to that nonjudgmental state of mind and shares his or her inner discovery, it frequently elicits an "aha!" moment in others. They say, "Oh, I *see*. It isn't *doing* anything at all. It is simpler than any doing." The impact of what people are learning can't be defined with words, but as they tell their story and share their insights, the energy conveyed behind the words transforms those around them.

We found that was true in a most direct way with the awareness cards. Some of the attendees said they placed the cards on their computer screen at work. Their colleagues noticed them and began to regularly ask, "What thoughts are we going to be aware of this week?" Soon their coworkers began to join them in focusing on the same thought for a few days. It turned out their coworkers had equally good results in shifting their awareness. Insights into freedom from the conditioned mind are contagious among those who allow themselves to be so touched. All it takes is willingness.

Since 1992, we have offered the Wellfolk workshops in a variety of formats with different names in the U.S., Argentina and Uruguay. We have learned that even people who do not think in terms of spirituality accept easily the Wellfolk understandings. When they hear them, they confirm it is more like an act of remembering than one of learning something new. They even describe it as something they have always known, but have forgotten.

Through these presentations, we have found people often have their own phrases to refer to the innate state we called our "wellfolk" nature. They describe it with terms such as joy, peace, contentment, bliss, vitality, oneness, unity, creative place, plenitude and harmony. In addition, they say when they live from that state they "make decisions with ease, redefine old problems so that they can be solved, are creative, communicate well, remain centered, enjoy silence and time alone, express themselves socially, and cultivate wholesome relationships." The different expressions all point to that common reality that precedes thoughts and words, the place where we are alive with happiness and joy, the place where we are connected with one another. No matter what name we give it, this is how we are all meant to live. And it was this awareness we wanted to introduce into people's lives.

I had a conversation with a man I'll call Ed, who told me about his eighty-five-year-old father's death from cancer. A year before he died, the elderly man had asked Ed to be his caregiver and stay at his side through the process to come. Ed gladly agreed. He told me how even though the cancer gradually reduced his father's body to little more than skin and bones, his eyes radiated joy, and his skin was as soft as that of a newborn baby. In spite of the severity of his illness, this man continued to radiate life.

The family was Catholic and the time eventually came to call the parish priest to administer the sacramental rite for the dying. After the priest had anointed the sick man and was ready to leave, he told Ed, "Your father is someone who really did not need the anointing. He is already one with his Creator." When Ed told me this, I understood that to mean that the sick man had let go of all ego attachments and was radiating pure peace and happiness—he was residing in the core of his being, and the priest could see that.

When we live from the peaceful center of our being, life isn't complicated. It moves organically and begins to unfold with unexpected twists and turns. Synchronistic events that seem to respond to our most sincere wishes become the norm. Life becomes a thing of delight, and all our energy is available to us for living, loving and creating. When we are entangled in reactive thinking and behaviors, life is more complex, generally empty of vitality, and often unmanageable. It isn't life at all, really, but rather a prison, even a waking death. Once we understand the difference, though it may not be easy to consistently remain in that center of peace, we recognize it as home and not only know what needs to be done to return to it, but are highly motivated to do so. We understand intuitively it is where we belong.

More than one person gave us feedback on how the Wellfolk workshop taught them to let go of prolonged feelings of emotional heaviness. Maria was one such person, and she provides an example of how the practice of accepting what is without judgment can change troubling behavior patterns that we have practiced much of our lives.

Maria loved sewing, mothering her two children and cooking for her family. Yet whenever her spouse gave her a compliment, she always saw it as a put-down. Instead of feeling pleased, she ended up feeling hurt and isolated from him. But it was not her spouse's words that caused her suffering, rather it was her interpretation of them. She was a victim of her own conditioned thinking mechanism.

As part of her conditioning, Maria believed she had to please her husband in every respect, all the time. As a result of such "heavy" belief, no matter what comments he made to her, what she heard was, "Maria, you're not pleasing me!" And it was to this that she reacted. What should have been a nourishing exchange between the two turned into a conflict that often resulted in hurt feelings.

It was an old and familiar pattern for Maria, one that she had engaged in throughout her entire life. Her reactive mind was programmed to understand present-day situations in light of the past. She repeated the past over and over again because she could not recognize that the situation was different. She felt she was just reacting the way she had to, the way her spouse was making her react. Her pattern was based on past experiences, probably from early childhood, before reasoned thought could diffuse them, and so they fell into the realm of a conditioned, and therefore automatic, response.

Finally, Maria's sister, Clare, who had attended one of our workshops, told her, "Maria, if you just accept your reactive feelings and urges as a simple, unimportant fact in your life, you will find relief. You'll feel better."

Maria told her, "That's not possible." But that same week an opportunity to try Clare's suggestion came her way. Her spouse made this remark: "Honey, you didn't go over our food budget this month, did you?" Her conditioned, reactive thought was, "He's putting me down!"

She felt hurt, as if no matter how much she did, it wasn't enough, and he thought she was inadequate.

This time, however, instead of reacting from those feelings of inadequacy, she stopped a moment to just observe and then accepted, without judgment, her hurt and her urge to run and hide. She calmly accepted her reactions and did not escalate the situation by responding defensively. A few minutes later, after the feeling subsided, she could tell she had passed through her usual reactive response as though it had never occurred. By observing and accepting what she felt without judgment, Maria found a way to break the pattern that had plagued her most of her life.

She told her sister afterward, "Gee, just observing and accepting my reaction sure beats all the suffering that comes from fighting it."

Weeks later, her husband, who had noticed the change in her, asked her what medication she was taking.

It wasn't drugs that had brought this change in Maria. She had discovered the principle of unconditional self-acceptance. She didn't fall apart emotionally as she usually did, and that, in turn, encouraged her to respond in the new fashion the next time a similar situation arose. By no longer identifying with inadequacy, and allowing herself to be as she innately is, she found her freedom. She discovered observing and accepting are not "doing" acts, but "allowing" ones, and they created dramatic changes in her life.

When others in the workshops chose to observe their impulses, they too, could see how arbitrary and groundless they were. Once that happened, past self-defeating behaviors began to melt away. Within a matter of weeks, and in some cases days, individuals learned to identify their anger or other habits and addictions of mind as nothing more than the impulses they were. They became free to act or not as they wished. When we live our lives from our "wellfolk" nature, we have a power that is greater than the restraints and aggressive reactions of egoic thinking.

Understanding that one does not have to give in to every impulse as if it were an order can be a powerful tool in a relationship. One couple, Helen and Frank, discovered how they were killing the life in their marriage and in one another through an unconscious and toxic pattern. They were driving down the highway to attend a retirement celebration for Frank's longtime supervisor. They had to take a particular exit. As they approached it, Helen noticed Frank wasn't slowing down. She said, "Here's the 35th Street exit!"

In response to her remark, Frank's face grew red with anger. "Don't you think I know this is 35th?"

"Yes, but I thought..."

Frank snapped back at her with even more anger in his voice, "Why can't you let me do the driving?"

"Look," said Helen, giving way to her own anger, "don't shout at me. It is your supervisor's retirement party. I'm only trying to help. I just thought you weren't slowing down—" She broke off her comment as Frank pulled the car over to the side of the road.

When he stopped the car, he looked straight at her, paused and stated with intensity, "You've been telling me what to do for years, so back off. I can't stand you trying to control my life."

When Frank paused to take a breath, Helen slipped in the remark, "Frank, why do you take everything so personally? Why can't we just cooperate and work like a team? I'm not attacking you."

Frank muttered under his breath as he looked out the window to his left, "You never let go, do you? You're always right, I'm always wrong."

This conversation is only one example of many that they had had over the past twenty-two years. They were locked in their ways of relating to one another, and it had all but drained their marriage dry of sensitivity, love or compassion for each other.

By becoming aware of the Wellfolk understandings, they both recognized they could step back and let go of the urge to act on their impulses. They moved beyond being victims of their instinctive, defensive and destructive reactions. As they shifted toward greater awareness of their impulses, their shared energy of waking to freedom accelerated their transformation. They learned from their own direct experience that the key was to let the impulses rise without judging them as good or bad. In time, the impulses themselves faded away like a bad dream.

Spirit or the Sacred Self is always present to nudge each one of us to awake up. It gives us clues all the time. The truth of this is both a fact and a force, but as long as we are locked into identifying with the confused conditioned mind and holding on to its impulses, the Self appears to be totally abstract and pure fantasy. Its nudges are ignored, and when noticed at all, they are reduced to the realm of coincidence. When we lay aside our pride and ask for help from Spirit, we find ourselves being changed in ways that we can't imagine until it happens. For the force to impact our lives, we must first be willing. Without that willingness, the conditioned mind maintains its dictatorship. The Wellfolk teachings helped people make the shift in awareness needed for this to happen.

On a personal level, formulating the Wellfolk understandings gave me great pleasure. I loved working out lesson plans and teaching the classes. When I put something on paper, it gives me clarity. In planning the lessons, I recognized my own conditioning, and could then see how to notice it, let go of it, and ask Spirit to undo its root errors in thinking.

In addition, teaching within the methodology I have outlined brought me a sense of harmony. I took delight in letting loose my creative imagination. Above all, I loved the feeling of adventure that attended this work. Spirit is unpredictable and often brought unexpected insights and experiences for all of us. Being involved in this kind of teaching, I always receive as much as I give—maybe more. It is both mystery and blessing.

The Wellfolk classes also taught me more about the *Course*. One of the central themes in the *Course* is that we are all a part of the "real" which never changes and cannot be threatened. Students of the Wellfolk understandings expressed this same basic truth in their own unique ways and with their own words. One young man, given to acting out his lust impulses, fell into trouble with the university he was attending. Three female students reported that he had inappropriately touched them and/or used unacceptable sexual language. By employing Wellfolk understandings, he discovered his lust impulse was not necessarily the dictator of his behavior. He learned he could witness his impulses without any need to act them out, and that the potential for doing so was present in every situation, all the time.

A middle-aged gentleman had been telling his lady friend how she should cut her hair, what colors were more appropriate for her, and what style of shoes to wear. This caused problems in the relationship. Though it was not easy, he too found that he could be the ever-present noticing field, and relate to his impulses differently, with the freedom to act on them or not. Both the young and middle-aged men found that underneath their impulsiveness there was a Self that never changes, a reality that can't be threatened.

One of the paradoxes of this work was that, even though I spent a lot of time in conversation with others, I also began to spend more time in silence. The silence was not associated with a schedule; it was more spontaneous in nature. I grew into it, expanding like a sail in the wind.

I turned to it because my heart bade me to. As I moved into it more persistently throughout the day, my body became still. The rattling and shrieking of ego, which I sometimes refer to as the monkey mind began to fade, and it was easier to witness it without a loss of calm. The ongoing emergence of the Sacred Self undid my conditioned mind's insecurities, anxieties and hesitations. I settled more into the soft blanket of being. I began to notice things as they were, instead of accepting my acquired interpretation of them, or obsessing on how I wanted them to be. I found pleasure in letting go of my focus on the future, and resting in the Now.

After teaching the Wellfolk understandings for six years, the vision became clearer and our method of presentation changed. We found the workshops themselves wanted to be different in scope, shape, and even physical layout. Because the work had drawn me into silence, we began starting each session with a period of silence. Whatever surfaced out of that became the point of departure for our exchanges. We wanted people to discover their inner reality without any push to label it. We changed the room arrangement from a classroom setting to a circle. We named our new gatherings "Dialogue on True Identity."

We worked with Wellfolk concepts in several formats from 1992 to 2000. Changes in format came about in part due to time spent with different teachers during this period. In the early 1990s, while studying the *Course*, I wanted to find a teacher who used a conversational approach rather than a lecture format. No sooner had I consciously articulated that desire when a friend gave me a tape and asked, "Will you evaluate this? Do you think it's for real?"

Unbeknownst to me at the time, the tape would lead me to the teacher I wanted.

Truth is a state in which there is no pursuing or seeking.

~Tara Singh

Expansion

The tape my friend gave me to review marked a turning point in my learning, one that brought several new teachers to me, and not all of them had an earthly form.

Tom Carpenter

The recordings were dialogues between Tom Carpenter, a teacher of the the *Course* from Hawaii and participants attending group sessions. Tom answered questions presented to him with words spoken by an internal voice he referred to as "brother." This "brother" was Jesus, who had spoken in a similar manner to Dr. Helen Schucman[1], the scribe of the *Course*. The format was simple: different members of the group asked questions and Brother/Jesus provided answers to Tom, who relayed the messages.

What struck me first and foremost was the reality of the words of Jesus coming through Tom. Throughout all my religious training, I had perceived Jesus as someone vastly superior and, from that perspective, separate from me. This image had an alienating effect on me. Hearing the dialogue on this tape, I grasped that Jesus could be something entirely different. He could be an intimate. I wanted to know more.

I picked up the phone and called Tom Carpenter at his home on Kauai

---

[1] Helen Schucman received the material through an internal voice while working as a professor of medical psychology at Columbia University's College of Physicians and Surgeons in New York City.

to see if he was offering any classes or workshops I could attend. He had one scheduled that was designed for therapists. A thrust of the class was that mental and emotional difficulties people face are often caused by identifying with the errors prevalent in egoic thinking. This was just what I was looking for, and February of 1992 was only a couple of months away. I signed up for the class. Berta, and Tom and Leslie Hatcher, also registered.

I later learned how Tom Carpenter began his work with Brother. When he and his wife, Linda, first moved to Kauai, Linda started a *Course* study group in their home. Tom Carpenter sat in on the sessions and soon noticed the difficulties that he and the others in the group had understanding the meanings of the text. The language was stiff, formal, often ambiguous, and somewhat archaic. Still, he felt as if it had something to offer even if it was not easy to understand. So, as he describes it, he withdrew inside himself to consider it. Since the information in it purportedly came from Jesus, Tom asked Jesus for help in better understanding the *Course* and expressed his willingness to teach others what he learned.

About ten days later, he began to hear a voice inside his head. At first, he found it quite disturbing. In the spirit of exploration, he asked the voice a question. To his surprise, it obliged him with an answer that he knew he hadn't put together on his own. He asked more questions, and answers were forthcoming. At first, Tom Carpenter called the voice "Brother," but later the voice identified himself as "Jesus." He told Tom that it was fine to refer to him as "Brother," but that in time Tom would be equally comfortable calling him "Self."

It wasn't long before Linda Carpenter began to ask questions of Brother through Tom, and he provided answers. Hearing what Tom and Linda were experiencing, their friends soon presented questions as well. Linda became so intrigued with the responses coming from Brother "through" Tom, that starting in 1989, she recorded the sessions. Linda eventually published these queries and their answers in the book *Dialogue on Awakening, Communion with a Loving Brother*, the first edition of which came out in May 1992. In the meantime, Tom and Linda were holding workshops centered on Tom's interactions with Brother and the principles of the *Course*.

That's when Berta, Tom and Leslie Hatcher, and I stumbled across them and attended their seminar. None of us had anything specific in mind when we signed up for the workshop. We were learning to let our inner spirit guide us at that point, and it was more as if something in each of us recognized this was a path to take. Certainly, it was still a new approach for me. By contrast, I always had clear goals and objectives in taking university classes and continuing education programs, but here I signed up for a workshop half an ocean away because something in me so urged me.

Upon our arrival in Kauai, before the workshop got started, Tom and Linda Carpenter received us with warmth and generous hospitality. They invited us for dinner in their home the night before the seminar. After dinner, all of us gathered in their living room. The four of us wanted to know what "Brother" would say to our personal inquiries. This is more than fifteen years ago, so I recall little, but that little is still important to me. He told me that I had guilt left over from my years of work in Brazil. He paused and added, "Thomas, it is important for you to stay open to connecting with beings who have passed over." I had not told him that my deceased maternal grandmother had connected a number of times with me in a supportive and loving way.

The next morning, a loosely structured workshop began with Tom Carpenter giving a short explanation and reading from the *Course*. He spent the remaining time in dialogue with those present. The discussion focused on the principles of the *Course* as they applied to the therapist-client relationship.

Tom Carpenter, with Brother's orientation, had a novel take on this. No meeting, he said, between any two people is ever a chance encounter, whether they meet casually in a hotel elevator or in the office of a therapist. In *Course*-centered therapy, the interaction is not treated as a hierarchical or one-way flow as may be found in traditional therapies. Each party influences the other in what is viewed as a predetermined and harmonious opportunity for learning. When both client and therapist are open to this concept, they are interchangeably teacher and student. This resonated with us, for it echoed the basic Wellfolk understandings.

It's a given that clients come to therapists for their own benefit. But in listening to Tom Carpenter, it also became clear that the relationship is as much for the therapist as it is for the client. Both are in the relationship to let go of some kind of wrong-mindedness and wake up to their Eternal Self. They are mirrors for one another, both with an opportunity to learn something specific. This idea turned the apple cart upside down for me. I had never so clearly encountered this perspective in any of my professional trainings.

On the contrary, in the traditional approach to therapy, one of the chief dangers for a therapist is burnout. It is also common for therapists to become overly or insufficiently involved with a client because the relationship is viewed as a one-way street. But when the relationship is viewed as a two-way dynamic, where each contributes something to the other, it transforms how each one responds. It becomes an exchange, a gift giving, if you will, and one never knows from client to client what the gift will be. As a psychotherapist, if I view every client as appearing precisely because of something I need as well as something I also provide, the process takes on the air of a blessing.

Tom Carpenter's insight into the client/therapist relationship changed forever the way I viewed my clients. It freed me to be open for that exchange instead of expending energy to accomplish predetermined goals that tended to drain me. This, in turn, changed my clients' experience of me as well. I've employed this approach for fifteen years as of this writing, and to some degree, it's made every client relationship an adventure in discovery.

I picked up a copy of *Dialogue on Awakening* when it was published a few months after we had our sessions in Kauai. It is one of those books I couldn't read straight through. Instead, I read a few pages every day and let them percolate before I read more. Ninety-five percent of the book consists of questions and answers from workshops or in private sessions with Carpenter/Brother. As I reflected on each passage, I saw every question and its answer as an invitation to drop the illusion of separateness and accept that we are all one at the level of spirit or essence. This, according to Brother, is what all of life is about. Spirit wants us to wake up to what we really are, joy, love and peace. Every life experience we have contains within it an opportunity to do so. This is true whether it is a short encounter with a taxi driver or the long-term relationship with a marital partner.

But there is another aspect that is powerful, and that is the way Brother knows a person's entire life history without the person saying a word. It seemed to me that he often responded not only to what people were going to say before they said it, but to their core issue, which may not have been spoken. I witnessed this on many occasions. One involved a friend from Argentina who attended a Tom Carpenter's workshop. Our friend does not speak English, so Berta planned to interpret for her. Our friend presented a lengthy explanation about what she wanted to know from Brother, but before Berta could interpret, Tom Carpenter, who does not know Spanish, was already providing a precise response.

The realm in which the conversation with Brother occurs appears to be without barriers of language. It is instantaneous and direct. The level of intimacy required for this kind of "conversational" exchange, where Brother talks to the person's inner self, had a big impact on me, spoke directly to my hunger for connection, and drew me into further study of Jesus' message in the *Course* and Tom Carpenter's book, *Dialogue on Awakening*.

The *Course* is a complete compendium on spirituality and contains far more material than is covered in *Dialogue on Awakening*. The issues Tom Carpenter covers are broken down into bites I could chew on, digest, and apply to each hour of my day. I cherished each sentence I read.

The lure of this material is hard to describe. My interaction with it elicited a yearning for Truth. The more I read, the more I wanted to read. I felt drawn into it by an invisible force, and it calmed and nourished me. The concepts I meditated upon resulted in sharp shifts in perception, not the least of which was the different way I came to view Jesus. I also viewed his teachings in a different light, one that appealed to my heart and soul in addition to my intellect.

In the short introduction to Tom Carpenter's book, Jesus states that we have a choice in remembering that we are whole. He states time is an invention of our mind that separates us from Divine Consciousness. It stems from our identification with the body, which is mortal. Once we understand we are not our bodies but spirit, we can grasp that we are never truly disconnected from others. When we remember who we are, we can make the choice to return to the infinite present. The choice, as it says in the following lines from a *Dialogue on Awakening*, is always ours:

> *It is not possible for it to be otherwise for that would be a contradiction of who you are. It is but you who must decide to wake. And you choose the time, while it still seems to govern you.*[2]

Brother's repeated reminders that we don't have to do anything other than ask for help to find salvation from errors in thinking was difficult for me to grasp. The following quotation from *Dialogue on Awakening* illustrates Brother's point of view.

> *There is only one choice for you to consciously make and that is the choice to recognize your being, to "wake up" to your Mind. Once the recognition again becomes the Reality in your conscious Mind of who you are, you will discover the natural thing is to simply be it. This requires no effort. It requires no doing. It is an activity of just reflecting who you are.*[3]

---

[2] *Dialogue on Awakening.* Tom Carpenter, Carpenter Press, 1992, p. x.

[3] *Dialogue on Awakening.* Tom Carpenter, Carpenter Press, 1992, p. 9.

With this difficult-to-grasp concept, I discovered the following: If something occurs that is challenging, I can ask the True Self for help, and then wait and see.

Tom Carpenter's teachings dovetailed perfectly with what The Wellfolk Institute promoted, so after we returned to Washington State, we decided to sponsor a presentation by Tom Carpenter in the Tri-Cities, Washington, area. The first meeting was later that year. Fifty people participated with many with questions for Brother. The sessions went so well, and were so well received, we subsequently scheduled others.

I told Tom Carpenter that I wanted to record *Dialogue on Awakening* in an audio format. Without hesitation, he replied, "Thomas, you can do that, and whatever else you want with the book." So, I organized my schedule in the following months to accommodate the project. Each week, I read several pages, starting from the front of the book. When I completed all but the last five pages of the book, I listened to what I had recorded. What a jolt that was. All I heard was the false drama and ego-driven quality of my voice. It filled me with acute discomfort.

I put aside the tapes and prepared to start over. Unsure of how to proceed, I struggled for inspiration. Finally, I remembered what Tom Carpenter did when he'd noticed the difficulties his wife's study group had in understanding the *Course* material. I settled into silence to address Brother directly. I said, "Brother, I will focus on pronouncing the words, please, you give them the energy and meaning." And I began again.

When I listened to the second recording, I discovered the force behind the words was totally different. Tom Hatcher listened to it and thought I must not have been reading from the book. He double-checked the spoken word with the written one, and to his surprise saw they were the same. When Tom Carpenter listened to the tape recordings, he said he was aware that a further richness in the text had come through.

What was the difference in the two recordings? In the first, I had been more involved in trying to make an impression on the listeners with how polished a performer I was. The message was secondary. My ego, trained with classes in drama and sacred eloquence, had a heyday with the first recording. In the second, I allowed Brother to impart his message. The difference was palpable.

Dialogue on Awakening teaches that we are motivated by ego when we focus on accomplishment. That was exactly what I had done in the first recording. It wasn't until I let go of my expectations that something else came through. It was transforming.

Brother makes the point in his teachings that this kind of "allowing" is the natural expression of our being. When we adopt a peaceful, loving, unconditional, and allowing attitude, our conscious mind is in closer alignment with the Self. Brother said in one of his dialogues with Carpenter:

> *...don't undertake this process of changing your mind with an attitude that says I must become something. Approach it more directly with a secure knowing on your part that the change is merely bringing you back into realignment with what you have always been. Think of it, if you will, as a process of bringing yourself out of a state of amnesia.*[4]

This was exactly the area with which I had struggled so much in my life. So many times I had been engulfed by a desire to perform and to become someone of importance. When I began to incorporate the practice of allowing, I found a new sense of expansion and ease. Self-imposed limitations and constrictions, feelings of inadequacy, guilt, and fear dissolved, leaving in their wake a deeper sense of connection to the real.

More often than not, it was the little things that contributed the most to the quality of my life. Often in the morning when I entered the kitchen to have breakfast, I fell into a form of unconsciousness where I was focused on the future. I felt pressured to rush and get the meal prepared so I could hurriedly eat it and be on my way. By noticing this urge, I learned to preempt it and deliberately focus on being in the moment, the Now. When I stayed present, time expanded, and I fully enjoyed preparing and eating the meal, adding a sincere pleasure to my life instead of additional adrenalin and anxiety.

In another situation, I approached the task of balancing the business account as if it were acid that would burn me if I slowed down. When I noticed how pinched I felt with this approach, I let that feeling rise up and let it go. Suddenly, the task was peaceful instead of painful.

Brother discusses how and when we can choose peace in our lives. He tells us as we go through any process or activity to let our intention be on attaining a state of peace. This is basic. All activities, even those as mundane as preparing breakfast or taking care of finances, are opportunities for finding peace. It is helpful to keep this intention in mind: "This I do to bring me peace."

---

[4] *Dialogue on Awakening.* Tom Carpenter, Carpenter Press, 1992, p. 86.

Do it first, he says, when it is easy to be at peace so that the pattern will be fixed in your mind for more challenging moments. The more you train your mind to remember it, the easier it will be to maintain.

As I read Brother's suggestions about being at peace, I resolved to have my intention be just that. I said to myself, "My intention is peace in whatever I do through assistance from Spirit." Then, with that thought firmly in mind, when my feeling flipped into one of disgust or frustration, I simply affirmed my intention. Then I waited. Shortly, I found myself feeling peace.

Through *Dialogue on Awakening* I discovered how "being" works in tandem with listening. When I am in a state of just being, I am open, and allow whatever comes in to come in. When I stay there, I go more deeply into it. As I remain in silence, I observe whispers from Spirit. When this happens, I know I have entered a realm outside of my individual self. I frequently find faint memories or echoes of past insecurities, struggles, fears and guilt, but by remaining totally accepting of Spirit's messages, it is easy to allow that voice to undo those echoes. In this state of being and listening, those passing memories are, without effort, transformed and released.

I readily admit that reading and studying the *Course* and *Dialogue on Awakening* is not for everyone. Linda Carpenter was eager to share the messages they received from Brother, but soon found some people had no interest in what Brother offered. She asked Brother about this and he told her this was natural, and he would work with those individuals in other ways, in a form that was acceptable to them. For me, though, working with Brother was and is precious. When he speaks, it seems as if I have been longing for eons to hear what he says. Through Brother, I discovered the choice of being peace. I learned I could choose peace as my permanent address, and that every situation I encountered was an opportunity.

Wayne Chenault and Jerome

Several years after meeting Tom Carpenter, I encountered someone who offered healing classes in our local community. Wayne Chenault[5] taught healing from a metaphysical standpoint, working with people in what he called the spiritual and karmic dimensions. He also worked with the ethereal realm, which is home to incorporeal entities. He saw people as being more than physical bodies, and he worked with beings from the non-physical realm as well as subtle energies that surround the body.

Wayne was more than an energy healer though. He was a guide on the shamanic path and helped others connect with their intuition so they could work with the forces of nature in the shamanic tradition. In addition, he was a medium, meaning he would allow an ethereal being to enter his body and speak through him. The entity that used his body was Jerome. Wayne organized sessions around the country in which Jerome told stories in response to requests from those present. The stories he told were often very powerful healing events for the person who made the request, and of interest to others who heard them.

Once or twice a year, Wayne accepted individuals for a two-week introduction to intuition through shamanism, a workshop he held in the mountains of North Carolina. I had heard about his workshop, but spending time studying with a shaman was a step beyond my cultural and religious conditioning. For years I'd been okay with the words from Jesus in the *Course* and through Tom Carpenter, but this was something else again. Nevertheless, when I recalled my experiences with Stephen Schwartz and Tara Singh, in which I learned to trust in and live from my intuition, I grew emboldened, stepped out of my comfort zone, and asked Wayne if I could take his training.

As with heading to Hawaii to take Tom Carpenter's class, it wasn't so much that I saw a purpose for such training as that I felt an urge and followed it. I didn't have enough experience with other paths to have formed something as definite as a purpose. I did have some anxiety about the prospect of involving myself with shamanism, for that conflicted with my traditional training. Shamanism, in my mind, relied more on the power of the individual mystical experience, whereas in Catholicism, as I understood it, individual experience is not emphasized and often discouraged. But the voice from within nudged me in that direction. I stayed eleven days with Wayne in the woods of North Carolina in August 1996.

Wayne and I worked with elements of nature. We walked in the woods for about two hours in the morning, afternoon and night, for a total of about six hours a day. We had no destination and just moved where the spirit took us. We opened ourselves to nature in a way I had almost lost in my "acquiring" and "doing" preoccupations. For the first time in years, I reconnected with the energies I had so enjoyed as a child. Wayne's dog accompanied us on our walks during the day. When he knew we were going

---

[5] The Way of the Spiritual Warrior, Rev Wayne B. Chenault, Third printing 2002.

for a walk, he spun around and jumped with joy. After two days of soul-stretching walks, I nearly behaved the same way.

During the first morning, Wayne explained how forces of nature, fire, wood, water, air and earth, each had guardian spirits. They, in turn, had a whole host of helpers. He tutored me in how to work with these five forces and their guardians, all of which had names.

Wayne talked about how the earth's energy systems worked. He taught me how to sense in my hands and body when we were approaching vortexes, the invisible fields of energy that maintain the earth's equilibrium. I was surprised with my sensitivity to these because I had never been exposed to the idea of earth vortexes as he explained them. He taught me to see the light energy that is always present. We never needed flashlights even though we carried them when we went out at night.

I presume that sensitivity is still with me, and may enlarge my enjoyment of nature, but I found I had no interest in pursuing a shamanic path. It became unimportant to me in light of what happened on my last day with Wayne.

On that day, Wayne told me I would have an opportunity to converse privately with Jerome. In these sessions, Jerome entered Wayne's body, and Wayne "stepped aside." When Jerome entered, Wayne's whole manner of expression changed—his vibration, his tone of voice, his gestures and even his posture.

I had listened to tapes of some of Jerome's sessions, so I thought I had a good idea of how Jerome worked. I was eager to experience it myself, for his stories fascinated me and I wanted to collect as many of them as Jerome would tell me. So before the last day, I racked my brain and came up with four items for him to address. My intention was to benefit as much as possible from our meeting.

The first was my drive to work hard. I knew it was possible to do the same work with a sense of joy instead of a great deal of effort, but I had not found out how, and I hoped he would offer something to guide me.

Secondly, I wanted him to show me how to tell the difference between my "ego perception" versus "vision," and how to choose the latter. It seemed my main method of perception was to see everyone as separate from one another. I wanted to learn how to see the light in everyone as a matter of course.

That led directly into my third issue: my pattern of holding on to intellectual understanding instead of trusting intuition. I was addicted to thinking. I had, and still have, a hard time letting go of it. I wanted to allow life to unfold organically, with every detail coming from intuition, from heart, from Self.

Finally, my work with Tom Carpenter, and now Wayne, had raised my curiosity about ethereal entities. After reading Tom Carpenter's *Dialogue on Awakening*, I was clear that it is possible to connect with the whole mind directly. I'd had some experiences with that, but they were transitory. I wanted a connection that I could be aware of with more consistency and hoped that Jerome could tell me what I needed to do to achieve it.

Hopefully, Jerome's answers to all four of those issues would help me break out of my prison of ego perception and the experience of separation, inadequacy, guilt and anxiety that it created. If I could break through this, I could move beyond wrong-mindedness and into a permanent vision of reality. I was ready for the promised interview with Jerome.

At the appointed hour, Wayne sat in a chair across from me. The only other person in the room was his wife. Wayne told me that he sensed Jerome's presence at his side and he closed his eyes. I could see the shift in Wayne's body. Within seconds, Jerome greeted me and I responded. He asked me what I wanted, and I described to him the four themes I hoped he would address.

Jerome let go a deep sigh, and said jokingly, "He doesn't ask for much does he? Behold, there is no separation. The question and the phrasing of the question make it sound as if you are separate from these things. But you are not. Nor are these separate things. They are all the same. You speak of powerful beings. Very well, if you wish them to be. Understand that everything in your world, in your space of linear time, is but the reflection of you. Therefore, who is it that helps whom? You are being of assistance to yourself.

"Always, human deception demands there is 'this,' and there is 'other.' This deception of 'this' and 'that' never has been. All are the same. All are the one manifesting as the many. Else, how should you become Consciousness unto yourself? Liken it unto a drop in the ocean and the drop understands it is a drop, but it is also the ocean. There is no difference between that which comprises the drop and that which comprises the ocean.

"And when the mind is increasingly aware of your true essence, what happens to the false notion? It disappears. It is as a cloud and it ceases to be. Rather than concern thyself with stories, concern thyself with awareness."

I had been thinking that the more stories I heard, the more "information" I would have. This was really just the ego-me in my typical acquiring, doing, and building aspect. Jerome spotted that right away and pointed it out to me.

Jerome then asked, "There is a flaw that holds you back. Do you wish to know it? I will not tell you." He continued, laughing, "Yes, I will. Of course I will. What is necessary and required is that there be less thought. One cannot, with the intellect, behold God. One can with the essence of the Self. For the essence of the Self is beyond intellect, beyond thought, beyond the physical form, beyond the emotion...Therefore, what is required will be the quality of utter simplicity, utter acceptance. As a child, go then joyfully as you have beheld in the animal kingdom. Nothing but the joy of going. Does this creature perceive any difference between itself and where it is? It is there for the gleeful experience. Then where shall you go? Nowhere! You shall go within. You are learning then to see, you are learning then to intuit, you are learning then to perceive more. Again, as Consciousness unfolds, it reduces the intellect.

"Allow then the Consciousness to unfold within, no longer thinking there is this other that you must be one with, but rather you are one now. Nothing else need be done. The unfolding transpires of its own accord. There is nothing that is required in the way of action, in the way of meditation, prayer or sacrifice. Nothing is in the way of that which already is. It is a reluctance that is largely flowing forth from that ego self, that personality which knows that when the essence comes, it will perish, it will cease to be. There will be a remarkable transformation. These things will be but dim echoes of the long distant past, no longer required.

"Why do those that you have mentioned—Jesus, grandmother, Krishnamurti—still present as a personality? Why do they still present as an ego form?" Jerome asked. He was referring to things I was thinking in my head, but I had not expressed out loud. He continued, "Why do they do that? It is a courtesy for that is what the mind of man can comprehend. Their essence is as of yet incomprehensible except in the way of knowledge. Knowledge about the thing is only words about the thing. It is as if you see a pencil drawing of the mountain and believe that you know the nature of the mountain. You do not. Likewise, thinking you are peace is not the same as knowing you are.

"No longer think that there is anything in the way. No longer think there is anything more that you must know. No longer believe there is something that you must do. It is only to be That. As you have learned, and as your powers unfold, is there not within consciousness the beginning of knowing that this is it? This is how you, the creature, would manifest. This is a beginning; allow the simple manifestation to continue.

"As to the intuition: Is there anything that such a creature cannot know? Nothing! You need only to have in mind what is desired. Is there effort involved in this? None whatsoever. What is needed comes. What is questioned is answered. No thing is beyond anyone. The only key is what you are willing to accept. Therefore, be open to accept all things. When you have received all things, you will then behold that which you have received. There shall be no difference.

"Yet you still struggle with the ego. What makes you believe that there is something else that you must do? Always there is yet another thing, and another, and yet another question to answer, another thing to learn. That is the ego expressing as the intellect. It always is demanding more questions and digging deeper. Answers are simply not there. They are already within. All of the stories you thought I might tell you will not serve you. What will serve you is acceptance, simply to be there. Where do you suppose that I dwell?

"Within," I said.

"Precisely so, and what is there?"

"Everything."

"Exactly," said Jerome. "Where do you dwell?"

"The same place. Within."

"Exactly," he said.

"And everything," I added, "is already there."

"Yes, waiting, waiting for you to wake up," Jerome said. "Wake up. You may wake up now. It is time. Then what else need be said?"

"Really, nothing," I said.

"Your questions are answered, are they not?" asked Jerome.

"The questions are answered," I said.

"It is all so simple. Then what is it that must be overcome? This is a test. We will review what it is that must be overcome."

"The thoughts of the false self," I said. "The intellect."

"Too many thoughts, too many questions. There is only one answer, and you have that already. Acceptance is all that is required. Acceptance of your True Self as you stand, that is it. How else could it be otherwise? Nothing more is required. It is ever so simple and yet there are those who seek this for lifetimes and never find it. It is an insight, a realization, in which you suddenly have a sparkle in the eye, a smile upon the face; you laugh until the front of your shirt is wet with drool. It is immaterial, for you have it at that moment. You have transcended all of the illusion and seen the fact. Thus, these simple exercises that you shall do will lead you inexorably to that."

I knew he was referring to the exercises on choosing peace from Tom Carpenter's *Dialogue on Awakening* and the lessons from the *Course* workbook. I could feel the connection between his words and the thought of these exercises in my mind. He had also "known" I had come looking for stories, though I had not said as much to him.

"So no longer is there any difference between you and anything. There is only you, beholding you, beholding you. Nothing else! Ever so elementary, and yet volumes have been prepared to complicate it. Nothing else need be done. This answer will then be sufficient?"

"Yes," I said, "thank you very much."

"You are most welcome. And bless you and the light that is in the heart of you and the light that goes forth from your eyes as you behold your new world. Long may the spiritual sun shine ever so brightly upon the pathway at your feet. So be it."

Before ending our conversation, he had a final suggestion for me. He told me that when I wished to speak to my grandmother, Krishnamurti, or Jesus, to address them as "Grandmother-Self, Jesus-Self, Krishnamurti-Self," and so forth. He addressed my unspoken thoughts by referring to history that I had not provided. Like Brother, he was teaching: we are whole, we are one. After his final suggestion, he asked, "Do you understand?"

"Yes. Thank you," I said, and our conversation came to an end.

During the eleven days that I worked with Wayne in the woods, I had slipped back into the mindset I had as a young Catholic. I felt myself separate from the guardians and forces of nature, as I had done with my guardian angel and the saints. I understood these things were available to me, but enveloped within that idea of my being separate and not worthy of receiving aid from such superior entities. I again saw the elementals and the guardians of nature as the same kind of entities, separate and superior, and I lost my focus on the oneness of creation. Jerome's words on that last day snapped me into alignment with the one True Self. There is no separation, he told me again and again. We are all one. And he showed me this in the most direct fashion possible: by being aware of my thoughts and my history without being told. I understood what he did, and I was overwhelmed with gratitude.

Jerome also showed me that I think too much. Waking up, he made clear, has nothing to do with thinking. Jerome, as was true of every other teacher I had, invited me to go within and intuit instead of think. I need not do anything, say anything, pray for anything, or sacrifice anything. I just needed to be.

After working with Wayne at the retreat, I carried away a deeper respect for shamans and other nature healers, but at that time I had little interest in working in that fashion. I loved nature, to be sure, but that was not the place of my calling. The sublime, transforming energy that accompanied Jerome's words set me ablaze. His words penetrated my every cell so that I felt what he said more than I heard it. Jerome's words "reorganized" me.

Since my conversation with Jerome, I have employed his suggestion to say "Self" when addressing Jesus or any other beings in the ethereal realm. And I found that it does evoke a stronger sense of connection to Spirit, to Self, to peace. The minute I think of Self as "other," I create the separation that disconnects me from "others" and from life. Through this shift, I found a greater sense of tranquility and harmony. I feel connected and content. To be sure, I do slip into old patterns, but having once found that connection, it is easier to recognize when I've stepped outside of it, and it is easier to retrieve knowing that it is never lost, only denied or forgotten.

For two months after my visit with Wayne, each morning when I woke up, life felt fresh, as if I were newly born. The feelings came and left without me doing anything to invite them in or to send them away. The experience reinforced the mystery of life, that it has the power to keep renewing itself in astonishing ways. Every action I took, whether kissing my wife or spreading marmalade on my toast, had a serene intensity to it. I felt as if I were doing these things for the first time. I paid attention to them, was completely absorbed by them. This time, all of me was engaged in the action, instead of the meager portions of myself that weren't tied up in fear, longing, regret, competing or doubting, all those things that bound my energy and capacity for joy, love and being in the Now.

Gangaji

The same year I made the retreat with Wayne in North Carolina, Berta and I read the book *You Are That* by an American woman named Gangaji. Several things impressed us about the book. Her words were clear and straightforward, without any "spin," and she echoed the ideas we were being drawn to from other sources. Among those was the idea that we are beings of pure consciousness, and the moment we accept and identify with that, we are free from all perceived restraints. We are free to choose to be peace, regardless of our bodies, thoughts, emotions or circumstances. Gangaji extended a perpetual invitation to the reader to trust the intuitive knowledge that rests deep within.

As a result of the way these things resonated in us, we signed up for a weeklong silent retreat with her in August 1997 in Crestone, Colorado.

The format of this retreat attracted me, particularly since I had developed a relationship with silence. As with the other things we'd investigated, we didn't have any preconceived ideas about what we would learn, but rather followed our own sense that it was something we wanted to explore. It seemed a fitting response to our intention of "waking up."

About 210 people attended. Twice a day, in the morning and afternoon, Gangaji conducted sessions in which she briefly presented a spiritual topic or read a letter from someone that contained questions or comments. Many times the authors of these letters were in the audience. If so, Gangaji invited that person to come up, sit next to her, and talk about whatever issues had been raised in the letter while the rest of us listened. Most often the conversation went into deep questioning and brought about discoveries of essential truths or the resolution of an issue. When one person finished, anyone in the audience could volunteer to sit in the vacated chair.

These interactions were lessons for the rest of us. In one case, a woman rose and expressed her confusion over the term "nothingness," which she had encountered in the works of several writers. She wondered whether it meant deadness or blankness, or whether it was perhaps another term for active intelligence. Gangaji asked her questions about the quality of this "nothingness" to which the woman referred, and the woman said it seemed intelligent, but was sometimes cloudy. Gangaji asked her, "That which is aware of clouds, and aware of some kind of intelligence that comes and goes, what is this?"

The woman paused a moment, then answered, "This is who I am." Just by asking the question, Gangaji had focused the woman's attention in a way that allowed her to discover and identify the witnessing in her, that constant presence that stood outside of the tidal pulls of emotion and circumstance. In this fashion, she could see that consciousness is always present and never changes.

Another participant, a young man, was concerned about what would happen to his marriage if he pursued his spiritual path, and his wife did not. "Is it a problem if my wife does not share the same yearning for truth I have?" he asked. Gangaji answered him in her usual direct style.

"Your partner will catch it from you, or the marriage will be finished. It is as simple as that." She went on to offer something from her own life. "When I met my husband, and before we were married, all I wanted was a husband. I thought that getting married would be total fulfillment. I caught the yearning for truth from him. His whole life revolved around truth. How lucky that destiny brought me to a man who loved truth more than he loved me. He served truth more than he served me. He was married to truth before he was married to me. For our marriage to be, I also had to meet truth. Once truth is met, one cannot help but fall in love.

"Let your marriage be in service to that and then, regardless of the problems, the discomforts, and the trials, it will be a true marriage. If marriage is in service to each other's ego, it is the usual, false marriage."

In situations such as these, and seemingly without effort, Gangaji had a way of illuminating the heart of whatever issue concerned the individual. Her answers were never complicated, contained no dogma or doctrine, and always focused on the truth behind the issue.

By attending these sessions with an open mind and heart, I received the purity of her insights, and the peace that flowed from and around her. In fact, the latter was really the natural consequence of being a "truth merchant." Speaking truth requires no energy for defense and leaves more energy available for love. Gangaji always radiated love. This sensation was so pleasant, so satisfying, that I knew I didn't want to go back to the seeking, striving mindset.

The experiences I had in the sessions percolated within me during the rest of the day, whether I was sitting in solitude, or Berta and I were hiking in the beautiful country around the retreat center. It was a passive process. I didn't do or think anything, I just stayed in the spectrum of consciousness that Gangaji's peace encouraged. I allowed consciousness to bring to me whatever it willed. I could see what I was feeling had nothing to do with ego. This retreat was a time to be totally open, and so I was.

Gangaji started off a session with a short talk that addressed how we are conditioned to close down our receptivity to information and how, in some cases, that is for our survival and growth. We simply cannot accommodate all information that is available to us from our environment. We must pick and choose what we will give reality to. Many of these decisions are made lightning fast and below the level of our awareness. Others are consciously made. For instance, if we hear of a new diet, we might choose to resist absorbing that information until we learn or feel whether it is right for us.

Gangaji described how as infants we have a natural capacity to receive; it is necessary for our survival and growth. We are wide open for love, attention, food and information. We do not know bad from good. Anyone who's ever watched a two-year-old move through his environment will quickly see that everything encountered goes in the mouth without discrimination. Eventually, between experience and guidance, we learn that some things we encounter, like scissors, a knife or a hot burner, may do us harm. We learn to discriminate and the full matrix of our discrimination is determined by the conditioning we absorb from our familial and societal environments, as I described in the first five chapters of this book.

If nothing in our environment supports us, we grow less open to receiving. We begin to harden; we automatically stop learning and growing. With time we may close out life all together.

Gangaji explained that the automatic closing down of receptivity to new information can become the problem. The ability to evaluate is necessary, whether one is judging data that comes from a neighbor, website, TV commercial or new book. The use of discrimination can be a matter of survival.

"My invitation to you in this retreat," she said," is to be open to the silence, rain, sunshine, everything. Lay aside your fears of receiving while we rest in the safe environment of the retreat. This retreat is not a time for gathering information on how to survive or to question what is given. It is a time to relax, to literally forget about the future. Now is the time to receive the truth, so we remember who we are."

As I watched Gangaji, she radiated peace, happiness and love, as did many others in the group. She consistently fanned the flame of desire in me to lay aside illusion and wake up to receive what Self or "being" offered. She did this through her presence, through the manner in which she approached each person with whom she spoke and in the explanations she gave. In that environment, my mind quieted. I took in what she communicated without effort and without intellectual analysis.

As with Jerome, she taught nothing new, but the electric effect of being in her energy field had a great result. She illustrated the possibility of waking up.

As a result of being in that sacred atmosphere, I had a most unusual experience during the morning session of the second day. It occurred spontaneously without design on my part as I sat in silence. My chest suddenly seemed to push out from my body to such a degree that I felt deeply loved, and I wanted desperately to extend the same to everyone and everything. I felt a fierce pressure in my head. It was so strong I thought my eyes would pop out like champagne corks. It seemed as if they strained to see the love I felt surrounding me. This was a physical sensation that permeated my entire body, and the love energy behind the phenomena was beyond words. The intensity caught me by surprise, but I surrendered to it instantly and without question, saying, "If my eyes are to pop out, if my chest is to explode, so be it." I continued to sit in silence and to accept the feelings. And, I'm happy to report, my eyes did not pop out, and my chest did not explode. Eventually, the feelings passed as freely as they came.

After the session, Berta and I walked to the parking lot. Out of the blue, my knees gave out as if I had been hit. The words, "the fruit has fallen," reeled in my head as I once again stood erect.

Those were the words that Gangaji's teacher, Poonja, had written to express how the knowing Self comes to a person without effort. The fruit falls when it is at its appointed stage, and so it is with each of us. We connect with Self when we are ripe.

At the time, my mind simply stopped. I suspended all judgment. After about fifteen minutes, the sensations subsided, though on a mental level I remained somewhat overwhelmed by the sheer intensity of the experience. I did not clearly grasp what happened, but I felt it was an invitation from Consciousness to accept myself as already awake, to allow Spirit to function in or with me in whatever way it chose. I didn't have to do anything with that. I remained silent and open, resting in my natural Self, accepting what it was, as it was.

That may have been the most important learning from that session: to allow whatever happens to happen without giving in to the compulsion to control. The false, limited "I" needed to let go and surrender to the mystery of life. Instead of making life happen, I was learning to let it live me.

At the next morning's question and answer session, I raised my hand and Gangaji called on me. I went forward and she greeted me with, "Namaste." I bowed and kissed her hand; she kissed mine in return. I handed her a letter and said, "I wrote this letter just in case you didn't see my hand."

"I've never seen your hand. Play your hand," she answered.

"It is being played for me," I said.

"Then you are winning."

"It has been a long journey to nowhere," I said.

"And from nowhere how long has it been?"

"Eons probably."

"That is what you would assume. From arriving to nowhere, how long has the journey been?" she asked.

I gestured my answer by forming a large zero with my fingers, meaning "no time." The group laughed.

"Yesterday," I went on, "in the afternoon session, my whole chest was bursting, and then it felt like my head was going to explode...my eyes were like corks on a champagne bottle. I said to myself, 'Go ahead and burst, pop out.' And of course nothing happened."

"Yes, spontaneous combustion," Gangaji said, "Give in to this force."

"What a wonderful force," I said. "A bit later, Poonja's words hit me like a hammer blow, 'When the fruit is ready, it will fall.' And then I was brought to my knees! I knew the fruit had fallen...from nowhere to nowhere, no fruit." In actual fact, there is no fruit that falls because it is and always has been ripe. We only seem to ripen as we grow to recognize the ego patterns of thinking. The more we see them, the less control they exert in our lives. Even the idea that we must wake up is an illusion because we already are—we just need to remember.

"And we all get to feast on it," said Gangaji. "There is enough for all."

I told Gangaji I had read Poonja's books, as well as hers. Someone in the group began to laugh. It was a contagious laugh, and soon the whole group was laughing. "There is nothing like a cosmic joke," I said. Then, I spoke about other experiences.

"Quite a love song, your story is," Gangaji said.

"The force is good," I replied. I was not being flippant here, but trying to convey the enormity of what I had felt.

Gangaji remarked, "If I would give out spiritual names I would call you 'The Big Banana.' There is this trick, when you have an unripened fruit and you want to ripen it, you put it next to a banana. Everyone benefits from this association."

The banana metaphor struck home with me. It echoed the same idea I found in the *Course* and in *Dialogue on Awakening*: .No one wakes up alone, we all benefit by the progress of each person as they succeed in undoing wrong-mindedness. When we let go of our allegiance to egoic thinking and allow Spirit to awaken us to what is real and eternal, it never happens without impacting the whole of Consciousness. If it didn't, then we would be separate, isolated beings with space between us. But we are not. We are whole. When we wake up to our True Self, we see that wholeness, and cannot help but see others the same way.

Eight months later, Berta and I attended a second retreat with Gangaji in northern California. This time, throughout the retreat, my ego-driven mind chattered nonstop, and the only rest from it came when we hiked in silence in the woods. Any attempt to stop this ego-based chatter by force only gave it vitality. The only solution was to step into the witnessing space and let it go. I did not do that.

I was agitated in this circumstance because I was attempting to free myself of the mental turmoil rather than accept it. Ego thoughts and values viewed the silent retreat as a threat. Silence raises the specter of annihilation to the ego, and it grows restive and reactive. I did not like what was happening, and I fought with it.

The negative chatter went on and on framing whatever any participant was sharing in a critical manner. My mind was filled with criticisms of the food, the retreat location, the weather. It judged how dense someone was who had spoken with Gangaji in public. Then it landed on the way I related to a particular client the week before. The trump card it played was that I had not dropped any errors in thinking. I had to admire its vigor.

In hindsight, I half-heartedly chose to see it as an invitation to be the impersonal witness of those ego thoughts struggling to win control of my life. Finally, after five days of rabid expression, it became silent, and a sense of outward and inward tranquility returned. I suspect it lasted that long because I had fallen into preferring it not be present, thereby instantly giving it energy to stay. If I had been wholly accepting and without any judgment, I am sure that it would have disappeared sooner. Once again, I had to learn the importance of allowing whatever comes into consciousness to be there without judging it as bad or good. The roots of the error in our identification go deep, and the unlearning is not a single action or decision, but a continuous process of recognizing how we block ourselves from entering into the unlimited realm of the One.

After the two retreats, I wanted to bring Gangaji's teachings to my home community. I'd found her approach to be so clear and so precise. She never imposed herself on anyone and was always respectful and caring. These attributes made her accessible to a wide range of people from almost any background.

Berta and I decided to sponsor Gangaji's retreat videos on our local public access television station. As a result, they have played almost continuously every Saturday since July 1998.

When we began to run the tapes, we established a weekly schedule for watching and discussing Gangaji's videos in our home. Every Thursday evening, about twelve people attended these informal sessions. We invited people we thought might be interested.

Often, our guests reported that after viewing the videos, they were more patient toward others and more peaceful in the following week and enjoyed more success in accepting what is. Through the repetition of accepting what is as it is, people have greater trust in the process and determination to consistently live from that frame of mind.

All of us who watched the videos enjoyed these sessions and felt the difference in our own lives, and so we continued the discussions for eight months. Then, by consensus, we decided it was time to bring them to an end. We had arrived at a kind of optimal understanding of the material for the time being and no longer felt the need for these discussions.

Involvement with Gangaji changed many things in our lives. It affected the way Wellfolk material was presented as mentioned in the last chapter. It helped me shed my addiction to searching and doing, and I rested more and more in the present moment. The more time I spent in the present, the more vigilant I became of thoughts, urges, and feelings generated by the false, egoic self that took me away from just being. When noticed, I could quickly let them go and return to the present. I found great enjoyment in living with a silent mind and cherished the cultivation of my intuitive mind. These are all great gifts, and I feel most blessed to have received them from Gangaji, Tom Carpenter and Brother, and Wayne Chenault and Jerome.

Summary

Looking back, I ask myself why I needed to connect with each of these different teachers. What was I looking for? In part, I was living in a state of trust, and had been doing so more and more since leaving Brazil. I followed currents moving beneath the surface that carried me to what I needed. I listened for the slightest nudges and moved in whatever direction they indicated. They took me first to Tom Carpenter, where through Brother, I learned to see myself as Self, and shifted my understanding of who and what Jesus was in a way most profound. I saw Jesus as he had taught—as Self. I learned to let my intention be peace in every environment, in every activity. Jesus's words in *Dialogue on Awakening*, have been a light that continued to shine away the darkness of my egoic errors in thinking.

From there, I was led to Wayne and Jerome. From Wayne, I learned it is a joy and perfectly natural to work with the forces of nature. Even though it was not my chosen path at that time, I still treasure what I learned.

It was my encounter with Jerome that resonated immediately with timely advice for me, "Stop asking all those questions, they only turn you into an addict who asks more questions. Wake up now! There is only the one Self." He demonstrated the reality that we are one mind, by knowing what was in mine before I could express it. He gave me an overview of spirituality that was lighthearted, joyous, and precise. Through his reflection, I saw that I dwelled too much in the thinking mind, and his invitation to cultivate intuition is with me to this day.

Gangaji's presence invited everyone near her to rest in being, to be open to receiving. Over the years of my association with her, I have noticed how fresh and alive she remains, even in the words she uses to illuminate a concept. I appreciated and learned from her special ability to deal with people from diverse backgrounds. She accepted the truth of who she is and thereafter extended to all who would listen the invitation to wake up. Over and over she emphasized that we are all equal, and there was nothing to do or say except to be still and discover our truth.

Living from a state of awareness isn't about a path of doing or becoming. It is about being. It is about knowing your Self that precedes all thinking and effort. This is incomprehensible to the conditioned mind. From childhood on, we are taught how to tie our shoestrings, eat with silverware, print our name, solve a math problem, and drive a car, use proper manners, and so forth. Many of us educated in a strong religious system were taught how to gain a far-off heaven and avoid a hellish condemnation. My struggle was a result of tenaciously hanging on to the idea that I had to know how to wake up. What these remarkable people mirrored to me, each in their own way was surrender to the Self.

This is an invitation to shift your allegiances from the activities of your mind to the eternal presence of your being.

~ Gangaji

Guidance

After I worked with Tom Carpenter and Wayne Chenault, it was easier to accept others who worked in a similar way. Years after my first meetings with Tom and Wayne, I met a couple who worked with entities of the spiritual realm. A friend of ours was the bridge to this next experience when she invited us to meet Andrew and Tamara Overlee.[1]

Andrew is a physical trans medium for a team of medical healers, physicians, scientists and researchers from the ethereal realm for many years. It has taken Andrew more than 40 years to accomplish the state of mind and pattern of thought to be at complete peace, to be developed, so that spirit can work through him, using his middle conscious, on a full time bases. In order for this to happen, his spirit family changes the molecular structure of Andrew's thought pattern which enables them to provide information from the ethereal world to the physical plane.

Andrew's wife, Tamara is also a devoted trans medium for automatic writing for the past 18 years, and she assists in all healing and counseling sessions. Their work is given to help all people with the internal thought of the God force of life so that the understanding of this physical life will help one prepare for transmission to the ethereal world.

Both Andrew and Tamara have dedicated their lives to this collaborative form of healing traveling throughout the United States and Canada for sessions, classes and workshops. In recent years, they have spent more time doing intensive healing work in their Montana home. All members

---

[1] Their website is www.joyofhealing.com. There you can also learn about their book entitled *The Truth of Life from the World of Love and Spirit.*

of the ethereal family with whom the Overlees work have at one time or another had a physical experience. Some have been doctors in the United States, Europe or China. One team member, Dr. Robert Koch, a bacteriologist, born in 1843 in Klansthal, Germany, was awarded the Noble Prize in 1905 in physiology or medicine for his work and discoveries concerning tuberculosis. He passed on in 1910. The Overlees refer to the healers they work with as their "spiritual family".

Berta sought out and benefited from a consultation. At the time, Andrew and Tamara were visiting Spokane and Kennewick, Washington, every four to six months. Berta and I attended a session with them in Spokane. The advice they gave Berta resolved her problem. Later, I followed in her footsteps and had healing sessions as well.

I had a problem with a tremor in my right hand that was addressed by an entity named Jesse Thomas. He was an English medical corpsman during World War II. During his life, he worked as a medium with Dr. Robert in the same way Andrew works with him. Jesse Thomas published his experiences in a book titled Psychic Surgeon. He passed on in 1965.

Jesse Thomas "worked" on my spine and told Berta to lay her hands on my back in specific places for thirty minutes each day for one month. This one session with the suggested follow-up treatment eliminated the problem, and it has never returned.

Because I so enjoyed my conversation about psychological and spiritual issues with Jerome when I worked with Wayne Chenault, I was curious whether there were entities in the Overlees's spiritual family who discussed these topics. I asked Tamara and Andrew about this and I was told they did indeed. They worked with Dr. Gregor, a psychiatrist in the Baltimore area who died in 1959, and a teacher named Lingrid. This sparked my interest. I wanted to learn about their psychological and philosophical perspectives, so I asked Tamara to arrange a consultation.

When the Overlees are on the road, their sessions vary in time depending on their clients' specific needs as they see several people each day. Because I wanted unlimited in-depth discussions, I met with Dr. Gregor and Lingrid at the Overlees's home in Montana on July 13 through July 16 of 2001. I approached this meeting not wanting to predetermine how the sessions would go just as I had done when preparing for meeting with Jerome. I remained open to whatever might come up and refused to build up expectations.

Berta and I checked into a motel a few miles from the Overlees home and arrived at their place on the morning of July 13 ready to start our conversations with Lingrid and Dr. Gregor. We started at nine in the morning and stopped for lunch at noon. Each afternoon, we had another long session, or two shorter ones, and finished by seven each evening.

Dr. Gregor

From the first moment that Dr. Gregor became present, Berta and I sensed his loving energy. He was straightforward and direct. He wasted no time and began the session by inquiring where I was in my thinking, professionally and spiritually. To do this, he asked me to define in my own words several concepts such as freedom, perception, religion and identity.

These concepts are "hot buttons" that reveal one's spiritual and psychological level of awareness. For my answer, I described freedom as that state of being where one is no longer entrapped by the limited mind's reactive thinking. Perception is formed by the interpretations and judgments we project onto situations and others. My own experience with the Church had left me with perhaps a keener sensitivity to the word religion. For that term, I responded that some organized religious groups use their traditional myths to engender guilt and fear to foster control, not freedom. As for true identity, I said that is when we recognize we are all One Consciousness.

I was surprised at how natural it felt to share these things with Dr. Gregor. He said that learning never ends, and that they, in the ethereal realm, learn as much from us as we do from them. This made me feel even more at home, echoing as it did Paulo Freire's methods of bilateral learning. It also fit the thesis in the *ACIM Manual for Teachers* that the roles of teacher and student are interchangeable.

After we had finished discussing these terms, Dr. Gregor asked Tamara and me to role play. The scenario he set was for Tamara to be a client of mine who was a convicted serial killer. I began the interview by asking why she was in prison. She disclosed that she had killed people because of the rage she carried inside. She described herself as "rotten through and through," and said she expected to "burn in hell" for the evil things she had done. I listened to her, and replied, "You are angry and hate yourself." She said that was it exactly. I told her, "I will work with you so you will discover that rather than being rotten and evil, you are really peace and joy." I met her expression of disbelief to my statement by assuring her that she was indeed peace and joy, but she had simply forgotten that fact.

Dr. Gregor concluded our role-playing session, saying, "Yes, yes, very good. Thomas, you think as we do in the ethereal realm."

Dr. Gregor had used this role-playing exercise to see whether I employed therapy from a traditional ego orientation or a spiritual one. Vastly different from one another, the two approaches yield different results. I use the latter because it is reality oriented. And I have found over the years that it is a gentler and far more profound approach. As individuals grow out of the fear-based, compulsive behaviors that drove them into therapy, they simultaneously prepare themselves to remember who they are in reality.

Next, Dr. Gregor moved into more personally challenging questions. He asked me, "Are you there in your heart all the time?" When I heard that question, I understood it to mean the same thing that Brother, Jerome and Gangaji had meant when they spoke of "being" consciousness, or the Sacred Self. They worded this question differently, asking, "Are you coming from the whole mind or True Self all the time?" I felt the resonance of it and knew in my heart what he meant. There was only one way I could answer the question.

"No, I am not," I said.

"What is your excuse for not being there all the time?"

"I don't know."

Dr. Gregor then pointed out how I hand out "cookies" to my clients. I knew right away that he referred to my drive to be the "nice guy" and never rock the boat. I often related to clients and others in a way that left them feeling good by avoiding conflict rather than speaking the truth, fearing it might provoke anger. This pattern reinforced itself because by indulging in it, I avoided the fear and acute discomfort of confrontation.

This, of course, meant I was not acting from True Self. I was not speaking my truth. Following the ego-conditioned mind, I placed such a high value on preserving my "safety" that if I did not continue to do this, I began to feel I had failed in some important way. This sort of loop caught me and kept me chained to unassertive behaviors. Over the years, I have learned to be more direct with clients and as a result, I hand out fewer "cookies."

After the discussion, Dr. Gregor brought the session to a close and told me that on the next day, I would meet with Lingrid.

At times during the conversations with Dr. Gregor, Tamara had writings from other members of their spiritual family who has been present but did not speak through Andrew.

The writings included many of the same elements that Dr. Gregor had addressed and included some additional perspectives. Following are a few of the messages I found special:

- "Do not continue with the expectations of society. Instead, do what you know is favorable to your soul, your true identity." This mirrored the previously encountered concept of "waking up" to one's Sacred Self. Mr. J. Krishnamurti stated the same thing when he discouraged following a given tradition to become someone special or important, but to seek out one's inner guides.

- "Do not deviate from your intuition. Embrace it, cherish it and act upon it every day of your life." Intuition is the way that Self communicates with Self. It is our pipeline to the whole of Consciousness, and it is independent of the split-mind. Its guidance always transcends any programming received from family, education and culture.

- "Awareness, my friend, is a key to the simplicity of life." Awareness was the message we taught as the third understanding in The Northwest Wellfolk Institute workshops. All those I had considered my teachers had said with varying words, "Be awareness, for that is who you are."

- "All souls are equal. The only difference between each is their personal awareness of life." Each teacher I have mentioned stressed that love and peace are available to everyone without exception. Love and peace are not awarded based on merit. They already reside within us. All we have to do is learn to access them. Anyone, anywhere, with any kind of history, can do that. Such is the equality of souls.

- "Let go of your fears about what you think you need to do. You have a great deal of work to do and you must move forward to the simplicity of your awareness. Allow your time and energy to be spent in fulfilling your desires as you relinquish your fears." I had heard this message about my fears many times, but yet on a day-to-day level, I was not aware of any fears. They had been so much a part of me that I did not see them. My desires could be distilled down to this: I wanted to teach spirituality as I knew it, learn the same by teaching and find joy in it. Within a few months, I learned how fear and teaching spirituality, were connected.

Lingrid

The morning after the session with Dr. Gregor, Berta and I again met with Andrew and Tamara. This time, Lingrid joined us. The session began when he introduced himself. He described how he had been what we would term today a mayor and spiritual leader of a small village in fifteenth century Iceland, and had considered himself to be a philosopher. He, like Dr. Gregor, was a noticeably attentive and caring presence.

Right away, he began to share his understanding of the reason for experiencing life on earth. He said the purpose for coming here was to learn the Constitutional Reality of the five elements of life: love, truth, honesty, humility and gratitude. Of these, love is the essence of life, the glue that holds the universe together. It is unconditional, extends to all without exception, and is the animating force in life. Lingrid encouraged us to live in such a way as to allow the love that resides within us to emanate to all—even those who are unkind or cruel.

Lingrid defined truth as that which is permanent and never changes; in other words you do not lie. It is, as expressed in the Course, what God created. What man creates is not real, not permanent. Our mission is to wake up to who we are and live in accord with that reality. We must, he said, "Relate as one to all life; feel the equality and connection to everything."

Honesty is the expression of revealing one's True Self in every situation. It means to live without lies, deceit or disguise. It means to be without judgment, prejudice or preconceived ideas about life no matter what the circumstance or situation. If one honestly exposes one's feelings and perspective, sincere listening must follow. Through sincere expression and sincere listening, people can discover their Eternal Self-worth and live life expressing that self worth in all times, places and circumstances.

Humility, which is not much discussed in our culture, is the expression in heart and action of the equality of all. It is the recognition that one is no better or worse than all others, regardless of what material gifts, deficits or behaviors they may adopt or have. One cannot have humility without also feeling gratitude. When one is truly humble, one easily sees that everything and everyone is a blessing of some sort, and a groundswell of gratitude pours forth. It also means standing up for who you truly are in all circumstances; standing up for yourself with conviction of strength.

Lingrid spoke more about the ethereal realm. I found this information had the paradoxical effect of shedding more light on the physical plane. He explained that if individuals still believe they are a body when they leave the earth plane at the time of death, they enter into a transitional domain where caring teachers and healers assist these souls in dropping their illusions, attachments and ego-generated emotions. If souls cross over and are trapped in expressions of anger, for example, it is understood that they are really feeling guilt, revenge or self-hate. They are helped to let go of their defensive anger so they can face the other emotions directly. Lingrid said he frequently worked with those who had recently crossed over from the physical plane and who were in a state of great confusion due to their enduring identification with wrong-mindedness. I had presumed that no one in the ethereal realm needed to develop a philosophy of spirituality. It had always seemed to me that one just "knew that one wouldn't need words to explain what the truth of life was." Likewise my assumption was that understanding would be complete, direct and immediate upon one's arrival to the "other side." It never occurred to me that there might be as many different levels of spiritual awareness there as here. I understood through Lingrid that a great difference exists among souls in their level of spiritual understanding. Thus, it is appropriate to help others see the truth of who they are whether they are in or out of the body.

Another aspect that made the ethereal world like ours is that suffering there has the same cause it does in the physical realm: errors in thinking. Heaven or hell is present wherever we are. They are not destinations so much as they are consequences of how closely we live in the truth of who we are. We create our own heaven or hell by what we think, no matter what realm we occupy.

At one point in our exchange, I told Lingrid about my friend Tom Carpenter and shared what Jesus taught in the book Dialogue on Awakening. He paid close attention as with everything we said and replied he'd like to meet Tom. This puzzled me because I had presumed that if he wanted to know more about Tom and his relationship with Brother/Jesus, he could just go to Tom's home and see for himself. Later, Tamara explained to us the reason for the meeting would be to teach and educate my friend Tom further on his enlightenment.

I had the impression when speaking with Brother, through Tom Carpenter, that everything in Consciousness was available to all ethereal teachers. When I probed this with Andrew, he explained that teachers exist at different levels of understanding. Andrew added that he could tell a difference in the level of awareness of the beings who had worked through him. Those on a higher level of wisdom will only communicate for short periods of time because the intensity of their presence taxes Andrew's physical body more. The discrepancy between physicality and their level of awareness is too great for the body to endure contact for any extended time without damage, and the entities he contacts never let that happen.

After Lingrid finished his introduction to the ethereal world, he asked for questions. Berta responded first.

"Last night I had a dream," she began. "It was a repetitive dream that I have had most of my life. I have dealt with it in therapy, and I thought I was through with it because I have not had it in about eight years."

Lingrid was clearly interested in this, and before she went on, he said, "Repetitive dreams have a lot of significance. In the ethereal realm, dreams are visions."

"In the dream," Berta continued, "I lost everything I had: purse, credit cards, passport, all that I needed to move from one place to another. I was lost in a city and didn't know how to get out of there. Also, somebody had painted over a beautiful wooden floor in my mother's home, ruining it. I was disgusted. Later, I was talking with my brother, and someone knocked at the door. I went into another room. When I returned, everything was gone and my purse was not there. I was naked; I was dispossessed. I could not function in the world."

"Berta," Lingrid said, "in another dimension you had an experience of being a person who does not like a sense of loss." By dimension, he referred to experiences in the ethereal realm that were like a physical life but without the physical manifestation of a body. "You had a lot of experiences of loss," he continued, "and for that reason you were protective. You brought that into the physical plane. You are very protective, are you not?" Berta was doubtful.

"Yes, you are," I interjected.

"Oh, about you," she said, "yes, I am very protective."

Lingrid laughed softly. "You don't want to get rid of lessons from other dimensions. The vision was a reminder that at this time being protective is necessary."

"I have to protect myself?"

"Yes, you have to protect yourself or something else around you. If this were not so, you wouldn't have had the vision."

The dream reappearing as it did, Lingrid said, was meant to alert her that something dear to her requires her protection. It is not prescriptive in nature in that it does not tell her how, or even who or what, it just alerts her to those instincts acquired in another dimension. How she fulfills her role is up to her. She has already learned how in those previous experiences. The more she pays attention to her recurring dreams, the more her life will unfold in a harmonious and stress-free manner because she is listening to her spiritual guidance.

In general, I thought of dreams as frequently expressing either disturbing or pleasurable ego-generated, suppressed issues. The idea that dreams could be visions or messages from other entities that care about us, or even glimpses of other lifetimes, was both new and provocative. During my doctoral studies, I had learned about dream analysis, but not this particular perspective. I have found that in working with this understanding of repetitive dreams, my clients have been greatly helped. I haven't noticed or devised any particular parameters, I just rely on my intuition as to when to present this as a concept for them to consider.

After Lingrid addressed Berta's dream, I told him about an experience I had while a student of past-life regression therapy. Berta and I had attended a conference that gave couples an opportunity to explore past lives they had in common. In one of the sessions, with guidance from the therapist, I went into a hypnotic state. I connected into another life where I found myself an infant in a crib, laughing joyously. The therapist asked me to look around and tell him what I saw. I looked around, laughed even more. Then I paused and told him, "Someone is here in the crib with me."

"Who is it?" he asked.

There was a long pause before I declared, "It's Berta, she's my twin." The joy of that recognition came bubbling up and out of me in peal after peal of laughter. I couldn't contain it.

When Lingrid heard this, he chuckled and said, "There are no past lives in a physical sense. Each soul has one life on this planet or in another planet similar to earth." The way he described it, we may experience other lives in different dimensions. In that unlimited realm of the thought pattern, he said, anything is possible.

I found it interesting that he did not believe in past lives in the same way I did. In reading various sources, I have concluded that some of us have had past lives on this planet and also imaginary lives in other dimensions. To be sure, from a practical point of view, it doesn't make any difference whether past lives exist or not, for healing only takes place in the present moment. Thus, if one accesses a past-life experience in which one had hate for another person, the healing of that hate can only take place in the Now. The "then" is already done and past; its effect can be undone only in the Now. Another point to remember is that if individuals affirm they have had past lives, there is danger that they see those lives as real and conclude their present life is also real. If some have had past lives, they were indeed illusions just as this present life is an illusion and represents thoughts in mind.

Compared to the importance of waking up to our true identity, the question of whether or not we have past lives is unimportant. If, through credence in past lives, we know that we have existed before this life and will continue to exist, such a belief is beneficial. But it can distract us from giving our full attention to the waking up process.

Lingrid explained the relationship that Berta and I have in this life as one that we had planned for in previous dimensions prior to our incarnation here. The two of us made a contract about what we would do together on this planet. "You two have found each other in the physical plane," he said. "You will assist each other to know yourself as the One and teach that to others. This is what you determined; it was not imposed on you. Thomas will teach like a bouncing ball of innocence. Berta will bring protection and anchoring in deep wisdom."

This idea of individuals planning in the ethereal world what they do together before coming to the physical one was not something I had ever been exposed to as a child, nor had I been exposed to it in the seminary. I had encountered it in my own spiritual reading, but it is quite another thing to hear about it directly from someone who knew it firsthand.

Lindgrid said everyone has helpers from the ethereal realm and introduced us to the members of our ethereal families. He described them by name, telling us their role in our lives and a little about each one. Berta recognized two of her family members right away. I did not know any of mine. In the last five years, I have become aware of them and their special tasks. One helps me with health issues, another protects me from physical harm, another guides me in teaching about spirituality, another helps me release my false identities and beliefs, and yet another is a student who is learning from the whole family and from me. While at times they feel as if they are something outside of me, I see them really as an example of what Jerome would call Self helping Self. I am equally comfortable calling these moments of assistance intuition.

Some guides, according to Lingrid, are always with us. Others come and go. Hundreds more may also, at any given time, be surrounding us. We have this magnitude of help because they want us to wake up to our true identity. They want the nightmarish suffering that we experience here to end and for peace to prevail. They also learn from us even as they help us. In spite of their goodwill and intentions, though, it is difficult for them to help us if we are not open to them.

I say a prayer every day upon waking. I use it as an invitation to my spiritual family members to abide with me during the entire day. I often repeat it just before seeing clients or when I am about to give a presentation. My guides help me stay focused on what is real, which keeps me from dissolving into what is not real. With their help, I stay in the space of the conflict- free mind. I have found I make fewer and fewer decisions that are dictated by the ego. This instruction to ask for help was the same issue I learned from the Course and Tom Carpenter.

From my training and conditioning, I learned to let much of my life be ruled and guided by thinking. Dr. Gregor and Lingrid gave me messages that paralleled Jerome's: "Stop the thinking and go with intuition." They did not mean for me to abandon thinking, but to refuse to let thinking be the dictator in my life. They told me to come from heart, or intuition, and to use thinking as a tool, not as my guide.

To help me develop intuition, Lingrid gave me an exercise. He suggested I go to a place where many people congregate, and walk around or sit for at least ten minutes. I was to notice what I saw without making judgments or interpretations. After doing that, I was to do the same thing again, only this time, I was to let the judgments and interpretations rule the day.

I followed his suggestion and once again discovered we have the ability to witness what is going on without becoming involved in it. Even in a busy mall, I found I could identify with the mind that is free of conflict and simply notice. All of us can be in the ever-present Now, completely free of judgment. When we are in that still point of the present, we are available to spirit, to the voice of intuition.

Doing this exercise helps create an inner disposition that is no longer addicted to ego-directed thinking. This frees us to receive and act from intuition. More importantly, we learn that being the conflict-free self is always an option. No matter how busy or noisy or stressful a dynamic may be, the choice is there to step outside of the ego-directed thoughts into the state of pure being.

Since our meeting with Lingrid, I have done this exercise many times in a local mall. What has become clear is that when I permit thinking to rule my life, I suffer, and my energy flows away like water down an unplugged drain. It is wasted in unnecessary struggles, doubts and insecurities. By contrast, letting intuition be the guide has created an increased sense of openness, peace and purpose in life.

The shift from ego-directed to intuitive processing did not occur overnight. It requires vigilance and patience. But as I do it, I gradually become aware that I am not struggling as I have in the past. I don't rush to accomplish tasks such as preparing a report or cleaning out the garage to get it over and done with. Instead, an internal attitude is beginning to bloom. Whatever happens will come about in its unique way and at the appropriate time. Instead of scrambling through life to accomplish a goal, I walk in leisure, relish each moment, bask in the sweet safety and security of knowing Infinite Love surrounds me with gentle care.

Fear Raises Its Head

One of the things Dr. Gregor emphasized in his sessions with me was the way certain fears were holding me back. I couldn't think what those might be, but shortly after my conversation with him, I had an experience that propelled those fears to the surface and I had a good long look at them.

It was Christmas time. One of my gifts to Berta was a simple story I'd written and illustrated with drawings and photos. The story was an outgrowth of our time with Dr. Gregor and Lingrid that centered around three themes we had covered with them: Berta's role in our relationship as the caring protector, my teaching from a state of joy, and my deep fears.

Berta was delighted with the story. She liked it so much, that she shared the story with our Thursday evening group at the first meeting after Christmas. These folks were caring and supportive friends, yet as she read the story to them, I grew achingly uncomfortable. I didn't know why, or even what I was specifically feeling. I just felt "wrong," somehow compromised, even shamed.

The next morning, after about ninety minutes in silent contemplation on this strange discomfort, tears sprang to my eyes. I realized I was immersed in fear. In one piercing moment, I understood what I had felt the previous evening: fear of being ridiculed and rejected. These feelings boiled foaming and frothing to the surface through the simple act of exposing my words.

In this expanded vision, I saw, too, why this fear had surged. The story I had written and given to Berta was about a truth as I understood it. I had no problem sharing it in an intimate fashion between just the two of us, but when she presented it to the group, it cast a large shadow. I would be defined by it, judged by it, and that made me feel naked and exposed. What if I were wrong? What if someone who heard it knew something I didn't? What if it made me look foolish? I was immersed in a dread of expressing myself to the public.

I had spoken before large audiences thousands of times when I was in the priesthood, but there was a critical difference. At that time, I spoke someone else's truth, not my own. Someone else's truth was actually a shield I had sought and wielded to protect myself from this visceral terror.

I saw too that this terror that had surfaced in my contemplation had come from some place down deep. Its roots lay in the very marrow of my bones. And yet it also seemed freeform, as if it came from outside of myself at the same time, and thus had authority. I hung onto it, though, and followed it back and back, sniffing for its seed. Then I got it. That fear had been born in the first grade when I experienced agony reading aloud. I had compensated for it all these years with my nice-guy personality structure and my single-minded focus on becoming adequate as a way to demonstrate worth. Of course, my feelings had nothing to do with any actions of others, for others did not "cause" me to fall into fear. That was my own doing. They didn't make me afraid; it was my own internal fear dragon that arose from judging myself inadequate.

This terror was like the eye of a hurricane. There I was, in the center of it, with fear whirling all around me, blinding my vision. I saw what a key factor it was in shaping my life. I saw how my earliest experiences in the classroom had devastated me and made me desperately afraid of ridicule. The children's laughter elicited by my poor reading ability crushed me, humiliated me, and made me afraid to expose myself further. A sense of inadequacy sprouted in me, took root, and grew as I grew. But even as I saw the source, I also received a gift. The problem was not my difficulty in reading; difficulty in reading was a fact. The problem was my interpretation of that fact. The cause of the suffering related solely to my judgment that I was inadequate, and not because of the actual reading difficulties.

As I saw this erroneous self-concept at the center of my fear, I also saw how the feelings of inadequacy it spawned had mingled with my ambition to prove myself adequate. Driven by this ambition, I had looked around the rural, Catholic community in which I lived and chose the profession that would most assuredly prove adequacy. I chose to become a Franciscan friar, priest and missionary. Who could reproach me then? Was I not God's emissary? Did that not sanction me, protect me and harbor me? In this moment of keen insight, I realized the decision, which affected my life, was not so much a calling, as it was a desperate desire to be safe. Becoming a friar, priest and missionary was the way I defined myself. "What I was" became the greatest hindrance for knowing "who I am."

The problem with fear, however, is that we cannot navigate around it as though it does not exist. We may think all we need to do is reroute ourselves and it will go away. It does not. It gets bigger. It goes into the protection racket and starts to make demands on the psyche, siphoning off more and more energy to keep from being felt. My response to that had been to develop my "good guy" personality to prevent any conflict that might expose my inadequacy. I avoided anger because that conflicted with being a "good guy." This worked for a while. But what I did not and could not realize was that I was cutting myself off from life itself. I troweled over any budding awareness with a load of wet cement and lost the capacity to feel many emotions, as it hardened into place.

As this vision unfolded before my eyes, I saw how being in this emotionally numbing state, I chose to be in a system that not only did not encourage inner, open-ended exploration, but to some degree actively banished it. That was good news at first. It enabled me in my flight from the demon of feeling inadequate. All I needed to do was what others directed. I never questioned this; it was not in my psychological script to do so. And frankly, the dread of discovering the full degree of my self-imposed inadequacy would have been overwhelming.

All this flashed across my mind, and I realized I did not have to run from the fear; instead I could face it. I neither judged nor interpreted it. I just accepted it as a fact in my awareness. In this witnessing and surrender, it was clear that I had created a whole life pattern associated with the story of being inadequate.

The feeling slowly faded. But it left behind an understanding that was permanent. I knew beyond doubt that the only problems I have are created by thoughts, and especially judgments about myself that I have taken seriously, struggled with, or avoided. I don't claim I have never again experienced fear. Part of being human is to feel fear. But each time it surfaces, I know I have the option to just notice it. I allow it to come and then leave. The only thing that gives fear its apparent "reality" is my thinking. When I welcome it as a normal part of my emotional symphony, it dries up. When I give fear some sort of reality, my energy is spent running from it, denying it or crushing it. I don't change the fear, but I change my relationship to it. I observe it as mere passing content in awareness. This has made all the difference in the world.

It was through the words of Dr. Gregor and Lingrid that the one Self extended me the invitation to know my fear dragon and release it. When I accepted it, I could at last recognize my fear for what it was and let it go. The moment I gave up my need to keep it hidden, interpret, or control it, I was able to accept what was, as it was. I lived with pure acceptance and with it, my life opened up to new and vibrant energies.

This wasn't a transformation that swept me forever clean of the ego and its compulsion to control and judge. It was only a step in the process of undoing errors in thinking. That continues to this day. The gift was the revelation that I did not have to take my fear seriously. The result was a sense of relief. Fear is so much work. What filled that space instead was a sense of safety and security.

This continues to manifest in my life as an internal shift whenever something arises that is of a non-peaceful nature. First, I see whatever it is and know it as a product of the limited, egoic self. This gives me the option of engaging it or of stepping aside and letting it go. Second, I request assistance from my True Self to be Peace with this too.

In a professional situation, I sometimes have clients who hold on to their victim role, acting it out again and again in new situations, and judging themselves harshly. Their judgments cause them to feel frustrated over this repetitive, destructive behavior. When I notice this, I have the choice of going along with the judgments that cause them frustration, or I can let them go and see my clients as the light they are. By not giving in to the ego-generated judgments and emotions, I create a space for my client and me to remember who we truly are.

An example of how I have inflicted judgments on myself is the following: I take down an important address over the phone, and then when I go to use it the next day, I can't find it. What's my first response? A judgment about being sloppy or careless and a flare of impatience. I can allow my energy to spiral down into denser realms of anger or resentment. Or, I see it as an invitation to remember that I have the choice of being Peace with that too. And I have learned to put important addresses in a special notebook.

No matter what the situation, we can use it to return to being Peace. Every time we accept that opportunity, we contribute to the expansion of Peace in the world; we may not see it actually happening, but that is what occurs, because we are the whole of consciousness.

Less Sleep and More Time for Being

A few days after meeting with Dr. Gregor and Lingrid, Berta and I were back home and soon immersed in our regular schedule. Something unique took place that has continued to this day. I began waking up each night after only three to four hours of sleep. Though awake, I am generally relaxed physically and maintain an internal state of witnessing whatever is in consciousness. When thoughts come up, I only witness them; I do not fight or invest in them. After a year of experiencing this resting wakefulness each night, I wanted to be certain it wasn't hurting or compromising my health in some way. I contacted Tamara and Andrew and requested that they ask their spiritual family if what I was experiencing was harmful. They replied that it was wholesome, and their spiritual family had in part brought it about. When I rest deeply, they come to assist me. They aid me in shifting my allegiances from the activities and preoccupations of the ego to those of the Sacred Self.

I am certain there is no amount of intellectual processing that can undo the deep ego thought and value system that kept me alienated from innate joy, peace, happiness and love. I have found that in being silent, though, ego patterns and the hidden illusions specific to me, as well as the universal ones, are burned away. I am left with a dedication to be in that eternal silence, residing in the eternal Now. It pulls me in; I do nothing except allow that to happen. Commitment to truth expands in periods of tranquility and even in those times of ego-generated upheaval. This experience is reflected in the following invitation from the Course:

> *Simply do this: Be still, and lay aside all thoughts of what you are and what God is; all concepts you have learned about the world; all images you hold about yourself. Empty your mind of everything it thinks is either true or false, or good or bad, of every thought it judges worthy, and all the ideas of which it is ashamed. Hold onto nothing. Do not bring with you one thought the past has taught, nor one belief you ever learned before from anything. Forget this world, forget this course, and come with wholly empty hands unto your God.*[2]

Summary

As a child educated in the Catholic doctrine of the communion of saints, I believed the saints and angels in heaven were "good" and the fallen angels or devils were "bad." I learned I was "bad" by nature due to original sin, and I could make myself "good" by following God's and the Church's rules. I saw residents of heaven as superior beings who would help us if we asked. I also believed there were poor souls suffering in purgatory that we could, in turn, help through our prayers and penance. Those who resided in hell were beyond our prayers; they were condemned to eternal hell fire.

The way I understood the doctrine, it focused on separation—specifi-

---

[2] *A Course in Miracles*, WB, Foundation for Inner Peace. Lesson 189, paragraph 7, p. 360.

cally, the separation relating to God's superiority and my inferiority. When I encountered the teachings described in the *Course*, I saw that the ideas of "good" and "bad" were arbitrary. They were, in fact, products of the split mind. Judgment of self and others is a heavy load energetically. It had never really felt "right" to me, and discovering a paradigm of innate joy freed me from that burden. We are all the totality of Consciousness and in that we find our individuality. We are the same except for our temporary diversity in awareness of truth. There is only Self beholding Self. The unreal evokes guilt and fear. The real extends love, security, peace, harmony and joy. As the Course says, "the real cannot be threatened, the unreal does not exist. Herein lies the peace of God."

In the last fifteen years, I have connected with several physical-bodied teachers and also with non-corporeal beings such as Brother and Jerome, members of my family of origin who have crossed over, and members of the Overlees' ethereal family. These experiences have provided me with a pervasive feeling of intimacy, gentle guidance and support. In the belief that there is only you beholding you, Self helping Self, I rest in the eternal presence of the One, the ultimate communion of all beings.

Concluding Reflection

This book began with a fable about an imaginary person named L28 who lived in 3001. L28 and his coworkers were highly conditioned to think, feel and behave in certain ways. To his credit, L28 was open, willing and, on one night, courageous enough to allow himself to stay with what he was discovering in spite of how it clashed with his conditioning. That was enough. When he allowed himself to discover and accept the depth of his own ignorance, the experience transformed him.

The fable was just a story, a creation of my mind. My own story is also just a story. I examined my conditioning from my family of origin, education, culture and religious formation. When I was locked into following my conditioned, complex mind patterns, life was highly predictable though often frustrating and confusing. My inner fixation centered on a decision that I was inadequate. To prove that I wasn't, I put myself on a road that would someday prove my adequacy, if not to myself, at least to others. I became a friar, priest, missionary and psychotherapist. In the end, it all led to more frustration and confusion. I longed for something, but I didn't know what.

When I showed interest in stopping the pursuit of becoming, True Self through the written word of J. Krishnamurti, opened me up to an unending parade of invitations to let go of my illusions. These experiences provided glimpses of a reality that offered intense, overwhelming joy even if only temporarily. It left me with an abiding sense of who I was, that had nothing to do with the body or my conditioned mind. The most prominent of these came like persistent, refreshing rain from studying the *Course* and *Dialogue on Awakening*, spending time with various teachers, and from every-day occurrences. By being the "allowing" presence that we all are, I found life growing resplendent with unpredictable twists and turns.

Through the cultivation of silence, I have been, and continue to be, drawn to consciously recognize that I am the Self that can always choose to let go of external or internal turmoil and return to the peace and joy that is my very essence. I see now how the highly structured, conditioned elements of my story cascaded into a harmonious sequence of events that led me to the grace of noticing and loving what is, as it is. I can and do, for the most part, choose to rest effortlessly in witnessing the contents of confused thinking. I allow whatever bubbles up from the conditioned mind to burst on the surface of consciousness without interference.

I continually learn at deepening levels, that I am never upset by any cause except my own thoughts. Furthermore, it is clear that nothing has any meaning outside of what I give it.

Though I have had wonderful experiences of Oneness, their emotional intensity has passed. Through seeking guidance from my true, Sacred Self, I am moving ever closer to a mindset of total willingness to see in everyone the Creator God, for everyone is indeed the perfect extension of Divine Love. This, I know as forgiveness. On this earth plane, the reality of Oneness is lived by seeing beyond the appearance of separation to perfect unity. In time, the peace and joy that arise from the Oneness will remove desire for anything else. In this there is freedom, freedom from subtle and gross mind conditioning, freedom from a complex personality founded on separation, freedom from past identities and roles, freedom from future worries and preoccupations, and freedom from my own story.

Part Two: Applications

The ever-present Self needs no efforts to be realized. Realization is already there. Illusion alone is to be removed.

~ Sri Ramana Maharshi

My only concern is to set humanity absolutely unconditionally free. Man cannot come to it through any organization... creed...dogma or ritual...or psychological technique. He has to find it through the understanding of the content of his own mind, through observation and not through intellectual analysis or introspective dissection.

~ J. Krishnamurti

As you survey your inner world, merely let whatever thoughts cross your mind come into your awareness, each to be considered for a moment, and then replaced by the next... Watch them come and go as dispassionately as possible.

~ *A Course in Miracles*

Introduction

Guided by many teachers, and through my own silent witnessing, I learned to allow the unfolding of awareness, so that I could understand my conditioning and awake to the ever-present Self. When we comprehend that we are awareness, we know ourselves as the conflict-free mind, as peace, as that which, in the words of Tara Singh, "precedes all thinking and conditioning."

Awareness, as I am using the term, refers to a state in which we observe the contents of our inner world of thoughts, judgments, interpretations, emotions and urges as well as our perceptions of the outside world without taking them as who we are, but rather as mere ego-content. This content automatically and involuntarily appears in the infinite field of being. When we understand that, we are free to allow the contents of our inner world to pass through without affecting us in any way.

As we are fully engaged in such nonjudgmental witnessing, we have no personal "I" or "me" separate from the totality. Because we are not separate, we have no mental conflict with "what is." Life is coherent and smooth. By contrast, when we act to accomplish one thing or another, we are consumed with "I" or "me," which to our ego way of thinking instantly banishes our remembering that we are the impersonal, witnessing Self.

With impersonal witnessing, we shift from being a victim of what happens around us to being free. We *become* peace and joy.

The story of Olga exemplifies the previous concepts. Olga is no one person; she represents hundreds of people I have seen, either as clients or as workshops participants, who all responded in a similar way to the same situation. The names of other persons utilized in the following examples are also composites of many individuals.

Imagine Olga is attending a workshop on true identity. She inquires about awareness. In answer, I ask her if she is willing to do an exercise. She is, and I ask her to close her eyes, go inside, and find a calm or neutral space. I tell her I'm going to say something to her, and I want her to observe her immediate reaction to my words. What she notices might be feelings, sensations, impulses or thoughts, I say. They might be pleasant or unpleasant. I tell her to just observe them. Olga nods, and closes her eyes.

"You are a good woman," I say. After waiting a moment for her to fully experience her reactions, I ask her what she noticed.

"I felt tightness in my chest," she says.

"Did you make that tightness happen or did you just notice it?" I ask.

"Oh, I just noticed it," she says. "It happened without any choice on my part."

I tell Olga that this exercise shows how she can know herself as awareness, as that field in which she can witness without any judgments. "You allowed what came up to be what it was," I tell her. "It does not make any difference whether the reaction is pleasant or unpleasant. You can choose to identify with being conflicted over what you felt, or you can be the awareness that isn't touched by conflict."

I ask her to close her eyes again. "You are a good woman," I repeat.

After another pause, I again asked what she noticed.

"This time," she says, "there was not any tightness, but a feeling of calm over my whole body...very nice. And I did not make it happen, I just noticed it."

Again, Olga sees she didn't create the tightness in her chest. She didn't create the feeling of calm. What causes suffering is our taking seriously the automatic interpretations, judgments, emotions and urges. What caused her calm was her True Self resonating with the statement. Olga was being awareness by just observing what comes up, whether pleasant or unpleasant.

Again I ask her to close her eyes, and I say, "You don't have to do anything, you are lovable just the way you are." After a short pause, I ask her what she noticed.

"I was going to say 'nothing,' but that isn't true. I felt sort of numb. It is like I was saying that can't be true. Oh, and again I simply noticed my reactions, I'm not consciously making it happen."

Olga has embarked on the great, internal journey of noticing her reactions without taking them personally. She does not have to analyze or interpret; she is free to accept them as facts of her experience. She accepted the fact that she felt tightness in her chest. She accepted the fact that she felt peaceful, or later numb. She was observing the contents of her mind.

I ask Olga, "Who is the one witnessing the content that arises in mind?'

She pauses, a smile washes across her face, and she remarks, "Yes, I am that." Her conclusion is precious. It is one that each of us can have.

One last time, I ask Olga to close her eyes. "You don't have to do anything, you are lovable just the way you are," I tell her again.

She waits a moment, and then says, "Very interesting. It was different this time. I felt a nice sensation in my hands. Then I noticed that I was really accepting the statement."

"Notice," I tell Olga, "that you did nothing to change your response except notice that it had changed." We don't have to fight worries, fears and guilt that show up in our awareness. They have nothing to do with the truth of who we are.

Olga's story reveals the following:

1. *We have the option to allow ourselves to be nonjudgmental awareness.* Olga did this with ease. She did not get into avoiding, denying or judging what she felt or saw. She just noted it.

2. *The unpleasant content of our thoughts in the early stages of the*

inner journey arises from the conditioned mind, and has nothing to do with who we are. Olga easily made the distinction between herself as the witnessing field and the content of what she observed.

3. *When we allow ourselves to be awareness, something changes inside, and it is always related to the change we make in our relationship to the contents of the ego mind.* Olga noted a change in her automatic response between the first and second time I said to her, "You don't have to do anything; you are lovable just the way you are." She had become the witness of her thoughts and reactions.

4. *When we allow ourselves to be awareness, we are living in the Now.* If we go along with reactive interpretations and emotional urges, we are responding to either the past or the future. We are not living in the Now, for the Now is free of projections from the past and the future.

5. *Through awareness, we know that which does not come and go, the immortal Sacred Self.*

On page 122, I relate an example from Gangaji that is similar to Olga's experience. A woman from the audience expressed her confusion over the term "nothingness." Gangaji asked her a couple of questions about the quality of this "nothingness." The woman said it seemed intelligent, but was sometimes cloudy. Gangaji asked her, "That which is aware of clouds, and aware of some kind of intelligence that comes and goes, what is this?" The woman paused a moment, and then answered, "This is who I am." Just by asking the question, Gangaji had focused the woman's attention in a way that allowed her to discover and identify the witnessing presence that she is.

In the chapters that follow, I examine various contents of the mind, presenting examples and exercises to help understand conditioned mind patterns, and let them go. You may use the material to fit your needs, and do so with the clear intention of remembering that all of us are innate peace, joy and love, the one Sacred Self.

Chapter 11, Allowing Yourself to be Awareness, uses exercises to help reveal the conditioning operating in our daily lives. We will see how the false self exerts its influence over life. The moment we see that, we have the option of letting go.

Chapter 12, Awareness Cards, offers a way of reminding ourselves to stay vigilant about specific issues.

Chapter 13, Silence/Peace, covers quieting the mind, choosing peace, so that we can live in the world with absolute acceptance of what is, as it is.

Chapter 14, Forgiveness, explains something that is in all of our minds, but has been blocked by ego beliefs. That thought is One-ness and is accessed through forgiveness.

Chapter 15, Knowing Self, shows how we can access our individual patterns of the false self, whose function is to persistently keep us alienated from the True Self. At the end, I include five heal-ing options.

Chapter 16, Relationships, covers the four stages in a marital or long-term, committed relationship, an explanation of the dynamics of each stage, and the healing processes for moving through them.

Our conditioning traps us in artificial, painful, and often toxic pat-terns. Each chapter focuses on specific content. You can go through all of them or only the ones that appeal to you. If done in the manner outlined, each offers an opportunity to shift from the conditioned mind to being in-nate happiness, joy, peace, love.

The intent is for each of us to use these varied focuses in our own unique way, so that we develop a clearer, more truthful understanding of what is happening in our minds.

Being innocently present in every moment allows you the fullest recognition of that which you are presenting to yourself.

~ Dialogue on Awakening

Being Awareness

In the fable at the beginning of this book, L28's experiences contrasted with what he believed to be true all his life. He could have shut down, denied them, gone insane, or died. But he did not. He accepted what was happening and dropped the ideas he had assimilated through his education and conditioning. He stayed present to what he was experiencing—he stayed aware—and thereby found a way to his own freedom.

In my own story, the first three chapters discuss the conditioning I experienced. Chapter 1, <u>Foundation</u>, described the way patterns in my family formed and incorporated me, shaping my sense of self and my understanding of the world. I learned to avoid anger and deny emotion without even noticing what I was doing. In Chapter 2, <u>Walls</u>, I described the second layer of conditioning provided by my experiences in school. These were harsher than those of my family, but just as thorough, and just as invisible to me. Through them, I concluded that I was inadequate, but that I could compensate for that by pleasing others and striving to become adequate. In Chapter 3, the <u>Roof</u> to my personality structure was nailed into place through intense indoctrination into the Church. My religious training included such concepts as: we are sinners and separate from the divine; salvation comes through the intercession of great beings; and there is value in suffering and penance. It never occurred to me to question these ideas. I accepted them as "facts."

These three areas formed the artificial structure in which I lived until internal pressures began to build and put a strain on my "house." It wasn't until bioenergetics therapy after leaving the priesthood that something broke through, and I allowed intense feelings of anger to surface. It was an entirely new experience for me. Through identification with the conditioned mind, I had kept both the source and the sensation of that anger hidden from myself. It was also one of my first experiences with witnessing unpleasant, intense emotions, and I learned how beneficial the actual experience could be.

Years later, I experienced a spontaneous and dramatic form of awareness expansion during the retreat I attended with Stephen Schwartz. While sitting with him and three other group participants in the center of a circle of twenty-five people. I suddenly saw everyone around me united in one grand light. They were still individuals, but in some mysterious but wholly real way, they were all of the same essence, all one. A glorious laugh erupted in me, and spread to all those present. This kind of experience had no logical explanation, yet it too, was the natural result of allowing an expansion in awareness to occur. I could not make it happen, but I could let it happen by being that allowing presence, which is awareness itself.

A similar experience occurred in my first retreat with Gangaji. On that occasion, I exploded with a sense of being love.

Awareness can also expand in a moment of severe emotional pain such as in the workshop with Tara Singh, when I answered one of his questions and he responded by saying I did not have what it took to understand spirituality, and that I had best start over from the beginning. I felt his words like a shotgun blast to the chest and was instantly filled with a brew of dread, worthlessness and inadequacy. But instead of collapsing into despair or boldly becoming defensive, I remained open and stayed aware of the sensations, allowing myself to feel them fully. I was free to interpret them in accord with the limited or the unlimited mind.

Did I feel dread? Yes. Was worthlessness flooding over me? Indeed. What was the next sensation coming? Ah, yes, inadequacy. I allowed each one of these nasty clouds to move into and across the screen of my awareness. I stayed with them, witnessed them without judgment or interpretation. I accepted what was, as it was.

As the emotions faded, I saw that Mr. Singh's comment had pierced decades of conditioning from family, school, society and religion, illuminating it in such a way that I could see how arbitrary it all was. Choosing to be the presence of nonjudgmental witnessing set me free. When I saw that, the chains of my conditioning and my interpretations broke, and I was filled with a clear understanding of freedom. It all happened with Tara Singh's slap to my spiritual "bottom," which forced me to gasp for air.

Awareness can also come quietly through the gentle opening of our senses, such as occurred with me in connecting with nature. In the forests of Oregon and Washington, surrounded by the grandeur of nature, my mind became still of its own accord. Empty of all conflict, I was free to experience each moment without impediment. My awareness expanded out into every leaf or passing breeze. The intensity of this awareness has, on several occasions, moved me to tears as Oneness became tangibly evident.

Awareness is always available to us because at the level of being, we are that! The content that moved across my awareness has fluctuated at times; sometimes it was pleasant and sometime unpleasant, but the impersonal "I" who observed it was ever the same. I was the awareness itself, the intimate witnessing field that is without conflict. No matter what the experience, we can return to ourselves through awareness. No aspect of our lives remains the same when we approach it with awareness, as the Self.

This chapter will examine different contents of awareness, starting with how words can shape our reality, and demonstrating what can happen when we remain in a state of innocent perception.

The Power of Words

Most of us have an understanding of the expression "the power of words," but what is less commonly understood is the way words actually shape our experiences in life. Here we will look at how our own words impact us. We will investigate three common phrases: "I can't," "I'll try," and "I have to." These all have the power to confine us and affect the quality of our reality in profound ways.

Each particular phrase twists experience, but by being awareness, a person can identify an unwholesome pattern in life, and let it go. Often the very act of seeing the pattern changes it. Our relationship to it is changed by the act of nonjudgmental awareness.

I Can't

Britney had been dating a man who frequently abused her verbally. In a counseling session she told me, "I can't let him do that to me anymore."

I asked her to participate in an experiment. "Britney, say these two sentences and note what you feel with each one: 'I can't let him do that anymore,' and, 'I won't let him do that anymore.'"

Britney agreed and repeated each phrase out loud, tasting each one. "Oh, yes," she said after a moment. "What I want to say, and will say, is,

'I won't let him do that to me anymore.' Wow, what a difference. That is a good one to be aware of. Thank you."

What Britney felt in her experiment was the way her energy shifted with each sentence. When we say, "I can't," we speak as the conditioned self. It is a learned response that comes from a position of weakness. It says we feel overwhelmed by what is happening to us. The truth is, we are not really standing tall and expressing ourselves with dignity when we say, "I can't." These words negate us, drain us of energy, and leave us feeling weak and helpless. It also speaks from a negative position of having no choice, for example: I cannot, I am unable/powerless vs. I won't/I will not, which is claiming a choice and speaking from a position of power. By stating, "I won't," we move into a position of strength. We communicate to ourselves the intention to protect ourselves from harm. Britney understood this just by noticing how she felt when she said each phrase. This required no effort, no practice, no penance, no punishment, no stick and no carrot. She simply noticed which phrase made her feel stronger.

When she first said, "I can't," she saw how she was speaking to herself from a position of powerlessness. With her insight into how the words affected her, she allowed herself to recognize what she was doing. In that moment she was free not to do it.

I'll Try

When Jake came to work twenty minutes late for the third day in a row, his supervisor, Frank, confronted him with these words, "Jake this is the third day in a row that you have been late for work by more than fifteen minutes. What's up?"

"Actually, nothing," said Jake.

"Okay, then. I want you to commit to getting here on time every day for the next two weeks," said Frank. "Will you do that?"

"I'll try," Jake said.

"Jake," said Frank, "this isn't a time to mess around with words. If you are only up to trying, you are fired."

No one had ever responded to Jake like that before, even though he had often used that expression. He was stunned. That moment of startled response was an opening into a new level of awareness. If he stays present to it, he will see how "trying" is blocking him from saying a clear "No" or "Yes." Another implication in his "trying" frame of mind is that when he does not do it or he does it, he will see it as the result of chance rather then his decision..

By saying "I'll try," he never really commits to cutting the lawn, getting the car repaired, or fixing the leaky bathroom faucet, as his wife has asked. He thinks he has, but "I'll try" means he has left the door open for failure. The action is not set in time—it never becomes concrete in his mind, and so it is never accomplished. At the same time, the expression excuses him if he fails. Because he said he'd try, he appears to have complied. It's not his fault if it doesn't happen. He does not see how by using those words, he has kept himself in a state of helplessness.

If Jake has the courage, he can look within where he may discover that he is afraid of committing himself. Without knowing it, he diminishes himself, makes himself feel less alive. This keeps him identifying with his little self or ego self and in constant denial of the grandeur of his innate state. The use of this phrase is of value to the ego because it keeps him in denial of his true dignity as happiness and joy. By cultivating an awareness of the emotional charge behind his choice of words, he can recognize ways in which he is sabotaging himself. When he sees with this new awareness the difference in how he feels about himself, he can expand his awareness.

I Have To

Leroy said "I have to" twelve times within the first fifteen minutes of his initial counseling session with me. Before the session was over, I asked him if he would be willing to do an exercise using five different phrases. He agreed.

I showed Leroy the diagram below and told him to complete each of the phrases. "As you fill in whatever it is you have to, should, need to, want to, and will do," I told him to observe his feelings and describe them in the second column, just as in the example given.

Statement to be completed	Feelings elicited by statement.
Example: I have to finish vacuuming the kitchen.	*Pressured, obligated*
I have...	
I should...	
I need to...	
I want to...	
I will...	

Leroy wrote the following responses in the column on the right:

I have to...: Rebellious, a bit depressed.

I should...: Ho-hummish, but I won't.

I need to...: Pressured.

I want to...: Good feeling, no pressure.

I will...: Assertive, empowered and a feeling of "It is done."

"If you used the phrase 'I have to' fifty times in a day, how would you end up feeling by the end of the day?" I asked.

"Yes, I get your point," he said. "I would feel very depressed and lethargic. What you are saying is that when I am aware of what is happening internally, I am free to choose to make myself feel depressed by using the phrase 'I have to,' or I can choose to state a fact about whether I will or won't do something."

"Precisely, Leroy," I said. "If we live out our lives on automatic pilot, we remain asleep to what we are doing to ourselves."

"Hey, this is good stuff!" Leroy said.

Phrases such as "I can't," "I should," and "I have to" seem simple and harmless. They creep into our mouths and solidify our thoughts without being noticed. But as they do, they deaden our energy and keep us confined in a box that limits the expression of our true Self. When Leroy took the time to notice what he felt as he said these things, it was instantly evident to him what was happening. He could see and *feel* the difference. Once he was aware, he could make a conscious choice to use a phrase that brought him life and created a sense of freedom. If he tried to stop expressing himself using words that weaken him only because I told him to, nothing would change. But with this exercise, he expanded his awareness to include how the words made him feel, and he experienced it for himself. As a result, he could choose not go back to those weaker methods of expression. His own awareness would prevent him from doing so. He now knew what the difference was. The power and relief brought by changing his words provided reason and incentive to remain aware.

As these examples show, the words we use can have a substantial impact. They can weaken us or give us strength. When we become aware, we can choose words that give us happiness and strength that resonate with our heart's deepest desires.

Innocent Perception

Innocent perception is an awareness focus that begins with learning to distinguish between judging and observing. For our purpose, observation is the viewing of a specific person, event, place, thought, feeling or urge in a manner free of any interpretation or judgment. It is the simple act of taking in data. A judgment takes in the facts and labels them with an interpretation that entangles the viewer intellectually and emotionally.

People can fall into the habit of judging without even realizing it, often leaving others or themselves feeling hurt due to judgment-inspired actions. Instead of spreading conflict, we can bring innocent perception into every situation.

The following exercise reveals the difference between an observation and a judgment. Place a checkmark next to each sentence that is an observation. The answers are provided below.

( ) 1. Mary is working at the computer.

( ) 2. Jim always tries to dominate others.

( ) 3. Those people are two-faced.

( ) 4. Francis never chews her food properly.

( ) 5. Bill can't sit still.

( ) 6. Jan always starts talking before I can finish.

( ) 7. Ray talks too much.

( ) 8. She's never here on time.

( ) 9. Jack said, "No one can trust that pair."

( ) 10. I saw you drive the red truck yesterday.

( ) 11. I prefer blue eyes.

( ) 12. Jenny always acts like she is superior.

[Answers: Items 1, 9, 10, and 11 are observations. All the rest are judgments.]

Again, an observation is free of any interpretation; it is noticing what is. The observations on this list were simple statements of fact.

Judgments, on the other hand, contain at least one interpretation. Number two above "Jim always tries to dominate others," says nothing about what it is that Jim does. It is an interpretation of Jim's behavior. In contrast, an observation of Jim's behavior might be: Jim moved to within inches of Alec's face, stood tall, and told Alec he had to do what he said.

Number three, "Those people are two-faced," contains no facts about what "those people" said or did, so it is a judgment.

Number four, "Francis never chews his food properly," is a clear judgment about Francis. It does not describe what Francis does while chewing his food, only that someone has interpreted it as improper.

In number six, "Jan always starts talking before I can finish," number seven, "Ray talks too much," number eight, "She's never here on time," and number twelve, "Jenny always acts like she is superior," the phrases use a word such as "always," "never," "too much," or "too little." These words imply an assessment of some sort and are good indicators of judgment statements.

Judgments can perpetuate old patterns, provoke defensive responses, be perceived as an attack, and may place blame on another or self. The energy they carry is heavy and aggressive, and often they elicit a reaction rather than addressing whatever the problem really is. They impede communication and perpetuate strife.

In this next exercise think of someone whose behaviors or mannerisms you don't like. In the space below, make two *observations* about that person's behavior that contribute to your dislike:

1 . _____

_____

2. _____

_____

Now, compare your statements with the criteria for an observation, or have a friend review them to see if they are observations or judgments. Did you succeed in keeping your statements factual, and thus neutral? Or did your judgments creep in and elicit an emotional reaction?

Next, think of someone that you like, and make two *observations* about that person's behavior:

1 . _____

_____

2. _____

_____

Check your statements out with a friend. Were these observations, or did you slip into judgment? Was there a difference between these statements and the previous ones? Was it easier for you to observe when you liked the person's behavior or disliked it? Did observing change the way you felt?

The experience of Kathy, who had learned about innocent perception in a workshop, illustrates how consciously applying innocent perception can make a difference in a tense situation. One morning Kathy, a supervisor, came upon Terry, one of her team members, who was yelling at Mark, a department clerk, in the corridor of the company where they all worked. Terry was berating Mark for an error he had made. Later, when Kathy spoke to Terry about the incident, her first thought was to say, "You're always acting like an attack dog with your fellow workers! You literally tore Mark apart this morning." Instead, she reminded herself about the differences between observation and judgment, and considered what she was telling herself about this event. She saw her words were actually judgments that carried their own payload of intense emotion. She would, she realized, be attacking Terry the same way that Terry had attacked Mark, thereby perpetuating the negative pattern of interaction.

Kathy made the conscious choice to stay out of judgment and asked herself what observations she could make. When she did this, she came up with: "At 10:30 this morning, I saw and heard you speaking with Mark. You wiggled your right index finger in front of his face; he put his hands up to his face. You told him, 'You are the laziest thing in this department.'" By speaking with Terry using observation instead of the judgment statements that had been her first impulse, Kathy gave Terry the opportunity to hear what she had to say and make an appropriate adjustment without being sent into a reactive cycle of her own. By this means, Kathy neutralized an intense situation instead of compounding it.

The following is a description of what happened with one group who practiced innocent perception while attending a spiritual retreat.

The group went to a mall and gathered in a central location. I told everyone to go for a walk or sit in one place and observe what was happening around them for fifteen minutes without any interpretations, judgments or elaborations. I encouraged them to notice what was going on with "inno-cent perception." If their mind came up with judgments, they were to just notice them and let them go.

When we reconvened in fifteen minutes, we compared experiences. Some found it difficult to notice without interpreting or reacting to what they saw. They were pulled into going along with their conditioned mind's chatter and judgments. It seemed that the line of least resistance was to follow the old, critical habits of mind.

I had encouraged them to treat their judgments as something to just observe, as facts in their awareness, and withhold judgment against them-selves for thinking them. Some succeeded in that for short periods, others did not. What everyone did do was discover how the mind was independent of their intention and came up with judgments automatically, and on its own. Even those who could not withhold from making judgments learned from this, for they became aware of how ingrained the habit of judgment was for them. They saw that they didn't even know they did it. Discovering what they did was the first step toward freeing themselves from the bond-age of their automatic and involuntary patterns of mind.

Some in the group reported finding a measure of peace in the exer-cise. They found they settled right into alignment with their true Self and stepped outside of judgment and conflict. They became themselves. They became peace. And when we choose to be peace, we extend peace to the whole of Consciousness, for we are the whole of Consciousness.

I sent the group out to do the exercise again, but this time with in-structions to go along with their mind's judgments and interpretations, and to pay special attention to how they felt as they did.

When people returned to share their experiences, they had marked-ly different responses. Some were displeased because their thoughts ap-peared to be constantly judging or criticizing. They reacted to how this person wore his hair, or how that one dressed. They became aware of how blindly they followed their automatic thinking. They could see how their behavior had been influenced by such judgments in other situations—with judgments they now saw as having no reality whatsoever. Others found they were uncomfortable allowing themselves to be critical and almost immediately returned to innocent perception. It didn't feel good to them to assess others negatively or to find fault with them. The more they did it, the more they didn't like themselves.

Many individuals who have used these exercises over time have re-ported two interesting phenomena. The first is the unfolding of heart-based common sense that allows them to maintain a calm presence under difficult circumstances. With the heart wisdom, they resolve difficulties in a direct, firm manner that clears the energy instead of compounding the difficulties. The second effect noted was the rise of an effusive sense of cherishing what is. Put in poetic terms, they feel their hearts swelling with love for everything they behold within and around themselves. They grow to see even the false thoughts of the ego mind as perfect, because when those thoughts arise, they are reminders to return to the state of peace.

Innocent perception isn't limited to mall watching. A mother in one of our workshops used the exercise to restore calm, and return to a loving presence with her eight-year-old twin boys. She had been greatly troubled by how quarrelsome the two were. They constantly fought with one another, and she always ended up shouting at them and using threats. The more they misbehaved, the more she struggled for control to prove she was a good mother. The more intense she became, the more they fought, which left her feeling more and more helpless.

She had tried different parenting techniques, but to no avail. Her self-esteem as a mother plummeted. Then she came to our workshop and did the innocent perception exercise. She began to see a pattern at work in the dynamic with her boys. She was getting caught up in her judgments of their behavior and of her own performance as a mother, and reacting to those instead of accepting what was.

As she cultivated her innocent perception, she broke through this cycle of reaction. With her vision no longer clouded by judgments, she saw how her boys were losing connection with who they were in reality. And, indeed, so was she when all she did was react in a judgmental way. When she remained as innocent perception, she related calmly to her sons, and this elicited a different behavior from them.

Without effort of any kind, she changed the way she spoke to them. She used softer tones and nurtured an attitude of accepting what was at the given moment. She relaxed, and stopped relating to them from her need to change them. When she spoke to them from her heart, using its clear common sense, her boys resolved their fighting. She instituted down time together with them where they could all be quiet. She asked for their cooperation instead of using threats. When they granted it, she thanked them. Instead of planning what she was going to say to them, she discovered that if she trusted herself to speak to them with innocent perception, the most appropriate words came of their own volition. Her peaceful presence became the catalyst for the boys to move into their own peaceful center.

A friend of mine shared this story about another parent, a father in one of our workshops, who used the practice with his son to handle a difficult situation from a place of love and clear-sightedness. The boy had been arrested after he'd run from an officer who had found him in possession of marijuana, thus compounding the seriousness of the offense. In a meeting that included the arresting police officer and a probation officer, this man told his son that no matter what he did, he could not change the love he felt for him. He told the boy, however, quietly and firmly, that because he loved him, if he brought any drugs into his home or did not follow the curfew set for him, he would report it to his probation officer. The probation officer was so impressed by the calm, clear way the parent had handled the situation that later he contacted him to ask how he had learned to speak with such authority.

The parent explained to him what it was to live in a state of innocent perception, where one did not become entangled in personal interpretations of a situation, but instead dealt with what was. He described how when he was in that state, he had a strong sense of who he was. His mind was free of conflict. He was not driven by fear or prejudices, nor was he concerned about future possibilities. This allowed him to be guided by intuition, he said, and then he could see clearly how to best relate to others.

As the people in the above examples discovered, the more we live from the state of innocent perception, the more we know with clarity and certitude that "I am that, the totality of Consciousness."

When we become aware of the words we use, we can see how they shape our experience of reality and how others react to us. If, with absolute acceptance we face things that plague us, we discover they dissolve under our dispassionate eye. In learning to look at life with innocent perception, we see situations as they are instead of as we think, want, or are afraid they are.

The two aspects of being awareness, "the power of words" and "innocent perception," when cultivated, lead us to knowing who we really are.

A separated or divided mind must be confused. It is necessarily uncertain about what it is. It has to be in conflict because it is out of accord with itself.

~ A Course in Miracles

Reminder Cards

We can initiate change in our lives by the tiny act of bringing awareness and acceptance of our thoughts, feelings and urges. Change is inevitable, and instead of being something to be feared, it becomes a natural occurrence, for the act of accepting is in itself transforming.

In this chapter, several homework assignments have been designed to allow us to know ourselves as judgment-free awareness in simple, effortless ways. Each of these exercises helps develop a more accurate perspective on how minds function.

These exercises use a set of cards prepared in advance and used for a week at a time. Each card works to expand accepting awareness in a particular direction. They are called "reminder" cards because they remind us to be attentive to what is happening in our mind. We have the option to turn off our automatic reactions and turn on our ability to make other choices.

Intentions for Today cards remind us to pay attention to what we are thinking. Urges and Impulses cards focus on ego-driven nudges to behave in certain ways and open the door to behavioral options. The last set, Delights and Joys, helps us discover pleasant feelings.

Students report that these cards have been highly practical in bringing more awareness into their lives. The cards provide structure to choices, offer something to focus on, and encourage one to be proactive about life and problems. By being aware of urges and impulses, one chooses whether to act on them or not. Noticing the simple moments of joy present in every day greatly expand the sensation of a life well lived. Most importantly, using these cards wakes up one to being a witnessing presence.

Daily Intention Cards

As we have discussed, unhappiness is due to being out of alignment with our Sacred Self. This is not caused by ego-driven thoughts, feelings and urges in themselves, but by our being enmeshed in them. The best insurance against such error is to allow awareness to fill every moment. Or, better said, to live life in a state of conflict-free consciousness. Since that is our natural state, we need to be aware of the contents of the reactive mind that blocks us from experiencing it.

Write each of the statements provided on four small index cards, something big enough to see, but small enough to be placed in a prominent place, so that you will have a set of four for each of the statements, or a total of twenty-four cards. Pick one of the statements and work with it for one week. Begin by placing each of the four cards in a strategic and visible place, such as the bathroom mirror, refrigerator door, your car's dashboard, in your purse or billfold, on your computer screen, etc. The point is to encounter them throughout the day in different settings and circumstances. Each time you do, make a point of reading the statement to yourself or out loud. For some, saying it out loud doubles their exposure to it, for they hear it, as well as see it.

This exercise is easy to do alone, but we have found that participants often get more out of it when they do it with friends who are also interested in remembering who they are. This allows for a little more discussion on insights that arise. If you do this with a "buddy," make another set of identical cards for that person to use. At the end of the week, share what you each noticed throughout the days as you focused on the reminder statement. Note whether any particular statement was harder or easier under certain circumstances. Give some thought as to why that might be so.

Read the cards with the intention of requesting help from your Sacred Self. The use of the reminder cards does not require deep concentration, rather, let it be a relaxed awareness that is effortless. Write out the cards, place them in strategic places, and let the rest follow, because you have given your mind a direction.

Each statement begins with "today." This is a gentle way of removing the burden of achievement. This process isn't about forcing yourself into a large project or change. It is purely about this day, and this day alone. Do not concern yourself with tomorrow. Most of us can manage something when we know it is short term. Each day, then, is the short term. By the end of seven short-term lengths of focus, chances are you will find that something has shifted inside you. You will have shifted from ignorance of the contents of your mind that have dictated your judgments, feelings and behaviors, to the ability to notice the contents as mere passing facts.

The intentions are as follows:

Today, I will be aware of my thoughts that are judgments.

Today, I will choose not to be a victim of my reactive thinking.

Today, I will be aware of the interpretations that cause me painful emotions.

Today, I choose to be peace in every situation that arises.

Today, I choose to see others as "wellfolk."

Today, I will notice my excuses for not being peace.

Many individuals have been surprised at discovering that their minds are making judgments about others all the time. In discussing it with another, the conclusion is often that it is automatic for the ego-driven mind to make judgments that block us from perceiving others as they are. Sharing this is helpful in understanding how the mind functions. Some have reported they have become aware of their minds running ahead in time, creating worries about the future that remove them from a sense of peace. Others find their minds are constantly going into the past focusing on things that are guilt inducing. In all likelihood they had been doing it for years without connecting the unpleasant feelings to the cause, the thoughts in their mind. In sharing, they often find others have similar patterns. This sharing opens up the door to a deeper friendship, joy in observing and willingness to change the pattern.

Many who reported having an intention to be peace in every situation discovered that the willingness to express that intention throughout the day elicited the grace to have and be what they wanted—peace. It often is a surprise that by starting the day with that intention, its power is present throughout the day. This joyful discovery, when shared with another, is often an incentive for cultivating that disposition as a way of life.

The grace of this exercise is that it can be done again and again until we know ourselves as witnessing Consciousness. In this, we see that nothing has meaning outside of what we give it, that only our ego-driven thinking causes emotional turmoil, and that freedom from the errors of the ego mind is always an option.

Urges and Impulses

While the Intention for Today cards are about noticing and accepting what is, as it is, the next exercise is helpful for those who wish to drop unwholesome or constricting behaviors. It is designed to bring attention to the urges or impulses behind those behaviors in such a way that we can choose whether or not to act on them. When we shift our perspective to such a degree that we can see our impulses as *impersonal* facts, we are in the best position to choose not to act them out.

Work with one pattern or habitual response at a time. Give some thought to which particular urge you find most plaguing in your life at the moment. It could be anger, saying nasty things, eating too much, or the compulsion to have the last word or interrupt others. Look for any behavior that seems to take control of you. Next, create an index card using the layout below. Fill in the blank space after the word "URGE" with whatever you want to focus on first. Carry the card with you as you move through your day, making a note of each time the specific urge arises. At the end of day, simply indicate in the column on the right how many times you acted on that urge.

In this exercise, the key issue is that *you have the innate ability to observe* urges and then to *choose not to go along with them*. Temperaments and preferences vary. Some find this card helpful; others can use the basic idea without a card. You might want to design a more elaborate tracking system. Go with your own intuition, or ask your Sacred Self how to best use this idea.

	Urge_____	How many times did you act on this urge?
Monday		
Tuesday		
Wednesday		
Thursday		
Friday		
Saturday		
Sunday		

The *Course* states that we are far too lazy about, and inattentive to, the thoughts we allow to meander through our minds. Just as a muscle that isn't used grows flaccid, without attentiveness, we are gradually lulled to sleep. We lose awareness of what passes across our mental screen, and we live on automatic pilot. The impulses become an invisible dictator that controls our lives. Our responses to stimuli become knee-jerk or programmed. We say the same things to the same cues. We indulge in mindless behaviors that range from the merely foolish to the downright destructive. We are cut off from ourselves, and we are cut off from others. We are in a prison of our own making.

The good news is we not only can be free, we are innately so. The first step is to return to a vital and authentic sense of who we are by noting and accepting what is, as it is. The second is being vigilant, giving no allegiance to ego-generated thoughts, feelings and urges. Every moment of every day offers an opportunity, if not an invitation, to do so. Every moment is a moment of choice.

We will begin to perceive how we are by nature, a calm, witnessing presence. With time, we see that our urges are not us at all. They do not define who we are, though they reflect *what we think we are*. And with time, those same urges we identified with the reminder cards will fade into nothingness. If they surface again, we generally notice them much sooner for having done so once already. If needed, using the cards again for a short time will quickly restore our sense of being judgment-free awareness.

Delights and Joys

The next exercise is beneficial for everyone. It shifts our focus in a delicate and subtle way, training our attention toward the pleasant moments in our lives.

I offer two different suggestions for tracking delights and joys. The first is for those who like to write about experiences, the second is for those who prefer tracking with minimal writing. For both groups it is important to know that the purpose of these cards is to *be the Presence that is aware of what is occurring in the mind.*

Use a lined index card. At the top, write "Delights and Joys." Write at least three delights or joys you notice during the day; give as many details about them as you care to. After several days, review what you have written, noting all the satisfying moments that enriched your life when you paid attention to them instead of discounting them as insignificant.

Delights and Joys
Day 1:
Day 2:
Day 3:
Day 4:
Day 5:
Day 6:
Day 7:

Examples we might observe, even if only on a T.V. screen, are: the peace a baby radiates as it sleeps, the abandon or comedy of squirrels playing; the comfort and intimacy of watching a father playing Frisbee with his son; the beauty of a sunset; or the feel of a loved one's touch. Our days are peppered with such things that are waiting to be noticed.

Our joys are generally more related to situations or sights that generate feelings than to concepts. They spring from connection, more than cold thought. Something we feel, or see, or hear touches us and opens us, letting in energy and light. Joy is not something we have to earn. It is always present. Always. Why? It is indeed God's will for his creation. This exercise is meant to help you discover where it is hiding in your life. Once you are aware of that, you can then expand your experience of it by allowing it more space.

At the end of seven days, take time to read over what brought you delight and joy during the week. Do you see any patterns? Did any of the situations require complicated orchestration? How many were "found" moments where you weren't occupied with other thoughts? Were any of your joys expensive? Ask yourself whether anything prevents you from experiencing these again. Do you think you could find other joys and delights if you kept looking? What would your life look like if you were totally open to all the little joys and delights?

These exercises are simple, and we have learned simple experiences may bring incredible tranquility, profound contentment, and even unforeseen healing.

There is peace only when there is no desire to become something. And, that is the only true state because in that state alone there is creation, there is reality. But that is completely foreign to the structure of society.

~ Krishnamurti

Silence, Peace and Absolute Acceptance

Many people find it difficult to be silent. Their minds are perpetually chattering, keeping them in a state of agitation or nervousness. They feel off balance; they cannot stem the tide of critical judgments, past memories, or preoccupations with the future. By inflicting random repetitive thoughts, their minds make them feel as if they are victims. Those individuals often feel they have no resources with which to tame the torrent. Some assume the only way to escape the constant assault is to remain occupied at all times so that the mind is diverted. While diversion appears to help, at least temporarily, it also hinders. We cannot know our True Self when we are diverted. We cannot rest in the peace that is ours by nature. It is impossible to override these pesky thoughts by brute force or to block them out entirely with meaningless or superfluous activity. The solution is to let them go.

Still Hands Exercise

This focus exercise, *Still Hands*, is meant to be used on a temporary basis, like crutches to be laid aside when no longer needed.

Through practice, individuals plagued with obsessive mind chatter can, within a short time, discover they don't have to be helpless victims of their thoughts. Over a longer period, they will learn to drop such thinking as soon as it begins.

This following script can be recorded on a cassette, CD, iPod, etc. It can be played in an environment free of distractions as often as needed. Be aware that each place that calls for a pause should be at least a 20-second rest. Do not listen to your recording when driving a motor vehicle.

Take a comfortable position in a chair. Place your hands, palms up, in your lap. [Pause] *Give your attention to both your hands. Notice what you experience.* [Pause]

Now shift your attention to your right hand. Focus on the sensations there. [Pause.] *Give your attention to the thumb on your right hand.* [Pause.]

Next, place your attention on your right index finger. [Pause.]

Turn your attention to your left hand. Notice what it is like without making any judgment; just notice and accept what is, as it is. [Pause] *Let go of that, and place your attention on your left thumb.* [Pause] *Now, move your attention to rest on your left index finger.* [Pause]

Give your attention to your breathing. Notice your body sensations of inhaling and exhaling; just watch your breathing for the next few moments. [Pause]

Let go of that. Now, without making any effort, notice the sensation of your breathing in your nostrils. [Pause] *If your attention wanders off that focus, it is okay, just bring it back to the sensation of your inhalation and exhalation in your nostrils.*

Notice what you are feeling in your body. Can you go deeper and deeper with each exhalation? [Pause] *Do you enjoy that? [Pause.] Do you want to be free of your conditioned mind's chatter and impulses?* [Pause]

Now, while remaining in that calm state of mind, open your eyes and silently look around. [Pause] *Close your eyes again and notice your overall sense of tranquility.* [Pause]

This is the end of the exercise.

While this exercise may seem deceptively simple, clients and friends have reported that after practicing it twice daily for about a week, they found they are more apt to stay out of the victim role in their thoughts. Furthermore, when they have the *intention* that nothing disturbs their relaxed state of mind, they easily drop obsessive thinking as soon as it begins.

Finding a sense of tranquility and calm is more than just a pleasant mental state. It can have quite remarkable effects on our physiology. When we are stressed, whether emotionally, psychologically, mentally or physically, our bodies tend to contract and stiffen. This reduces the even flow of blood and energy to all parts, which fatigues muscles and compromises the function of our kidneys, lungs, digestive system and other organs. If we can return to a state of peace, even if only for a few moments, we counteract the effects of stress. This affects general and specific health problems.

But this isn't a question of training the body. It is a question of learning to be vigilant to where our thoughts take us. With the clear intention that nothing disturbs our peaceful state of mind, we drop obsessive thinking as it begins.

The exercise offers a way of changing our state of mind. It disturbs the status quo of how we have been living. When opposed, the ego thought/value system will quite likely raise all manner of clever and creative reasons for not continuing with a practice that threatens it. It will tell us that we don't have time, or that the practice doesn't work. It may even tell us that we look ridiculous. By knowing its tactics, we have a better chance of evaluating which condition we prefer: the one where our mind is riding us with spurs, or the one where we are being peace.

In Steven Spielberg's movie, *ET*, the lost extraterrestrial says, "I want to go home." That line resonated with viewers of any age because we all long to go home, to a place that brings us comfort and happiness. This exercise of just sitting and focusing on one hand and then the other, and then on the breath itself, is an effortless way of returning to the center of our own universe. That place is soft, gentle and nurturing, and when we touch on it, we know we are home.

God's will for each of us is that we enjoy perfect peace and happiness. He created us in pure joy and peace, but many of us are stuck in the illusion that peace is inaccessible. Divine will remains intact; it is our understanding that is misapplied.

Choosing Peace

Choosing peace may sound like a passive way of being in the world. It can be seen as an excuse for not participating, or for letting injustices go unchallenged. But that is not real peace. It is only when we are peace that we have the presence of mind to follow our inner voice for the proper action.

We may think of peace as something that we stumble upon, a random and rare occurrence. But it is always available to us, and as our lives grow more complex, it becomes more important to wake up to the truth of who we are. Without knowing that, we are left vulnerable in a time of rapid change, where even the tiniest shift can topple us if we are not living from our center. If peace becomes a priority in our lives, however, we can cope with all the pressures brought to bear by modern life. Before long, others recognize the peace we bring to everything that we do, and we, in turn, spread peace as a balm to the lives of everyone.

It is often hard for people to know what peace is. The word itself is seen as ambiguous or soft, and people can't recognize when they do or don't experience it. Its most recognizable form is that state of being wherein we are no longer impacted by the past or worried about the future. We are at rest and have the strong sense of being anchored in ourselves even as the world around us is changing. We are not striving to become this or that, and mentally we are conflict free. Once we have found that place, we know it for the permanent treasure it is and increasingly refuse to give it up for something that comes and goes.

As peace expands, it changes the shape of our lives. When we live from our center, we move through life differently. We feel calm and relaxed, and possess a strong sense of humor. We see things from a clearer perspective, often appreciating the absurdities present in many situations. Sometimes, we may seem strangely non-responsive, but that may be because we are not playing the societal games that others remain accustomed to.

A number of techniques exist for creating a sense of peace around ourselves, including breath work, self-hypnosis, calming music, yoga or gentle stretching. All are beneficial and support the desire for peace, so long as one does them with the clear intention of returning to the True Self.

Peace, however, does not require a complicated regimen. The simplest way to become peace is to begin the next time you are faced with a decision. At that precise moment, consider only which alternative extends and fosters peace within you. No matter what the circumstances, one possibility will engender more peace than the other, and you'll feel it in your body. Choose that option. That is the simple practice of choosing peace.

It doesn't matter how mundane the task or how stressful the dynamic, we have the choice to move through it from the calm center of our being. Whether we are shopping, taking out the garbage, waiting in the doctor's office, sitting in the dentist's chair or stuck in traffic, closing a big contract or experiencing criticism, we can use every single situation as an opportunity to be peace. When we do so, we affect not only ourselves, but the totality of Consciousness.

Often we slide out of peace without realizing it. The moment we feel our peace slipping away and conflict or irritation beginning to replace it, we can retrieve it with a simple reminder, "I intend to be peace with this, too." Then we wait and see. We let the situation unfold in its own time without exerting effort to change anything. We don't form any expectations about when things will change because that immediately takes us out of the present moment and into the future. We don't think back to what happened the last time we were in a similar situation, for that takes us into the past. Stay present and surrender to the real Self with total trust. What unfolds will be peace.

To be peace is to have peace. In the spiritual realm, there is no distinction between having and being peace. It is not something we dress up in, it is who we are before, and who we are even when we are entangled in the dynamics of the ego world. These things are arbitrary and external. They have only as much power over us as we ourselves give them.

Absolute Acceptance

As we suffer from longstanding, intense emotions such as guilt, fear, worry or inadequacy, it is common to want to avoid those feelings. We run from them, mask them over, or try to ignore them. But if we go inside, become silent and face the demons with absolute acceptance, without the associated story, judgment or interpretation, something remarkable happens.

When we totally accept the feeling, witnessing what is, we see that the physical sensation of the emotion sometimes moves about in our body, shifting from one location to another. As we follow it with absolute acceptance, in time the feeling begins to fade without us doing anything. It fades because it is a phantom produced by ego that only comes when we do not accept what is, as it is, and instead struggle with the emotion. That is what happened with me and my fear dragon described in Chapter 10.

Take, for example, Ryan, who had battled for decades with oppressive feelings of worthlessness that made his life miserable and finally drove him to seek counseling.

After considering his situation, I asked him if he was willing to do an exercise to hold himself in a state of absolute acceptance. He agreed. I told him to close his eyes, go inside himself and connect with the sense of worthlessness that so distressed him.

"Stay away from all the stories relating to the emotion," I said. "Experience the worthlessness. Don't run from it; let it be. This is a time for allowing and accepting." By his changing facial expressions, I could see he was following my suggestions.

"What is happening?" I asked after a moment.

"I found a sensation," he said. "It started in my chest, but now has moved. It is like a slight headache right above my eyes."

I encouraged him to keep witnessing. He continued giving me commentary, saying at one time that he felt hot all over. A little later he reported he felt pain in the back of his neck. Then he grew quiet.

"What is happening?" I asked. "Do you still feel pain?"

"Oh, I don't have the headache anymore," he said, "and...it's like magic. I'm calm and I don't understand clearly what has happened. The worthlessness is gone."

This surprised him. He almost couldn't believe that a feeling that had been so much a part of him had disappeared in front of his accepting attention. I told him the key was always awareness. The content of our confused, conditioned mind, in Ryan's case a sense of being totally worthless, has nothing to do with the reality of who we are.

"When you don't fight that emotion, but simply allow it to be, it fades," I said. "Another way of expressing this is, when we choose to be absolute acceptance, we are living 'in the now,' which means we permit whatever comes into awareness to be as it is. If we refuse to judge or fight it, we are choosing to be the impersonal witness, to be as we were created."

"It sounds too simple," Ryan said, "but it worked. Worthlessness faded. What a great tool!"

I cautioned Ryan about thinking of it as a tool for his toolkit. If we do that, we fall back into trying to "get rid" of the feeling. That leads to judging it and attempting to accomplish something, which means we are right back in the ego mind. Instead, when we stay with the feeling, let it be, without judging it, we are being our real Self, the infinite field of Consciousness. We are not really doing anything, we are just being. The feeling fades on its own.

Each of us can make the choice to be peace. When we do, we let go of ego perceptions of separation, and rest in being the totality of Consciousness, the One.

Forgiveness is the only function here, and serves to bring the joy this world denies, to every aspect of God's Son where sin was thought to rule.

~ A Course in Miracles

Forgiveness

Forgiveness, from an ego perspective, is an act of charity, where one committing an offense is granted pardon by another who is generally recognized as morally superior. Ego perception believes that one can be injured by another. I declare, "someone hurt me," and then judge that individual to be the victimizer, and I the victim. In the ego world, the fundamental belief is that bodies are real, and the physical world is real, too. Therefore, individuals are distinct, separate and different from each other.

To talk about forgiveness in the context of the *Course*, we must remember its basic premise: "Nothing real can be threatened, and nothing unreal exists." What we see taking place in the physical world is illusory, a dream projected from the ego mind, a split-off mind determined to prove that we are separate from one another and God, our common source. Our bodies, and what we see outside of ourselves, are no more than projections of thoughts in mind.

The "real" is God's creation, manifested in the Oneness of all, the Sonship. Therefore, conflict, separation, and injury are not possible. Forgiveness is offered as a process for us to heal the pain and guilt generated by the idea of separation. With forgiveness, we look beyond the events that seemed to have occurred, and acknowledge the holiness of each one involved in the situations, no matter what actions they may have participated in. We see ourselves and all others as the Creator sees us.

Obviously, when we are entangled in ego perception and judgments about others, ourselves and the world, we have no chance of understanding or practicing forgiveness. If we want to do that, we have to ask for assistance.

Seeking Help

To maintain an awareness of oneness, it is necessary to ask for help from Spirit, because as individuals who have identified with separation, we will not give it up. Spirit knows nothing of separation, except that it is an illusion. One method of asking for help is with the practice of intentions. Early each morning, I express certain intentions to remind myself what I want. Examples:

- Divine Self, grant me the grace of total willingness, so that I might live the truth of Oneness through forgiveness.

- Divine Spirit, today, I intend to see my brother as myself. Help me.

- Today, my intention is to have others show me the face of God.

- My intention is to allow the one and only God-Self to make all decisions.

Intentions are not mindless distractions from uncomfortable thoughts. They are requests to Spirit to help focus our thoughts. The intention gives direction to what we want to occur, and Spirit gives us the grace to fulfill them. It is not the frequency of their use that is important. It is the sincerity of our request and complete willingness to follow what is granted. Spirit is always present to undo errors in egoic thinking and move us in the direction of true forgiveness. With dedicated application and vigilance, we begin to notice that we see others in more accepting and loving ways. With awareness of our shifts in judgments about others we come to understand how intentions and forgiveness work.

In my own daily practice, I use the generic statements of intention mentioned above to set a certain tone, but I also use more specific requests. As I began to use intentions relating to forgiveness, I experienced their power and I noticed more possibilities for their use. For instance, when I sit down to watch the television news, I often say to myself, "Spirit Self help me watch this as you would." Then I wait. Soon, I see beyond the appearances, to the truth of the figures that represent only thoughts in mind. This allows me to extend forgiveness, which is my only function. I am not suggesting that anyone attempt to intellectually abdicate the way they perceive what they see, taste, or touch in their physical experience. That cannot be done, because the ego will never, never let go of its belief in separation which the physical world symbolizes. However, one can be fully functional within the dream world, and choose to be open to seeing differently.

In a workshop with Stephen Schwartz (described in Chapter 7), I wanted to see differently. I perceived all present as one and the same light, the same essence, with no space between us. Though the emotional bliss faded after a short time, the most important blessing that stayed has been greater clarity and certainty that we are all the same essence.

I use intentions in simple social situations as well, such as when Berta and I have friends over, or are invited to someone's home for dinner. I may ask, "Spirit let me be present in this event, with you in charge." I want to avoid merely playing the social role of being nice, as I have done in the past. I want to be the presence of joy and love, and follow intuition. The consequences are pleasantly surprising. I might tell a story or ask a question without a sense of where it will lead, and the results are a fruitful exchange and a relaxed environment. Through such intentions, the apparent mundane becomes a sacred moment. Without this intention, my interactions with others are directed by the ego's automatic patterns. With intentions, unexpected moments of tranquility and joy unfold because I am allowing the True Self to direct the interactions.

When I have a session with a client, I say, "God-Self, let me see beyond appearances to the truth of this client, and let me use only the words that you choose." With every decision, I ask the Sacred Self to take over. A long-term effect of using intentions is that my sense of ego identity is pushed into the background, and I come to know that my spirit guide/teacher is the Sacred Self. And I am that.

Healing Past Traumas, Wounds, and Fixations through Forgiveness

Most of us have deep wounds and scars. Many arise from traumatic events in childhood. Individual responses to such events are diverse. They can leave us with a mind set that others disapprove of us such that, even when we receive positive feedback, we interpret it as disapproval.

A situation may have occurred in which we became fixated with the belief that we are inadequate. Then, we relate to others in such a way that our inadequacy is proved valid in our eyes. Many times, the individual is oblivious to the fixation, and sees it as reality. Other fixations take the form of how people identify themselves: I am ugly, guilty, unlovable or unworthy. Out of fixations arise injunctions. Some common injunctions are the need to be perfect, work hard, please others, not feel, not question authority, seek approval, or be the life of the party.

When we are stuck in a fixation, or have been abused by others and are suffering because of their actions, we may choose to heal those hurts through forgiveness. Three simple steps lead to forgiveness.

First, ask Spirit for help in healing through forgiveness.

Second, picture the other persons involved in the event, and look beyond what they did or said to you—see them as God's perfect creation. Use whatever imagery works for you. You may visualize light emanating from and gradually encircling their whole being. Stay with the image and observe the feeling associated with the image. When you feel a sense of peace, or even relief from the anger or heaviness associated with the memory, you will know you are forgiving the individual. For some, the visualization process seems contrived, and it may work better to express a sincere desire to behold the others as the Creator does; thus resulting in a sense of relief and calm. If these methods do not provide peace or relief, simply say, "Spirit Self, I don't yet appear to be in a place of forgiveness. Give me the grace of total willingness that I might see differently."

Third, once you have sensed peace or relief, acknowledge that what took place occurred only as thoughts in mind, and then wait and see. If you find a pleasant shift in your emotional state of mind, end there without analysis. If you find you are balking at this idea, then whisper, "Spirit Guide, grant me total willingness to grasp that all of this has occurred as only thoughts in mind." Don't punish yourself for holding on to illusion. The True Self knows what is real; and in time, you will allow Spirit to correct the egoic illusion.

Following are two examples of the above process.

Ryan was the second son in a family of three brothers. He perceived that his father always put him down by saying, "Why aren't you like your older brother? You will never amount to anything!" He saw his father as always angry with him, and felt he was always being persecuted and judged. This evoked a deep sense of sadness and shame in Ryan. He carried around a constant feeling of failure that affected many of his choices. In high school, his coaches encouraged him to go out for varsity sports due to his natural athletic ability. He held himself back precisely because his chattering mind told him he would fail, because he was not good enough.

As an adult, though Ryan had a successful career, he always worked hard to offset his pessimistic thoughts. His wife thought he was depressed and should be on medication. For years he avoided examining his past, for it was simply too painful to go there. He took a course in spirituality and began to learn ideas he felt at home with.

He related to this concept: What people believe they are, and who they are, are not the same. What people believe they are relates to ideas they have assimilated. Who they are refers to who they are before any conditioning took place. Through forgiveness, they are given the opportunity to undo blocks to remembering who they are. Ryan knew that he wanted to find innate happiness, and he asked for it in his prayers. When he became familiar with the concept of spiritual forgiveness, he took time to quietly and calmly go through the three steps previously noted, in his own unique way.

First, Ryan asked the True Self for help to be free from his traumatic relationship with his father. He easily admitted that he was unable to let go of the past on his own. He felt unable to resolve the issue with his father, so he sincerely asked for help. Second, he found himself picturing his father as he remembered him from childhood. To his surprise, Ryan experienced his father in a different way. His attitude changed. He saw him as okay, as God's perfect creation. He knew nothing actually changed historically; the only thing that changed was his perception. He also realized, he did not actually do anything, but was open to forgiveness, and that is what he experienced. He felt calm and relieved. Without any doing or effort on his part he felt joyous. He remained very still for a few minutes as he experienced the feeling of joy.

Third, he said to himself, "Sacred Self, help me grasp what it means to affirm that this whole experience never happened, except as thoughts in mind." He remained in silence for some time. There was not even a whisper of a thought, only stillness. He waited. He didn't move, and he found the silence filled with joy. In that joyful stillness, he somehow knew that what was real did not change. What did change was his judgment about his father being evil and a victimizer; what changed was his emotional reaction to recalling the scene. It was evident that what he wanted was given to him. In that stillness, his memories of a past trauma were no longer emotionally upsetting. His perception had, as he requested, been altered. In that stillness, no ego thoughts arose to question or analyze what had happened. In the following days and weeks, he related to his father in a kind and lighthearted manner. Previous to his experience, he habitually felt uncomfortable speaking with his father. Now, he saw his father in a different way. Ryan was delighted with the change. He knew that what he desired with his whole heart, and what he had requested, had been given. More than that, he did not care to know. He chalked it up as grace requested, and grace given. He realized that dissecting it would not be beneficial. By not questioning the experience, he stayed with what he learned about being Peace itself. Perceptions, thoughts, urges and judgments driven by ego come and go. Ryan knows he always has the option of not taking them personally. The intensity of the peace and joy of that forgiveness experience faded, but what remained for Ryan was the knowledge that he was now free of past erroneous perceptions.

Forgiveness is a process that has to be lived from the heart and guided by Spirit. If forgiveness is done with an ego idea of accomplishing something, it will never happen. If done in the spirit of total willingness in allowing healing to unfold, it will. The following story shows how someone related to the three steps in forgiveness in a different way than Ryan did.

Anita was the eldest child in a family of four. Her mother was an alcoholic and unable to consistently give tender loving care to her children. She was seen as a cold and negative woman most of the time, and her role was that of the controller who could do whatever she wanted. Because her mother always put Anita in charge of caring for her younger siblings, from an early age, she felt she had no right to take care of herself. Her needs were always sacrificed on behalf of her younger and more helpless siblings. Resentment built up in her. She felt depressed for being treated unjustly, and perceived her role as servant, without any right to have fun. She became a grade school teacher and loved her job, but was nervous and preoccupied, and always worried about the quality of her work. She spent a lot of energy worrying about the future. Her peers saw her as a conscientious teacher, though some thought she was a workaholic. Her close friends thought she often took on the role of rescuer.

Anita was an avid reader of self-help books. Through them, she made contact with groups that helped others find their inner, True Self. Some of the issues she faced were: inability to relax and slow down, an ongoing critical mind that kept her preoccupied with the future, and a need to be perfect. The most crucial issue was her anger and frustration in relating to her mother. Like so many, she was conditioned to believe that by the force of her will and sheer determination she could heal that relationship and find peace and happiness. Over the years, she intellectually came to know that was impossible, but she did not know any other way of addressing the issue until the following occurred.

Her intention was to heal her relationship with her mother. The intention brought her to a study group that focused on inner healing through forgiveness. The first step in forgiveness was to acknowledge her inability to heal the relationship using her ego resources. This was less challenging for her to accept because she had tried unsuccessfully for years. Admitting this, led her to ask Spirit for total willingness to see things differently, to heal the relationship with her mother.

A month after Anita had gone through the first step in forgiveness, she felt it was time to sit quietly and go through the second. Anita closed her eyes and remembered various images when her mother was intoxicated. She felt numbed by the memory and a bit sick to her stomach. As she stayed with the image, she felt helpless to do anything about it. So she once again asked her True Self or Spirit for assistance in the healing process, and then she silently waited. Slowly, she began to see a light radiating from within her mother. She felt her own inner numbness and sick feeling dissipate. In its place, there was tranquility. For several minutes, she stayed with the new image and inner feeling.

As she remained in silence, the third step in forgiveness unfolded. She recalled her often repeated prayer, "True Self, give me total willingness to accept the idea that what has taken place has occurred only as thoughts in mind." She stayed silent for ten minutes. No thought stirred in her mind. She had been touched by her inner voice for truth—strong in silence and absolutely certain in its message. In that silence, she came to know what was true.

In the days that followed, the emotional intensity faded, but more important to her was that the old way of relating to her mother was finished. How? She didn't need to ask herself such a question. She knew it in her heart. It was clear to her that if she analyzed the experience she would be back where she had started. She continued to accept what was given. Ego thinking interprets events to prove its thesis that we are not one, that we are bodies, and that physical world is real. Truth, which is of Spirit, is a quiet power, and does not attack or even defend itself. It is. Because of her intentions and willingness to allow her True Self to bring about the transformation, Anita experienced spiritual forgiveness.

These two examples have some things in common. Both Ryan and Anita felt they had no control in their childhood, which caused them to feel like victims. In each situation, they felt their parents made them feel bad. Their early experiences translated into a conditioned belief that they carried into adulthood. Others controlled their feelings, making them feel like victims. This acquired belief was a reality for both Ryan and Anita. Their perception was that others made them feel what they were feeling. In all likelihood, their parents felt precisely the same way. Their children were making them feel bad, and so they fell into the habit of attacking or blaming the children to protect themselves. Indeed, this is the insane thinking of ego. Thinking in this way is an ego value, because it proves we are separate from one another (victim/victimizer) and keeps us from knowing ourselves as innate joy, peace and happiness.

Few escape this egoic way of interpreting situations. Ryan and Anita identified with being anything but joy and peace and carried that false sense of self into adulthood. Through the healing of spiritual forgiveness, peace, love and essential sameness was extended to others in their families. The mechanism was the desire to see differently, asking for assistance and allowing Spirit to correct errors in thinking.

Spiritual forgiveness is our only function. Through it, we allow the undoing of thinking that has clouded the truth of our connectedness. Such forgiveness is a paradox. We overlook what is not there, forgive all things that never existed, and let go of nightmares that we never had.

Are you not speaking with a relative or friend because of something that took place in the past? Do you hold any grudges against another whether living or dead? Are you vengeful with someone? How would your life be different if these relationships were healed?

You are, of course, free to hold on to unhealed relationships. Healing will never be imposed upon you. Are you at least willing to ask for the *desire* to heal these relationships? If so, you have begun a journey of spiritual forgiveness.

Acceptance is all that is required, acceptance of your True Self as you stand, that is it. How else could it be otherwise? Nothing more is required. It is ever so simple.

~ Jerome

Unveiling the False Self

As noted in the previous chapter on forgiveness, by the time we reach the age of seven, most of us have probably experienced some kind of traumatic or intense emotional pain. Because we lack the awareness and the brain development in those early years to see such wounds in a larger context, they often cause a shift in our relationship to life from that point forward. We acquire a scar in the form of a conclusion about ourselves, that is not accurate, and that conclusion becomes the foundation for a false sense of identity. It is a fixation.

Over time, through what we perceive to be corroborating experiences, and lack of information to the contrary, that false identity builds up walls that actually mask or block out the truth of who we are. We lose sight and forget. This false identity is a specific expression of the universal bank of thoughts and values that represents the ego belief in separation. This belief generates guilt and fear.

Such distorted interpretations about the nature of our being can be damning in their simplicity. They stick in our minds like unwanted ad jingles: I am bad. I am guilty. I am unlucky. I am always picked on. Everyone hates me. I am unlovable. I am lacking something. I am not good enough. It is played out when we experience the slightest stress and also when we are rejoicing. These insidious refrains often play below consciousness, where even if we can't hear them, they are the engine that determines how our lives unfold.

We think we are in control of choices about what we like or love, but that is not usually the case. Our "preferences" are far more reactive in nature.

What we do or don't react to, what we do or don't choose, can often be traced back to some kink in our sense of self. It may control who becomes our friend, who we fall in love with, and who we develop a violent dislike for.

Consider this example. Let's say I was a victim of physical abuse as a child, and later in life, I meet someone who tells a story of physical abuse. What happens? Right away I recognize, I have been in a similar situation. Chances are I will "identify" with the person, because I assume my interpretations of the experience are the same. This person may not actually have interpreted the abuse as I did, or may have healed from the experience, and is now in a totally different mind set. Yet, I "rest" on my fantasized similarity, and stop really seeing the other. All I see is my projection onto that person.

Perhaps more influential than defining the kind of people we choose to associate with, these internal scripts become self-fulfilling prophecies. For instance, if I think I'm a failure, I will interpret events in my life as proof that I am, even though others may have an entirely different take on a given situation. In another example, Kevin decided early on in life that he wasn't adequate. In high school, he put forth effort to excel, and did well. However, he commonly interpreted the remarks and looks of teachers and coaches to mean that he wasn't adequate. He pushed himself even more to become "enough." He believed that by striving and working harder he would someday be adequate.

These kinds of patterns are called reactive cycles, and because they are born out of who we think we are, they are tied to our false self-image. It is almost impossible to break these patterns, until we learn to recognize them and the false identification that created them in the first place. Below are two diagrams that help reveal these patterns, "The Reactive Cycle" and "A Question of False Identity." Once you understand these two diagrams, you can work with a third diagram, "The Story I Tell Myself," either alone or together with two or three friends. The advantage of working in a small group is that it provides feedback from others in the form of comments and questions, which facilitates greater honesty. Vulnerable emotions are elicited as each participant verbalizes how he or she filled in each of the boxes. The caring, supportive presence of others makes sharing safer.

Not everyone finds working with the diagrams useful. Some individuals have already moved in their awareness of life beyond those learnings. Others may have issues too fearful for them to face in this informal context or other personal reasons for not wanting to do the exercise. Acceptance of each individual, at whatever level, creates a nonjudgmental environment and fosters respect.

The Reactive Cycle

This diagram illustrates how a particular thought produces a corresponding set of feelings. Our feelings encourage us to engage in certain behaviors which, in turn, produce results that reinforce the original reactive thought. Thus, our reactions form our experiences, developing a pattern of how we interpret what happens.

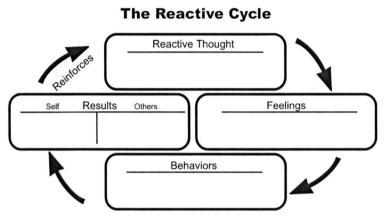

The Reactive Cycle

Guilt - Judgement - Punishment

Sometimes individuals are aware of their wounds—they know what caused their hurt or fear—and it is easier to untangle the threads of unwholesome behaviors that developed from the wounds. However, some individuals may not have any idea why they feel the way they do, or why they are drawn to certain things. Because the pattern is a cycle, by knowing some part of it, such as the feelings and their results, it is possible to trace back to the reactive thought in the cycle.

The Reactive Cycle diagram begins with the top box labeled "Reactive Thought." The arrow to the right of that box points to the "Feelings" box. This indicates that the false self-concept generates a certain spectrum of feelings. The arrow below the "Feelings" box points to the "Behaviors" box, which contains the things we do that are the result of the items in the two previous boxes. The arrow to the left of the "Behaviors" box leads to the "Results" box, which is the fruit of the contents of the three boxes that precede it. The thought we have affects how we feel. These two things together affect our behavior, and all three affect how we act in the world. This, in turn, affects how we are treated. How we are treated often reinforces what we think, thus launching a self-perpetuating cycle.

The last line under the diagram consists of three words: guilt, judgment and punishment. As we live a reactive cycle, it is common to feel as if we have done something wrong. It is not guilt in the common usage of the word, but a lack inside, or a feeling of imperfection that holds the belief that a full and joyous life is not deserved. It is this feeling that prevents knowing the True Self as innate joy, happiness and security. The ego, seemingly outside of conscious awareness, makes a judgment that the person lacks something or is imperfect and, therefore, needs punishment. The fixation and reactive pattern is the punishment. Does this sound crazy? It is. And it is all based on the delusion that we are not who we are.

To demonstrate how the cycle works, the following diagram shows an example of a young college student, Ted, whose self concept was that he was stupid. In the top box of this diagram, his self-concept is explained as, "I am stupid." As a result of having this opinion of himself, Ted often felt anxious and fearful, and that's what he described in the "Feelings" box. For the behaviors that resulted from these feelings, he wrote in the bottom box, "don't study or do homework, can't concentrate, skip classes." The result of this behavior, which-as the chart shows-grew out of his belief and feelings, was that he earned poor grades and experienced criticism from others. This, in turn, made him feel inadequate and reinforced his belief that he was stupid.

The more stupid he felt, the less functional he was in life, and the more frightened he became.

A Question of False Identity
Subtitle: How Life Unfolds

Guilt - Judgement - Punishment
The Story I Tell Myself

The more fearful Ted became, the more it influenced his behavior; the less able he was to perform adequately or make responsible judgments.

The more immersed he was in his story, the worse his grades were and the more he felt stupid. Ted went round and round in this cycle. It was a self-fulfilling prophecy. The guilt he felt was wrapped up in his self-imposed label of stupidity. He believed that he was rightly judging himself, which resulted in punishing himself in his reactive pattern. This fixation or pattern did not need to exist; all of it was caused by thoughts in Ted's mind. This cycle proved his version of the universal ego's thought that we are separate and not united in love and joy.

As a objective outsider to Ted's situation, consider the following questions:

1. Is there a connection between Ted's belief about himself and the emotions that he has repeatedly felt? If so, describe it.

    _____

    _____

2. Explain the relationship between Ted's false concept about himself and his behaviors.

    _____

    _____

3. How is it that living within this reactive cycle reinforces his idea that he is stupid?

    _____

    _____

4. Ted's employer has sent him to five-day computer training. What is the story Ted will likely tell himself?

    _____

    _____

5. How would Ted experience his life if he believed deep inside that there was nothing wrong with him?

    _____

    _____

6. What words might describe his feelings if he believed he was not broken but whole?

_____

_____

7. What behaviors would he have?

_____

_____

8. What might general outcomes would Ted experience as a result of this?

_____

_____

9. What is the true story about Ted that he could tell himself?

_____

_____

As you can see from Ted's diagram, he had been feeling defeated and worthless. Once he identified his reactive cycle, the door opened for him to initiate a healing process described later in this chapter. If Ted worked to change his belief from "I am stupid" to "I am smart," he would be attempting to turn things around. But this is not a process of turning things around; rather, it is dropping the whole idea of the false self. There is no need to establish a new identity. Healing takes place in letting go of the false identity, so that the truth is revealed.

Who we are has been clouded over. By undoing this false self-concept, a block that interferes with remembering who we are is removed. This is done by being aware of the elements in the reactive cycle, and asking one's True Self to undo the pattern. This is not replacing one thought with another; the knowledge of who we are has never been lost, only denied. Healing is a return to an unconflicted state of mind, or who we are, and finding that we never really left it.

Knowing Your False Self

In the following diagram, "Unveiling the False Self," you fill in the boxes with answers from your own life. You may not be immediately aware of any particular reactive thought, but if you start with a feeling that troubles you, you can work your way around the diagram from there. It is easier for most people to start by filling in the "Feelings" box, because we are often more aware of how we feel than why.

Take a few moments to think about unpleasant emotions you typically experience. Allow yourself to feel the sensation of them. Then, fill in the "Feelings" box with three examples. Ponder these for a moment, and start with the strongest one. Let the sensation take you back to a memory of one of the first times you experienced it. Answer the questions below the diagram:

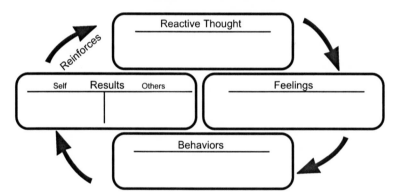

Unveiling the False Self
Subtitle: How Life Unfolds

Guilt - Judgement - Punishment
The Story I Tell Myself

How old are you?

Where were you?

Who else was present? How did the incident start?

What happened next?

What did you do?

If someone else was present, what did they do?

How did it end?

What was it that you felt?

As a result of the experience what did you think about yourself?

When you have an answer to that last question, write it in the "Reactive Thought" box. It will be something along the lines of: I have to do everything. I'm clumsy. I'm stupid. I can't sing. I'm terrible at baseball. I'm a bad person. I can't do anything right. And so on. Once that is done, you can complete the other two boxes, describing the behaviors and results associated with the thought. If you follow this process with the other two feelings you listed, you will likely find that they take you to the same historical scene.

In the last line of the diagram are three words: guilt, judgment and punishment. The denial of who we are is always accompanied by guilt; however, ego often keeps that specific emotion hidden by suppressing it. We tend to experience guilt as a human weakness or imperfection. What specific word describes your guilt? At times, guilt is present, not because I am bad or have "sinned" in some way, but because I have judged myself as imperfect or lacking some skill or asset. For example, people may see themselves as inadequate in sports or mathematics, or feel they lack physical beauty. This "guilt-imperfection" leads to an internal judgment about not deserving a wonderful life filled with joy, peace and never-ending love. This judgment, as formed in the ego mind, must in turn be punished. The cycle of reactive thoughts is the punishment.

As you review the entire diagram, allow yourself to feel the story that you automatically tell yourself. That story is an expansion of the false identity. For instance, the reactive thought of Alissa is, "I am ugly." Her story springs out of the thought that "Lovely clothes, makeup, and friends are not made for me, because I am ugly and always will be." Whenever situations occur in which she ends up feeling less than others, or that she is lacking something, it is because she has interpreted the situation through the lens of her story. This process normally occurs just below conscious awareness.

In another example, Nathan's reactive thought is, "nobody really cares about me." He formulates his story as, "I always end up with the hardest, dirtiest and poorest paying job because no one really cares about me." Whenever he feels depressed, angry or isolated, it is because he has interpreted what is going on around him through the lens of his story.

Once a cycle and the story are identified, they can be interrupted and "rewritten" by healing the original false identity with the following procedures. All of them have been discussed in previous chapters. All encourage and depend upon our developing awareness, unearthing our innate ability to witness what is, without taking it personally. All of their power comes from Self; in themselves they are no more than words on paper. Any one of the procedures has the potential to be sufficient and effective if diligently applied and done with total willingness to wake up.

Four different procedures are provided, because different ones appeal to different people, or at different times to the same person, depending on their stage in their process of undoing ego attachments. With the guidance of your Sacred Self, pick the one(s) that feel most natural to you for healing the reactive thoughts, feelings and behaviors you have identified.

The first healing procedure begins by examining your thought stream. Notice what it is you are actually thinking. As you become aware of any thought, feeling or urge that is not reflective of peace and joy (which means it is instead associated with your false identity), declare your intention: "With the help of the Sacred Self, my intention is to be at peace with this, too." (See Chapter 12.) You may want to use a reminder card to increase your vigilance. (See Chapter 13.)

As long as you are aligned with your false identity and rely on it to define who you are, you cannot change. With this procedure, however, you shift your point of reference to outside of your enmeshment in the ego's thoughts, and so gain perspective on them. The goal is to stay aware of what you are thinking as you think it, so you can catch your old false-self pattern the moment it arises. This is what it means to be vigilant.

This vigilance is a powerful help in itself. When we state our intention is "to be peace with this, too," we invite the True Self to give us assistance. After you declare your intention, just wait and see. Trust that what needs to take place will happen. Soon you will feel lighter, calmer, more at peace. You will feel life is more possible. This will automatically result in your defining more clearly what it is that you want. You will also see more clearly how to get it. You will then have greater willingness to use the procedure, because it works.

The second healing procedure is to pause for a moment whenever you feel racked with the emotions you wrote in the "Feelings" box of the "The Story I Tell Myself" diagram. After you have recalled your fabricated story, move to the second step, and tell yourself the truth about who you are. Word it however you like. One suggested formulation is: "I am as God created me, His perfect creation." Then, turn over the undoing of the fabricated story to Spirit.

A third healing option is the practice of absolute acceptance. (See Chapter 13.) When a feeling or urge arises out of the false self-orientation, don't run from it or judge it, instead, just let it be. Remain one with it in absolute acceptance. The uncomfortable feeling around it exists as a product of your egoic or conditioned mind. It will dissolve, if you approach it with the absolute acceptance of the witness, that is, without judging, interpreting, analyzing, or telling any story about it. In Chapter 7, I used this method of absolute acceptance to process the intense emotions I had in reaction to Tara Singh's words.

The fourth healing option stands out among all four procedures because of its particular focus. "Spiritual Forgiveness" corrects the foundation of ego thinking. (See Chapter 14.) The procedure works on two levels. The first level involves healing the relationship with the individuals involved in the event, by seeing them as God sees them. The second level involves letting go of the egoic belief that something happened that was more than mere thoughts in mind. Both levels are addressed with these three steps.

First, recall the original event that created the disturbance in your life and ask Spirit for help in healing it.

Second, see the other person(s) involved in the event as God's perfect creation. Also see the younger you in that same way.

Third, look at that event and state, "None of that ever happened, except as thoughts in mind."

In working with people over the years, I have discovered that many of us frequently don't recognize we have the option of turning things over to our Sacred or True Self, or we forget to ask for help in the heat of the moment. Perhaps it doesn't feel real, or it doesn't seem as if it will really make a difference. This, of course, is the defense the ego uses to keep us stuck in an old repetitive pattern. From the ego's perspective, asking our Sacred Self for aid raises the fear of annihilation. That is why it is so important to ask for help, because the conditioned mind will not change or let go of its errors on its own.

By surrendering everything to our True Self, we instantly stop nurturing egoic thoughts. When we pull our support of these, the ego control over our lives fades, for it only thrives when we give it power.

Above all, remember you are not designed for misery, but for joy and peace. If you are not feeling these, it means you have slipped out of alignment with both Divine Will and your Sacred Self. When that happens, you can use the diagram to identify the erroneous thought and its self-imposed story. You can choose to be peace, harmony and oneness again.

---

[1] In our presentation of healing procedures in this part of the book I do not wish to exclude more traditional approaches to psychotherapy. At times, they may be necessary and beneficial. I find "Thought Field Therapy" particularly effective and in line with the theoretical bases of what I present here.

I, you, he, she, we...in the garden of mystic lovers,

These are not true distinctions.

~ Rumi

Relationships

There is one Spirit alone manifested in its entirety in each one of us. That is our essence, the wondrous permanent presence, our only identity. Who we are, is that one, the whole, the Sacred Self. We are connected to each other. Therefore, we can have no discussion on establishing a true identity that does not address relationships with others. All relationships offer moments for undoing conditioned thinking. For example, we may have little to no patience when a store checkout clerk chats unnecessarily with those in front of us. Or, we may feel irritated when a golf partner gets upset over a poor shot. By being a witnessing presence to such internal automatic reactions, we free ourselves from taking them personally or acting out on them. In this chapter, however, we will focus on committed relationships, married or otherwise.

We do so not because they are more important than any other relationships, but because they provide an excellent milieu for understanding hidden agendas of the ego. Most of us spend a great deal of time together with our partners, and unpleasant feelings and judgments caused by the story we tell ourselves, inevitably surface. Facing those gives us repeated opportunities to invite the Sacred Self to undo those feelings or judgments. Spirit's goal for us in every relationship is to wake up to the truth that we are endlessly extending love, joy and peace.

No matter what partners bring to the relationship, most successful relationships follow the same general process, which can be broken into four stages.

Stages in Intimate Relationships

1. Initial Stage
   - The Romantic Phase (with hidden dependencies)
   - The Blaming Phase (unexpressed and unmet expectations)
2. Individuating Stage
   - Diminished or no communication
3. Practicing Maturity Stage
   - Listening: giving the other a sense of being understood
   - Honesty in all areas of the relationship
   - Healing procedures
4. Maturity Stage
   - Total commitment to being the presence of love
   - Radiant peace and love toward each other, and outward to all others
   - Acceptance of physical events as thoughts in mind

As you become acquainted with each of the four stages, you can easily identify the stage of your relationship.

Initial Stage

The initial stage consists of two phases. "Falling in love," or "finding one's true love," is associated with the romantic or first phase. Both parties are pulled into relationship by strong feelings and often an inexplicable attraction. Each has a sense that the other is "right" for him or her. The second phase is the blaming phase.

Romantic Phase

Falling in love frequently takes its "charge" from ego thoughts and values, where we see the other as the answer to our needs, and settle into depending on them to make us happy. We are often unaware of our real needs, yet we depend upon the other to meet them, and thus, the platform for the unfolding of the relationship is set by these hidden dependencies. The common denominator in those needs is that we secretly hope the other will make us happy.

In reality, the other cannot make us happy. It is impossible. First of all, happiness is our natural state, and it is never really lost. Secondly, no one else can confer or create innate, enduring happiness for us. When we fall in love through ego neediness, we tend to idealize the other person. In the romantic phase, we do not really see the other as they are, but rather we see our idealized image of a mate projected as on a movie screen. In time, reality begins to interfere with the illusion and rosy overtones that we painted both the other and the relationship. The person begins to disappoint us. He or she fails to meet our expectations, fails to make us happy. We may feel betrayed, hurt, even deprived of something we thought we were entitled. The blaming phase arises, and relations can turn acrimonious.

What takes place, in both phases of this initial stage, is often automatic and outside of conscious awareness. Many do not really know why they were attracted to the other person. As noted before, we often do not have awareness of what expectations we brought into the relationship, or those our partner brought. When these expectations begin to clash, or simply go unmet, we think the source of the unhappiness is the other. It looks like the other person is intentionally hurting us. We feel betrayed, and our behavior toward the other changes to reflect that. We may attempt to control the other to prevent the other from controlling us.

All of us have heard stories, read books, and watched movies about the romantic phase in relationships. Falling in love is a joyous and light-hearted sensation, and it makes us feel good even to see it happening to others. When it happens to us, we may feel more alive than at any other time. For many, the experience is beyond words and can't be compared to anything else. Where does this come from?

When we are young, if we don't receive the tender loving care that we need and want, we begin to feel we are missing something and we lose connection with our innate happiness. We respond with a hope that someday, someone will be there for us, and make us happy. This hope is what we believe is being fulfilled, when we fall in love. We say to ourselves, "I have found the right person...Now I will be forever happy." Our partner becomes the great hope for the future. We feel that rush, and think we have arrived home to a permanent place of lasting happiness. Our hope has been realized.

Some individuals do receive unconditional, tender loving care at an early age. They may believe at that time, due to the influence of ego thinking, that their parents have made them happy. They grow up thinking their happiness has been bestowed by another. The same dependency thoughts and values that occurred for the child who did not receive unconditional love fill their minds. Thus, when they are older and looking for a partner, they too, may go through the strong emotions and hidden dependencies that accompany the romantic phase in relationships.

They may look for a mate with certain characteristics or personal style. When they encounter someone with those traits, they project onto him or her the image they have crafted of the person they hope will love them as their parents did, and they will then be forever happy.

More frequently, the dynamic is much deeper and apart from conscious awareness. It is related to the false self discussed in Chapter 15. As noted there, individuals formulate a concept that they are ugly, unworthy, guilty, stupid, etc. These self-imposed false identities are self-fulfilling prophecies that they experience in many areas of their lives, often surfacing in intimate relationships. For example, individuals might see in another, someone who will listen and validate them, and their fantasy of finding enduring happiness will be realized. Others may search for someone who sees them as beautiful, and they anticipate they will find the long-hoped-for happiness they have been seeking. And others may feel they are on the road to being permanently happy when their feelings are validated.

Whether the expectation is based on something superficial, such as "I am too fat," or a deeper intra-personal dynamic, "I am unworthy of love," the loved one becomes a blank projection screen upon which we place the image of what we hope for and want. As long as we hold on to this image of the loved one, and to the belief that they will make us happy, we set ourselves up for disappointment. Happiness is an inside job; it is not something we get from another person or the outside world.

This romantic phase can last days, weeks, months, and in rare cases, years. Younger couples tend to feel the emotional pull of this romantic phase more than older couples. This is because many older couples have, at some time in their lives, gone through these early stages in relationships, and intellectually and emotionally already know that their happiness is not dependent upon another person. Some older individuals often enjoy the energy of falling in love, but because of their level of experience and maturity, they are not blinded by what is happening. They simply enjoy the fun of it.

Blaming Phase

One characteristic of dependency is seeing the other as responsible for creating and securing our happiness, and subsequently our sadness and disappointment, as well. The romantic phase ends and the blaming phase begins, when one party in the relationship feels their partner is no longer "making" them happy, and even perhaps has lost all ability to do so. One, and more often both, blame the other for "making" them angry, sad, hurt, disgusted and depressed. The ego thought and value system relies on this. And so long as we maintain this attitude, it keeps us stuck in the illusion of being a victim.

When asked if they are depending on their partner to make them happy, many say they know no one can make them happy. At the conscious, intellectual level, they are telling the truth. The level where the dependency expectations arise is often below conscious awareness. It is a thought/belief structure that they may be entirely unaware of. Until people uncover their hidden expectations for their partner, and recognize their dependencies, they remain in some form of blaming cycle.

The following exercises help identify the presence of hidden expectations and dependencies in a relationship and help us recognize and define things about ourselves that we do not realize we do or think. Once aware of them, we can see the ways in which we are controlled by them, and we can release them. Answer each question as honestly as you can.

Exercise: Revealing Hidden Dependencies

1. What emotional need did you have as a child that was not met by your family of origin? (Some common responses have been: to be listened to, be respected, be myself, be loved and so on.)

_____

_____

2. Take one of the phrases you wrote down, and fill in the blank space in the following statement with that phrase. For example: I give up the hope of ever finding someone to truly love me.

I give up the hope of ever finding someone to _____

_____

3. Read the sentence you just completed out loud as a statement of fact, and consciously give up the hope. Notice what you feel as you do, and write it in the following space.

_____

_____

Responses to this exercise vary greatly. At one end of the scale are those who say they would never honestly make such a statement, because they wouldn't have anything to live for. Others feel sad, hopeless, empty or scared. Such strong emotions are felt because these individuals intensely believe others make them happy or sad.

Some who are rigid may resist allowing any feelings to surface, because, while emotionally dependent, they steadfastly deny it. Some actually find relief when they make the statement, because their awareness of this dependency has been growing, but they never had the opportunity to face it so directly. When they do, they feel as though a burden has been lifted.

With any of these reactions, I suggest repeating the statement out loud twice each day for a week, keeping track of emotional responses. At the end of the week, notice any changes in reactions to the statement. For example, the sadness felt when first making the statement may, after a week now be delight at an awareness of letting go of that belief, as we realize how it has influenced our lives.

The goal of this exercise, as with all the awareness exercises in this part of the book, is to undo errors in thinking which are obstacles to remembering who we are. Often this repetition releases the ego's deeply held illusion that happiness is dependent on others.

As we repeat the statement, and then wait and see, our True Self will undo the illusion that another can bring us permanent happiness. How do you know if this happens? Simply wait and see, and pay attention to your feelings; your feelings will give you the answers.

Cynthia, a well-educated woman, had been married three years. She cried in her session with me saying, "I give up the hope of ever finding someone to love me the way I want." Each day during the next week, she repeated that same statement, and by the end of the week, she was laughing at having been caught up in that way of thinking. Through awareness, she let go of living life as if controlled by the automatic pilot of dependency. By repeating the statement, Cynthia faced her belief that her innate happiness was dependent on her finding the right man.

Once we recognize our hidden dependencies and expectations, we tend to rapidly release them, and have a strong desire to learn how to relate in a mature way. The key is always awareness of the belief or expectation that another is going to bring us permanent happiness. Without awareness, we are victims of our past or imagined future.

Individuating Stage

The romantic phase ends with the decline into the blaming phase, but couples can only take that path so far, before it also comes to an end. They have exhausted the good feelings of falling in love, and it soon becomes counterproductive to keep blaming the other for the nasty things they feel. At this point, they enter the individuating stage, called so because the focus of each partner falls away from blaming the other for his or her lack of happiness. In this sense, it is positive. They want their partnership to work out, but are without knowledge or skills to make that happen.

At this juncture, there may be some talking, but neither one is really listening in such a way that the partner feels understood. They generally have little communication with one another, and the interactions they do have are characterized by guardedness.

Some couples might accept the fact that they simply can't communicate and resign themselves to living in a marriage that is far from satisfying. Some become like partners in a business, where their lives function together in a relatively smooth fashion, but there is no emotional investment. Those who have children may choose to stay together until the children are raised. Staying together affords them, among other things, the external appearance of being married. It gives them status, keeps them from the terror of living alone, and avoids the stigma of a failed marriage. Since the relationship is not their focus anymore, the partners are freer to devote their time and energy to their professional lives, children, social interests or financial endeavors.

The influences that impact the choices couples make are as broad as life itself. Some may reach a kind of satisfaction with the stale status quo, because it helps them avoid intimacy, or keeps them from the responsibility of taking their own internal journey of self inquiry. Others may fear getting a divorce due to cultural or religious injunctions, or because they are afraid of being alone. The length of time individuals stay in this stage varies. Some may separate at this point, unable to stay in the half-life of together, but not together. Some move through it and onto the third stage, while others remain there for the rest of their lives. The reasons why couples move out of this second stage vary from couple to couple. In my experience, they often develop an ability to express their wants for a more meaningful and intimate friendship without getting caught in old games like, "Let's fight," and opens the door to further sharing and searching for answers as a couple.

Practicing Maturity Stage

In this stage, the primary issue is giving one's partner a sense of being understood, and also being a presence of love oneself. In the individuating stage, in general, neither partner has the knowledge or ability to do that.

One goal in this stage is to learn to be present to our partners in such a way that they have a sense of being understood. The basic rule in communication is to remove behaviors that clearly block our partners from feeling understood and validated. This means we put down the newspaper or book that we are reading, or mute the television, so we can give them our undivided attention when they speak to us. When our intention is to listen in this way, we notice that old habits, such as labeling, questioning, arguing, judging, and so on, are barriers in giving our partners a sense of being understood. Facing patterns that have interfered with real communication in the past, and letting them go, is an enriching transformation in this stage.

For example, Jay is a building construction supervisor, who habitually thinks in terms of defining things as problems and then creates practical solutions. His wife Carla tells him she feels like a worker that he supervises. She wants him to be a friend, to know him as the presence of love. She perceives that he interprets most of what she says as a problem, and immediately gives her a solution. She feels like one of his subordinates. Lately, he has been noticing his habit of defining what she is saying as a problem, and he is backing off. Instead of giving her a solution, he listens attentively. In doing this, he is one step closer to being Carla's friend, giving her what she wants, being a love presence.

With that basic rule as a guideline, some develop a feel for being the presence of love and relating without judgment, so that their partners feel understood. For others, that guideline is not adequate, because they have no idea what it means or how to apply it to their situation; they need more specific suggestions to know how to create conditions in which their partner feels understood.

The following section illustrates how to give your partner a sense of being understood and how to be a love presence.

Giving our Partner a Sense of Being Understood.

When we interact with another, we do so for one of two reasons: we want to extend love, or we want to receive it. We may not consciously be aware of it, but this is a universal truth, even though to the ego's perception it is not. Deep down, we all want to extend love and to receive it, for that is our essential nature. When we don't, it might be because we feel hurt or fearful and don't want contact with anyone for the moment. We might be wrapped in intense guilt and feel temporally paralyzed.

This dynamic is part of the ego thought and value system. It may look like individuals who are worried or vengeful do not really want love, because by all appearances they are extending negativity in some form. Knowing that others approach us desiring love, we are more likely to be alert in giving them what they want. If every time a spouse or another person comes to us, we recognize which of the two reasons brought them, we are more prepared to give an appropriate response.

This example shows how Josh avoided responding defensively by having the intention to perceive Krissy as coming from a space of wanting love. The two had been dating for more than a year. One evening when they were having a meal, Krissy said, "Honey, when we go on a trip together, I really get nervous when you drive." Josh immediately became aware of his defensiveness and the impulse to tell her she had no basis for her nervousness, because for two years he had raced cars and made good money at it. In his mind, he was an exceptionally safe driver. But he did not choose to go with that impulse. Instead he replied, "You're really scared with the way I drive." Krissy said, "Yes, that's right. Thank you for listening." They continued their conversation and resolved the issue. Because of his explicit intention, Josh recognized that Krissy wanted love, and he responded by giving her a sense of being understood, which was the form of love and validation she wanted.

For some, like Josh, successfully mirroring and expressing feelings to their partners in an honest and direct fashion is the first step to breaking out of the non-listening dungeon.

Below, is another example of a spouse giving a partner a sense of being understood.

Todd and his wife Brianna had been married for a year, and their relationship was deteriorating. When they came to counseling, I invited them to sit in chairs facing each other. Brianna initiated the discussion with a comment on something that was a problem for her. Todd responded in a manner that gave his wife a sense of being understood.

"Todd, most mornings when I get up, the kitchen table is still covered with your dirty dishes. You have left for work an hour or so before, and have once again left me with your mess. I have asked you kindly several times to at least put your dirty dishes in the sink, and clear the table."

"You're frustrated with me," Todd responded, choosing to give his wife his attention and show her she is being understood.

Brianna nodded her head in agreement and continued, "Yes. But more, I am angry. You never seem to really pay attention to what I have to say. You physically seem to hear me, but you are out to lunch; it is like my words go in one ear, and then right out the other. Sometimes I'd like to shake you."

Todd was tempted to defend himself, but didn't. Instead, he said, "You are really angry with me."

"Yes," said Brianna, "I want you to listen to me, so I have a sense that I matter to you."

"Above all things, you want me to pay attention," Todd said, "So you have a sense that I am respecting you."

After a pause, she said, "Yes, yes! Will you do that?"

"Yes, I will...and from now on, I will put my dirty breakfast dishes in the sink, and clear the table before I leave for work in the morning."

"Thank you for listening to me, Todd," Brianna said as she gave him a hug.

Let's review what took place. Brianna started by saying clearly what she disliked about Todd's behavior, and what she wanted from him. The brief form of what she said is, "Most mornings you leave your breakfast dishes on the kitchen table. I want you to put them in the sink." Todd was not defensive, though he might have been tempted to be. He told her, "You are frustrated." That gave Brianna a sense of being understood, and she communicated that with a nod of her head.

She went on, expressing more of her feelings. She said, "I am angry." Todd was really tempted to defend himself, but he knew that would only perpetuate past ineffective communication. He gave her feedback about her being angry with him. That too elicited a sense of her being understood, as indicated with her "yes" response.

Next, Brianna expressed what she wanted from Todd. He again gave her a sense of being understood with the words, "You want me to pay attention so you have a sense that I am respecting you." From there, Brianna asked him if he would do that, and he responded in the affirmative. She got what she wanted emotionally, and he also promised to put his breakfast dishes in the kitchen sink.

The following exercise helps couples learn to give each other a sense of being understood.

Sit with your partner so that you are facing each other. Determine which of you will be the speaker and which the listener. The speaker will focus on some issue about which he or she has strong opinions or emotions, and will begin by describing in three of four sentences the nature of the feelings.[1] The listener will respond using the following format, "You are feeling _____ _____ _____ _____," with the blank being the feelings the speaker communicated directly or indirectly. The listener may include other ideas, but the format must be respected. To do this, the listener focuses on the feelings behind what is being said.

The listener only follows and never leads the conversation. Examples of leading instead of listening are: asking questions, solving the problem, disagreeing or labeling. Once the listener has spoken, the speaker can continue talking. Frequently, as the dialogue unfolds, the speaker confirms the listener's response by saying "yes," or nodding, and then immediately moving on to further expression of feelings. This is what Brianna did in the example above.

After expressing some feelings, speakers often make direct or indirect statements about their wants. This, too, is a natural process, and Brianna did just that. When this occurs, the listener should respond with, "What you want is _____ _____," where the blank is the speaker's desire. Notice that is what Todd did.

Use the structured format of the dialogue for five minutes unless the emotions are too intense. If they are too intense, don't force it. If both want to continue the exercise for a longer duration, do so as long as that is what both want. When the dialogue is finished, share with one another what the experience felt like.

The speaker will be the first to describe what the experience was like, noting whether he or she had a sense of being understood. The speaker also comments on whether or not the exchange offered something of what was wanted from the other, as well as what advantages or disadvantages the format offered.

The listener should then describe what the experience felt like. Note

---

[1] For ease in communication, I have used a single pronoun here and elsewhere in this section. The speaker may be a man or woman. Likewise, the listener may be either gender, depending of the situation.

whether the exchange was difficult or easy, and whether any old patterns surfaced. In particular, the listener should address how the format helped or hindered the whole process.

In using this exercise with hundreds of couples, I've seen that the listener often finds it intensely challenging to stay focused on giving the other a sense of being understood. Frequently, driven by ego impulses, listeners are tempted to be defensive rather than give their partner a sense of being understood. The ones giving the feedback often think if the other only knew the facts, the problems would disappear, so instead of listening they have a strong urge to provide information. Many men have told me, "Listening in this way is the hardest thing I have ever done; it is one thing I don't know how to do." The best way of intercepting these challenges is a clear intention and commitment to give your partner a sense of being understood.

Both speakers and listeners can respond to the idea of incorporating this form of relating into their lives as a couple. The essential element is to be a loving presence for your partner; whether you actually give the verbal feedback in the manner suggested is not crucial. For when you relate as the presence of love, you will avoid pitfalls such as the urge to be defensive, give out correct information, or offer solutions to perceived problems. Many couples stumble on these pitfalls, correct them, and move through the gates of the practice of being mature stage.

Once we have a feel for giving our partner a sense of being understood, and know what it is like to be understood, we may discover common behavioral patterns that are barriers to true communication, such as interrogating or commanding. As you read each item in the list below, place one of the following three numbers in the blank space to indicate the frequency with which you indulge in the behavior:

> 1: *Never or hardly ever*
> 2: *Occasionally*
> 3: *Frequently*

_____ Command, direct or order my partner or others

_____ Give solutions or advice when they aren't specifically asked for

_____ Lay "shoulds" and "have-tos" on others in a preaching fashion

_____ Interrogate and probe the actions or motives of others like a prosecuting attorney

_____ Divert attention to something else when feeling uncomfortable by changing the topic being discussed, or by joking about the issue

_____ Deny what others are feeling

_____ Agree with the other, when in actual fact you disagree

_____ Label or indulge in name calling

_____ Analyze, interpret or diagnose behaviors of others when they haven't requested it

_____ Give logical arguments when the other only wants a sense of being understood

If you marked any of the statements with a "3," and you want to let go of that habit, use the following diagram over the next week to build awareness of when and how you use the statement. At the top, fill in the habit you want to focus on. On each day of the week, note the number of times and circumstances when you had an urge to use the pattern. In the column to the right, indicate whether you succeeded in dropping the behavior or succumbed to repeating it. Remember, to drop a habit, you have to first be aware of it when it occurs. Whenever you become aware of the ego-generated urge, you can choose again, this time in accord with the inner voice for truth, your Sacred Self.

	Behavior pattern _____ **Number of times and cicumstances**	**Did I choose differently?**
Example	*Pattern: Label. Twice, had urge to call spouce stupid.*	*Yes, twice.*
Monday		
Tuesday		
Wednesday		
Thursday		
Friday		
Saturday		
Sunday		

Being Honest in All Areas of the Relationship

Being honest has two sides: being honest with ourselves and being honest with others. To be honest with ourselves means we live as innate peace, joy and love. Being honest with others means we behold them as equal to ourselves as innate peace, joy and love.

Once we are able to give our partner a sense of being understood, by really listening to what the other is saying, we will be less compelled to respond with automatic reactions, and we will no longer be prisoners of judgments, interpretations, and of our story. When we are free from such judgments or interpretations, the innate self is revealed, because the innate self is the presence that precedes all judgments and interpretations.

If we used to judge a partner as too emotional, and that idea resurfaces, we refrain from acting on it because we are totally committed to giving our partner a sense of acceptance. If our interpretation is that people are out to get us, we will lay that aside too, in order to fully listen to our partner. If our story is "I am always rejected," we will put that aside, and instead offer the other a sense of validation. When listening this way, we discover a way of connecting with others that is more personal and meaningful. This is to be the presence of love.

When we relate more consistently as who we innately are, we can acknowledge our imperfections, mistakes and limitations, for we know they are not who we are. When coming from innate peace, we come with innocent perception, perception that is free of judgments and interpretations.

The ten statements below have been designed to assist in the awareness of any beliefs or attitudes that tend to block us from honestly accepting ourselves as innate peace. Read over each statement, then circle the number on the scale that best describes the degree to which you agree or disagree with it. Mark "0" if you feel neutral about it.

1.   I am never upset or frustrated by anything but my own thoughts.
   Disagree = -3, -2, -1, <- 0 -> +1, +2, +3 = Agree

2.   There is a state of mind that is innate happiness.
   Disagree = -3, -2, -1, <- 0 -> +1, +2, +3 = Agree

3.   Freedom from the conditioned mind is ultimately a choice.
   Disagree = -3, -2, -1, <- 0 -> +1, +2, +3 = Agree

4.   Accepting what is, as it is, is essential to finding inner peace.
   Disagree = -3, -2, -1, <- 0 -> +1, +2, +3 = Agree

5. I feel others are equal to me rather than superior or inferior.

    Disagree = -3, -2, -1, <- 0 -> +1, +2, +3 = Agree

6. I am equal to others even if they have more money and authority.

    Disagree = -3, -2, -1, <- 0 -> +1, +2, +3 = Agree

7. I do not find fault with my spouse, family members or others.

    Disagree = -3, -2, -1, <- 0 -> +1, +2, +3 = Agree

8. I am at ease with the opinions or attitudes of others that are different than my own.

    Disagree = -3, -2, -1, <- 0 -> +1, +2, +3 = Agree

9. I do not need praise from others to feel good about myself.

    Disagree = -3, -2, -1, <- 0 -> +1, +2, +3 = Agree

10. I do not brag about my accomplishments.

    Disagree = -3, -2, -1, <- 0 -> +1, +2, +3 = Agree

This exercise helps us become aware of what makes it difficult to honestly accept ourselves, our partners or others as innate peace. Hence, if you circled a -3 or -2 on any of the ten statements, showing a strong disagreement, it is likely that you will have difficulty being honest with the truth of who you are, and the truth of who your partner is.

If you want to let go of a pattern that you have marked with a -3 or -2, you can use awareness cards, as we have described in Chapter 12. Make four copies of the statement and place each of them in a critical place where you will encounter them throughout your day, to heighten your awareness of the issue. Here is an example.

Today, my intention is to accept what is, as it is.

Healing Procedures

Practicing the following three healing procedures move us into the maturity stage. Each procedure is meant to accomplish the same thing—undo ego-generated errors in thinking, so that we remember who we truly are.

The first procedure is to choose to be peace whenever feelings arise in our relationships that are not peace. Simply declare, "Sacred Self, my intention is to be peace with this, too." Then we wait and see—letting Spirit fulfill the intention. What are the effects of this intervention? On a physical level, any stress, tension, or churning in the stomach will lift. On the level of the intellect, our minds will be calm, and conflicts will dissolve. On an emotional level, we will sense peace and tranquility.

The second procedure involves the story we are telling ourselves that is actually causing disturbing feelings. Whenever we become aware of strong feelings that are not reflective of innate peace and joy, we can do the following:

1. Identify the story we are telling ourselves.

2. Tell ourselves the true story of who we are: "I am as God created me, innate peace."

3. Turn over the correction of the false story to Spirit, and then wait and see.

If we have used the suggestion concerning a false self-identity in Chapter 15, we will, with a little practice, see that the unwanted emotional states we experience are caused by the story we repeatedly tell ourselves. By identifying the fabricated story, we have a choice about whether to keep reacting like a robot, or begin living in the truth of who we are.

Consider the case of Jennifer, who had a situation in which she caused herself emotional pain with a story she told herself. . As she waited in line at the grocery checkout counter, she reached for her wallet, so she would be ready to make the payment. She realized at that moment that she had left it on the kitchen table at home. She felt embarrassed and disgusted with herself, and quickly left the store. As she sat in her car before starting the motor, she remembered a childhood scene. In that scene, she concluded: "I am incompetent." In reflecting over her life, she recalled several situations when she had forgotten something, and she concluded that it proved she was not competent.

On this occasion, when she remembered telling herself that she was incompetent, she realized she caused herself to feel embarrassed and disgusted. Once she was aware of this, she affirmed that she was still as God had created her, the Divine Self. She turned over the correction of the fabricated story to the Sacred Self and waited. A little later, as Jennifer drove home, she felt a sense of calm and peace.

The third healing procedure is to learn to be in a state of mind so that we can easily assess whether our partner is either extending love or asking for it. When our partner greets us at breakfast with a smile and says, "Good morning! It's a great day to be here with you!" he is extending love. If he wants love, he might say instead, "I had a bad dream last night."

Or perhaps we have just returned from the store and our partner communicates her love by saying, "I am so pleased we did the shopping this morning, I am a bit rushed." If she needed love, she might say, "Did you forget again to buy the two-percent milk?" If you have just fixed a nice dinner and your spouse says, "That was a great meal, thank you, I loved it," you know you are being given love.

I have repeated many times that awareness is the key. This exercise is about the awareness of the other extending love or wanting love. Knowing this, we can respond in an appropriate way.

When we encounter love, we bask in it, accept it with gratitude, and respond in kind. If we encounter any of the emotions or behaviors described as requests for love, we respond with the love that is being requested. We go to the heart of the need, and bring a balm to it by recognizing the individual as God's perfect creation. Sacred Self may have us express that with words of affection or tenderness, or without words. In general, it is rare that the inner voice will tell us specific words to use. We know how to respond by staying open to what we are feeling. It is reflective of being the presence of love. Each of us can have the following intention at all times: "I will be the presence of love, and let the inner voice for truth guide me." As we allow the True Self to guide us, we are aware of everyone we meet or see as coming from a mindset of extending or wanting love. In watching the television news, we can learn to see the people in the stories depicted as either extending or wanting love. We are free to respond to them in the same way as we respond to our partners: if they are extending love, gratefully return the same, if they want love, see them as God's perfect creation.

Maturity Stage

As we allow the Sacred Self to undo errors in thinking, peace and joy become the default drive, and we remain awake to who we are, and who others are. When we know we are the Sacred Self, there is nothing to do but be it, which is what the maturity stage is all about.

Togetherness based on essential equality with one's spouse and others takes on a sense of reality that can't be spoken. It precedes intellectual understanding, and is more akin to direct and immediate knowing. It is associated with peace and a still mind.

There are times when one behaves in ways that do not reflect joy and peace. Those reactions, however, do not diminish the certitude of knowing the Sacred Self is who we all are.

In finding freedom from the ego's domination, we realize what it is to live in the now, rather than in a mindset contaminated by past guilt or future worries and fears. With time, we grasp that following the ego is a choice, just as following the gentle voice of the Spirit is a choice.

When both partners recognize the eternal reality of one another, their love cannot be confined to the marriage. The healed relationship becomes a source of healing for every person with whom they come in contact. It pours love and joy into the whole of Consciousness.

Do not struggle to come out of the mud of your concepts,
you will only go deeper. Remain still.

~ Nisar

The mind is a television with a thousand channels.
I choose a world that is tranquil and calm
so that my joy will always be fresh.

~ Thich Nhat Hahn

Christ's vision has one law. It does not look upon a body,
and mistake it for the Son who God created.
It beholds a light beyond the body...
a purity undimmed by errors, pitiful mistakes,
and fearful thoughts of guilt.

~ *A Course in Miracles*

Afterword

Each time we notice, without any interpretation or judgment, frustration, anger, hate, impulses, etc., we choose to set ourselves free of egoic conditioning. When we refuse to take seriously the conflicted mind's contents, letting whatever is there come and go, we know ourselves as that which never changes, the Self.

Contact

For further information, comments, or to purchase copies of this book please visit www.youbeholdingyou.com or e-mail to:

Thomas: at talpax@charter.net and Berta at bcanton@charter.net

Dr. Leenerts is available for presentations, leading dialogues, or conducting retreats on any of the subjects presented in the book. Topics include, but are not limited to the following:

- *Introduction to ACIM*
- *Understanding Intimate Relationships*
- *Unveiling the False Self and Healing*
- *Cultivating Silence*
- *Being Peace*
- *Approaches to Healing*

He is also available for private consultations and therapy.

Berta S. Cantón, a Master in the Usui System of Reiki Healing, is available for consultations and classes.

Thomas A. Leenerts, Psy.D. and Berta S. Cantón

2007 W 35th Ave.

Kennewick WA 99337

Phone: 509 586 2333. Fax: 509 582 6506

Printed in the United States
201138BV00003B/163-261/P

9 781934 248843